History and American Society

History and American Society

Essays of David M. Potter

 Edited by

Don E. Fehrenbacher

NEW YORK   OXFORD UNIVERSITY PRESS   1973

PREFACE

Plans for this book were made in 1969 by the author, David M. Potter, and the publisher, in the person of Executive Editor Sheldon Meyer, with initial encouragement and valuable advice from the author's Stanford colleague, Barton J. Bernstein. It is in many respects a sequel to Potter's *The South and the Sectional Conflict* (Louisiana State University Press, 1968), a selection of eleven essays reflecting his sustained interest in the cluster of themes associated with the American Civil War. Potter's scholarship of course extended well beyond even that immense subject, and the scope of his interests seemed to militate against thematic unity in any second collection of essays. Yet, as he himself realized, most of his other writings pertained either to the functional thought of American historians or to the distinguishing characteristics of American society, viewed in historical perspective. Thus it was the author's decision to organize this book in two parts—one on history as a discipline and the other on the study of American society—which, together with *The South and the Sectional Conflict*, appear to designate rather accurately the three principal categories of David Potter's unique contribution to historical knowledge and human understanding.

The categories, to be sure, are arbitrary; for in the patterns of his thought there was much interlocking and overlapping. Often, for example, in seeking to illustrate some theoretical problem of historical method, he turned to the Civil War period he knew so well. That is why there are in Part I of this book certain echoes of

The South and the Sectional Conflict, why it has in fact been necessary to include one of the essays (Chapter 5) published in that earlier collection. Similarly, the critique of Frederick Jackson Turner's frontier hypothesis (Chapter 6), which has been grouped with studies of three other historians in Part I, might just as reasonably have been placed in the second part of the volume, where the Turner formulations are repeatedly used as a point of departure in Potter's explorations of national character (see especially Chapters 11–13).

The book now presented is in several ways different from the one originally conceived. It does not contain the two presidential addresses that David Potter expected to deliver in 1971 before the Organization of American Historians and the American Historical Association; for he died on February 18 of that year without having written either of them. On the other hand, Chapters 14–16 go beyond the original plan by including material on alienation and social disaffection which Potter, if he had lived, would have reserved for incorporation in a separate study of major proportions that he managed only to begin. One further difference, perhaps, is that the author himself might have decided to revise or even rewrite some of these essays, but as his surrogate in the publication process, I have confined myself to minor corrections and alterations of the kind that constitute refinement rather than revision of a text.

In addition to the two men named in the first paragraph above, preparation of this book was aided in various ways by the author's daughter, Catherine Potter; by George H. Knoles, Director of the Institute of American History at Stanford, and by Betty Eldon, its secretary; by Witold Sworakowski of the Hoover Institution; and by the office staff of the Stanford Department of History: Patricia Bernier, Nancy Ray, Barbara Richmond, and Loraine Sinclair.

Stanford University   D. E. F.
September 1972

ACKNOWLEDGMENTS

The following chapters were published previously. Thanks are due for permission to reprint them here.

Chapter 1 "Explicit Data and Implicit Assumptions in Historical Study" from *Generalization in the Writing of History*, ed. Louis M. Gottschalk, The University of Chicago Press, 1963.

Chapter 5 "The Historian's Use of Nationalism and Vive Versa" from *Generalizations in Historical Writing*, eds. Alexander V. Riasonovsky and Barnes Riznik, The University of Pennsylvania, 1964.

Chapter 6 "Abundance and the Turner Thesis" from *People of Plenty* by David M. Potter, The University of Chicago Press, 1954.

Chapter 7 "C. Vann Woodward and the Uses of History" from *Pastmasters*, eds. Marcus Cunliffe and Robin Winks, copyright © 1969 by Harper & Row Publishers, Inc. By permission of the publishers.

Chapter 8 "Conflict, Consensus, and Comity: A Review of Richard Hofstadter's The Progressive Historians" from *The New York Review of Books*, April 29, 1969. © David M. Potter.

Chapter 9 "Roy F. Nichols and the Rehabilitation of American Political History" from *Pennsylvania History*, XXXVIII, pages 1–20, 1971. By permission of The Pennsylvania Historical Association.

Chapter 10 "Is America a Civilization?" from *Shenandoah*, X, no. 1, pages 18–22, 1958.

Chapter 11 "The Quest for the National Character" from *The Reconstruction of American History*, ed. John Higham, copyright ©

1962, Hutchinson & Co. (Publishers) Ltd. Reprinted by permission of Harper & Row Publishers, Inc.

Chapter 12 "American Individualism in the Twentieth Century" from *Innocence and Power*, ed. Gordon Mills, University of Texas Press, 1965.

Chapter 13 "American Women and the American Character" from the *Stetson University Bulletin*, Vol. LXII, No. 1, January 1962.

Chapter 14 "The Roots of American Alienation" from the *Emory University Quarterly*, Vol. XIX, pages 194–218, 1963.

CONTENTS

II AMERICAN SOCIETY

I

HISTORY

1

EXPLICIT DATA AND IMPLICIT
ASSUMPTIONS IN HISTORICAL STUDY

*This essay was David Potter's contribution to an important
book published in 1963 on some of the processes of historical
thought, a category of scholarship that W. H. Walsh has
labeled the "critical philosophy of history." Edited by Louis
Gottschalk and entitled* Generalization in the Writing of History, *the book culminated six years of discussion and study
by the Committee on Historical Analysis of the Social Science
Research Council. Potter was a member of the committee and
at one point prepared a commentary on its progress, which he
entitled: "A Memorandum on the Applicability to Historical
Practice of the Essays Gathered by the Committee on Historical Analysis." The published essay was an outgrowth of
the memorandum, from which one sentence may be quoted
as an indication of the direction of Potter's concern: "If few
historians employ high-level generalization, and do so option-
ally because they prefer to and because they believe they can
cope with the methodological problems involved, while all
historians must perforce, consciously or unconsciously, employ low-level generalizations, because such generalizations
are inescapable, then is not the problem of low-level generalization far more important functionally for historians in their
work, and therefore more important to our committee, which
is, I take it, concerned with the improvement of practice in
the historical profession rather than with theory as such?"*

IT IS CHARACTERISTIC of priesthoods that, although claiming to know the truth, they modestly disavow any personal function in determining it. Instead, they profess to have special access to the sources of truth and to be mere passive channels for communicating it from the repositories where it lies awaiting discovery—in the entrails of birds or in the cryptic phrases of Holy Writ or, if they are a legal priesthood, in natural law or in precedent and *stare decisis*.

In this practice the priesthood of historians has been no exception. During the era when "scientific history" was in the ascendancy, historians disclaimed any initiative in interpreting the past or ascribing meaning to it. Their only role, they insisted, was to gather the data of the past and arrange it in chronological sequence, whereupon its meaning—or, in other words, the truth—would reveal itself.

This faith of the devotees of scientific history that some embodiment of truth lay buried in the sources, waiting only to be unearthed and exposed to the light, has now been pretty effectively shattered. It is at least thirty years since the oracles of this faith spoke with undisputed authority. But though scientific history has almost passed from the scene, it still casts a long shadow. For during the era of its ascendancy, it shaped what we call "historical method," and this method has survived, more or less unchanged, long after the historical philosophy which gave rise to it was swept away.

Orthodox or formal historical method was shaped at a time when men believed that a body of data would reveal its own meaning and would interpret itself, if only it were valid or authentic and were arranged in time sequence. The central problem of method, therefore, was to validate the data rather than to interpret them. Hence the problem of historical interpretation was neglected; indeed, its very existence as a problem was denied at the theoretical level, and the principal questions which the problem of interpretation ought to have posed were left to non-historians. Thus, the problem of causation has been left to the philosophers; the problem of human motivation has been left to the psychologists; the problem of social organization has been left to the sociologists. Historians dealt every day with questions involving causation, motivation, and social organization, and often by virtue of their qualities of personal sagacity they handled these topics extremely well. But the anomalous fact remained that the chief problem which historians recognized in their method was the validation of data, while the chief problem which they actually encountered in their daily work was the interpretation of the data. Thus, the most important achievements of historians were attained in spite of their method rather than by means of it.

After living for a long period under the dominion of scientific history, historians at last threw off this creed and embraced historical relativism. As they did so, they passed from the belief that they could attain truth without troubling themselves about theory to the belief that they could not attain truth even if they invoked theory. The result was a sharp reaction, in which historians atoned for their previous pride by professions of self-abasement. They not only repudiated all their former claims to objectivity and to absolute knowledge but also insisted on making repeated confession of their subjectivism and even renounced their right to talk about the ultimate questions of history. If truth could not be attained and if the belief that it could was now in disrepute, the best way for a historian to avoid the imputation of harboring such a discredited belief was for him to abstain from even discussing what might be regarded as the ultimate questions.

This reaction showed up in an especially diagnostic way in the attitude of historians toward what had previously been called "causes." Causes, it was now agreed, did not reveal themselves. The historian still might try to hunt them down, and, of course, in practice historians did continue to seek them, but since they could not be attained in an absolute sense, a prudent man might avoid needless exposure to criticism if he would refrain from speaking of causes as such. Accordingly, one eminent American historian, in the preface to an important and intensive book which cannot be overlooked by anyone who is studying the causes of the Civil War, said that his work "is not intended to be a discussion of the causes of the Civil War." It was "only an attempt to state a few general impressions as to how events got into such shape that they could not be handled by the democratic process." He went on to complain that "some people cannot see the difference between such an effort and attempting to state causes." [1]

One of the people who apparently cannot see this difference is J. H. Hexter, who in his essay "Personal Retrospect and Postscript" writes:

> In the nineteenth century, the word "cause" in either its noun form or its verb form would have done the work done by "factor." . . . But somehow, "cause" got into trouble with the philosophers and the scientists and was dropped by all

1. Avery O. Craven, *The Growth of Southern Nationalism, 1848–1861* (Baton Rouge: Louisiana State University Press, 1953), p. x.

the best and some of the less good intellectual clubs. The work the word had been doing had to go on being done, however, since everyone found it necessary to go on talking about the species of relation which "cause" had formerly designated. So "factor" was slid into the slot which "cause" had once filled in the vocabulary of rational discourse, and this made everybody very happy. Thus the human mind progresses—sideways.[2]

But the historians' scrupulous avoidance of the word *cause* did not arise merely from the fact that the word got into trouble with the philosophers. Rather their avoidance was symptomatic of what had happened to historians after they gave up their faith that objectivity was attainable. If they could not attain it, they must not even make overt use of the concepts that had pertained to it.

Thus both the cult of scientific history and the reaction against the cult placed a barrier between the historian's practice and his theory. The cult told him he could find what he sought without theory, and the reaction told him he could not find it even with theory. Hence, the development of theory has been inhibited in history as much as in any branch of learning. This neglect of theory did not mean, of course, that the historian really confined himself, as he often professed to do, to the mere compilation of data. In practice, he was constantly attempting to work out answers to the questions of causation, motivation, etc., but the assumptions of scientific history told him that he found these answers in the data and therefore did not need analytical tools—other than those for validating data—to assist him in working them out. After the decline of scientific history, he usually went right on, just as before, trying in practice to work out the answers to interpretative questions. But his belief that it was impossible to work them out in an absolute sense stifled his impulses to

2. J. H. Hexter, *Reappraisals in History* (Evanston, Ill.: Northwestern University Press, 1961), p. 200.

formulate any systematic theory. Consequently, for the better part of a century now, the historian's assumptions concerning the nature of his own work have prevented him from attempting a systematic consideration of the concepts which he uses constantly in the course of his work.

This gap between theory and practice has created a situation which might seem quite extraordinary—indeed, almost incredible—if we were not so accustomed to it. Here, in the field of history, is a profession which has several thousand members in the United States alone. These people produce one of the largest bodies of published literature issuing from any branch of academic study. They are represented in every university in the country, and they are constantly engaged in the training of new historians. This training process, leading to the doctoral degree, requires a minimum of three years of intensive work after the baccalaureate. Historians do not agree on whether their subject is a science, but they do virtually all agree that it has a discipline, and they are, on the whole, as proud of their discipline and as jealous of it as any other group of scholars.

Essentially, what all of these people are engaged in doing is converting the raw data which pertain to history, to past human experience, into statements, which we also call "history," about this experience. In the process of formulating these statements historians constantly work with the relationships between separate items of data—relationships which pertain to the effect of one thing in leading to another (what we call "cause") or to the effect of a given condition or event in inducing a particular impulse or purpose (what we call "motivation") or to the degree of similarity or dissimilarity between given units of time in a chronological sequence or given individuals in an aggregate (what we call, respectively, "periods" or "groups") or to many other kinds of relationships. In a certain sense this consideration of relationships is the chief part of their work. Yet the literature of their method and the procedures of their training give so little attention to the systematic analysis of such relationships that a majority of those trained in history have never confronted the general question of the nature of causation or of motivation or of group identity. This may seem singular, but what is really singular is that many who are being trained are not even aware that they have not confronted these questions, and many of the men who train them are not aware of it either.

Such historians, when asked why they have not concerned themselves with such questions, will reply with a double-barreled answer. They do not need to become entangled in theory, they will first assert, because they are not engaged in interpretation; they confine themselves to facts. And then they will add that theirs is a pragmatic approach—that is, one free from a priori generalizations—rather than a theoretical one. In a battle between pragmatists and theoreticians they will fight to the end, they announce, against the warping of facts to fit ideological formulas. They intend to keep on chopping away at the facts and to let the chips fall where they may. They make these assertions with great sincerity and in a way that sounds most convincing.

But is it really the function of the historian to confine himself to mere compilation? And can he so limit himself, even if he would? It is by no means agreed that he should accept any such narrow and limited role. Indeed, we have had two brilliant recent statements—by E. H. Carr[3] and J. H. Hexter[4]—which, if they are symptomatic, indicate a trend toward reasserting the larger responsibilities of the historian. Carr makes a refreshingly dogmatic reaffirmation of an old axiom when he states, without qualification: "The study of history is a study of causes." Hexter shows how heretical an old belief can be made to sound when he says:

3. Edward Hallett Carr, *What Is History?* (New York: Knopf, 1962), p. 113.
4. *Op. cit.*, p. 189.

In fact, truth about history is not only attainable but is
regularly attained. It is true, for example, that at Waterloo
on 18 June 1815 Napoleon I and his army were decisively
defeated by a coalition army commanded by the Duke of
Wellington. This is true in the simple sense that it is an *accurate* description of something that happened in the past,
and the accurate description of things that happened in the
past is one of the ends of history writing. But is it an adequate description? The answer to that question is another
question: "Adequate for what?" The statement as it appears
is quite adequate for a dictionary of dates. It is not adequate
for a historical study of the era of Napoleon; and if by "adequate" is meant a narration of everything thought and said
and done at Waterloo that June day, no historical account
of any event can ever be adequate. The whole issue has been
confused by a failure to make some rudimentary distinctions,
the most important being that between knowing something
and knowing everything. To prove that there is nothing
about which a finite mind can know everything, is not to
prove that there is nothing about which a finite mind can
know something; and to demonstrate that all human knowledge is incomplete and all human truth partial is not to
demonstrate that all human knowledge is ignorance and all
human truth false or some ambiguous thing between true and
false. That this is the working conviction of historians as
contrasted with their inept excursions into theory is easy to
demonstrate.

Still, many historians will deny the goals which Carr and
Hexter set for them and will continue to assert that theirs is a
pragmatic consideration of facts, happily remote from the
pitfalls of theory. If this assertion were true, their position
would be a difficult one to assail, and the need for theory
would indeed be doubtful. But the vital question in historical
study is whether this choice between a pragmatic approach
and a theoretic approach really exists. Or is the actual situation
one in which the historian inescapably applies theoretical
assumptions to his data, as the only possible alternative to
leaving them in chaos? If such is the situation, then the real
choice is between the conscious application of reasoned and

stated assumptions and the unconscious application of un-reasoned and unrecognized assumptions.

The historian, in his compulsive wish to be pragmatic, has been very arbitrary in his readiness to recognize the role of theory in the forms in which he can abstain from it, while refusing to recognize its existence when it appears in the im-plicit forms in which he cannot avoid using it. Thus, historians have always agreed that (to state in other words a point that Hans Meyerhoff makes)[5] an investigator who seeks to find the principles which apply as universal laws throughout his-tory must resort to theory. If a historian is going to look for the cycles which regularly recur or for the basic sequences which always repeat themselves or for the parallels between various civilizations, of course he must reckon with theory. In other words, historians do not deny that the class of generalizations which Gottschalk defines in his fourth, fifth, and sixth categories[6] inescapably involves a use of theory.

5. Louis Gottschalk, ed., *Generalization in the Writing of History* (Chi-cago: University of Chicago Press, 1963), pp. vi–vii, 129.
6. *Ibid.*, p. 113, where Gottschalk, in an essay entitled "Categories of Historiographical Generalization," writes as follows:

> At least six categories seem to be implied: (1) those who make generalizations only if they are unaware that they are doing so and try to eliminate the ones of which they are aware; (2) those who make generalizations knowingly but intend to limit their generalizations strictly to the exposition of the historical subject matter under investigation and of that subject matter only in its own setting; (3) those who make a deliberate effort to go beyond the historical subject matter in hand in order to indicate its inter-relations with antecedent, concurrent, and subsequent events and who thus risk broad interpretative syntheses but still limit their interpretations to interrelated trends; (4) those who with a similar readiness to go beyond the subject matter in hand draw parallels and analogies to it in other times or places of the past, whether or not otherwise interrelated; (5) those who venture propositions about past trends or analogies in such general or abstract terms as to leave the implications, if they do not indeed state explicitly, that their propositions may well be extrapolated to events in the future; and (6) those who propound philosophies that are intended to provide a cosmic understanding of the course of human events past and to come.

But also, most historians make it a matter almost of pride to avoid generalizations at this high level of analogy, abstraction, or universality, and to confine themselves to more limited statements. Often such statements merely set forth two or more items of "fact," with, of course, an implied relation between them. Many historians fondly believe that such statements are factually pure and free of any infection of theory.

Yet even statements which appear to be most "factual" and most limited are often based upon assumptions so broad and ridden with implications so extensive that when one recognizes these aspects the whole distinction between high-level generalization and low-level generalization, or even between factual statements and theoretical statements, tends to break down. Two or three examples may serve to illustrate this point.

Take the statement "The pro-slavery wing of the Democratic Party blocked Van Buren's nomination in 1844, and in 1848 he ran for the presidency on the Free Soil ticket." [7] The facts that are stated here are relatively solid; no one is likely to deny their correctness. But there is implied a relationship between them: what the proslavery Democrats did to Van Buren in 1844 had a bearing on his attitude toward Free Soil in 1848. Indeed, a motive is implied: perhaps because they defeated him, he turned against them. But to ascribe this motive alone is to minimize other possible motives, including especially his sincere ideological commitment to the antislavery cause. In broader terms, a theory of motivation is involved and is applied to the data—a theory which stresses the importance of considerations of self-interest rather than the power of ideals. Yet the historian who writes such a statement may never have formulated in his own mind a coherent attitude toward the problem of human motivation. The questions must arise, therefore, whether it would be possible in

7. This statement and the two which follow are invented by the writer but are believed to be fairly illustrative of well-known types of historical affirmation.

his training to make him more aware of the kinds of unconscious assumptions which he and his fellows are most likely to use and, if this could be done, whether the quality of his historical statements would be improved.

Let us look at another statement: "The Radical Republicans defeated Lincoln's mild program and inaugurated the era of drastic reconstruction." This relatively simple sentence, though apparently devoid of theory, contains at least three very broad generalizations, each one treacherous in the extreme. First is a generalization which ascribes to an unstated number of individuals a common identity strong enough to justify classifying them as a group—namely, the Radical Republicans—and ascribes to this group a crucial role in defeating one policy and implementing another. Yet, in terms of analysis historians have had great difficulty either in defining what constituted a Radical or in proving that any given aggregate of individuals formed a truly cohesive Radical bloc. Second is a chronological generalization—that a certain time span was pre-eminently significant for the process of what is called "Reconstruction"—setting up new regimes in the Southern states and restoring them to the Union—rather than for other developments, such as industrialization. Yet, that process lasted for very diverse intervals of time in various states, and the long-range problem of the relationship of Negroes and whites continued to be important long after the so-called Reconstruction was "ended." Third is a generalization about the degree of severity of Reconstruction, which involves not only a verdict on the over-all effect of a whole series of acts of Congress but also an opinion on what kind of settlement can be regarded as drastic in the case of a defeated belligerent. Many of the measures adopted during Reconstruction are now regarded as salutary—for instance, the establishment of public education in some states—and other measures, such as the Amnesty Acts, do not conform to the generalization that Reconstruction was drastic.

May I offer one more example of a seemingly "factual"

statement with little apparent infusion of theory? Suppose it is said that "John Wilkes Booth shot Lincoln at 10:30 P.M. with a derringer, at point blank range, behind the left ear, the bullet moving through his brain toward the right eye; and Lincoln died at 7:22 A.M. the next day." In formal terms this is a recital of a series of facts, but it is, in its implications, almost inescapably also an explanation of cause—the cause of Lincoln's death. In this statement there are several assorted items, all assumed to be part of the causative complex but unanalyzed concerning their relative part in the total result. These factors include an assassin (Booth), a ballistic weapon (the derringer), and a physical injury (Lincoln's wound). A physician would explain Lincoln's death in terms of the wound, and a ballistics expert would explain it in terms of the weapon; the historian in our culture would probably take the wound and the weapon for granted and would explain it in terms of the assassin. But this choice is culturally conditioned, for if the death had been caused by a special, previously unknown weapon or if Lincoln's assassin were being described by a writer in a culture which did not possess firearms, probably the derringer would receive primary attention. This observation is not meant to suggest that the historian ought to discard his cultural assumptions and to spell out every one of the infinitude of circumstances, from gravitation on, which are taken for granted in any situation. But it is to suggest that he might well have a more carefully reasoned basis for selecting as significant the factor which he does decide to emphasize.

Probably the historian would place the focus upon Booth individually not because Booth pulled the fatal trigger but because Booth planned the killing and without Booth it would not have happened. Without the derringer, presumably, it would have happened anyway, with some other weapon. If the killing had been planned by the Confederates and Booth had been a mere instrument for them, as his derringer was for him, he too would be de-emphasized by the historian. Implicitly, it would seem that to the historian, faced with a multiplicity of factors, the significant ones are the ones without which the event would not have occurred. But this is by no means a firm criterion, for usually a multiplicity of circumstances are necessary to the event (for instance, Lincoln's presence at the theater, the negligence of his guards, the physical layout of the presidential box and the anteroom beyond it),[8] but the historian is likely to treat most of these as being either understood or insignificant, without ever defining, either for himself or for others, the bases of his selection.

The point here, however, is not to settle upon the cause of Lincoln's death but rather to recognize that it is almost impossible to make a simple "factual" statement about the circumstances of his death without basing it upon assumptions about the nature of causation and what makes particular facts significant or insignificant.

If the above statements about Van Buren, the Radical Republicans, and Lincoln should be taken together, the striking thing about them is that in form they all resemble one another to a considerable degree. All appear to be mere narrative statements about what occurred. In terms of Gottschalk's six categories of historical generalization, all fall into either the first or second, the lowest levels of generalization, for there is no broad comparison or analogy or abstraction or universalizing about them. At first glance, they would hardly be regarded as involving generalization at all. But though they seem alike in their factuality and in their avoidance of overt or explicit generalization, actually they are all suffused with implicit generalizations. These generalizations, although similar in level, are extremely diverse in kind, for one involves

8. These are, it may be argued, merely conducive factors, while Booth was an active factor, but this argument raises the questions: Can one systematically use this criterion to distinguish what is significant, and do historians do so?

assumptions about motivation, another about classification, and the third about causation. Even in a pure narrative, therefore, where interpretative or explanatory or analytical discussion is most rigorously suppressed, the mere inclusion of items of "fact" in a particular sequence will suggest one relationship rather than another for the individuals involved in the events, one motivation rather than another for their acts, one cause rather than another for the course of events, and even one criterion rather than another for making an evaluation of what happened.

But if these simple statements are indeed enmeshed with assumptions of the broadest theoretical kind, we must then conclude that the historian really cannot abstain from generalization and cannot escape theory. The choice before him is not between a "factual" and a "theoretical" approach but between, on the one hand, theoretical assumptions which have been recognized and, so far as possible, made rational and explicit and, on the other hand, unrecognized, half-hidden assumptions which remain unordered and chaotic.

If the true choice lies between the latter pair, it would seem to follow that one of the most important questions for historians today is: Can their common, working assumptions be systematized and refined to some degree and raised above the threshold of the subconscious? If there is to be a method for the practices which historians actually engage in and not merely for those which they imagine that they engage in, such an ordering of the historian's interpretative procedures would seem to be of the essence.

When I state this problem as a question, I intend it as a question—one to which the answer is really in doubt, for there are immense difficulties in the way of reducing the almost infinite range of operative historical assumptions to a system.

At one stage in the work of the Committee on Historical

Analysis, I attempted to draw up an abstract statement of what historians write about, with the thought that if one could state in comprehensive terms what themes they deal with, it might then be possible to make at least a tentative inventory of what kinds of generalizations they use in connection with these themes. My effort resulted in the following statement, which I set down here not because I believe it to be adequate but because it may serve to illustrate the problem of identifying various kinds of generalizations:

> Historical writing, in all its various forms, deals with people, as individuals or as aggregates, acting in relation to other individuals or aggregates, responding, with more or less freedom of response, to forces in the primary or secondary environment and motivated to follow a course of thought or action, often in preference to alternative courses of thought or action—with the result that certain developments become manifest. These manifestations, taking place in a context of specific culture and institutions, modify and are modified by the context, and historical change occurs. Historical writing also frequently offers conclusions, if not on the virtue and wisdom, at least on the effectiveness and suitability of given courses of thought or action.

In this statement, what kinds of generalizations may one identify? The term *aggregate* certainly points to the frequency of classificatory generalizations which involve the tricky question of deciding when a pattern of associations shows the existence of an organic group such as a faction, a school of thought, or a nationality—entities whose existence is commonly assumed without analysis. The concept that "historical writing . . . deals with . . . individuals . . . responding, with more or less freedom of response, to forces in the . . . environment" would place a focus upon examination of the generalizations about the extent to which events are deterministically controlled, without real choice on the part of the participants, and would also involve a scrutiny of concepts about the nature of the impact of environment. Historians who stress environmental forces frequently describe these forces in detail and then simply make assumptions about their impact, without real analysis of the data pertaining to the impact and without much attention to the character of the society upon which the forces impinge. It is sometimes asserted, for instance, that Frederick Jackson Turner's frontier had upon people with an Anglo-American, nineteenth-century culture a certain impact which it has not had upon other peoples with other cultures.

To continue: If my statement regarding the content of history is at all valid, historians are constantly concerned with the motivation of people in past situations, as such people follow one course of action or another. Historians constantly ascribe or at least imply motive in specific situations but without any general theory of the nature of motivation and without adequate recognition of what the behavioral scientists know about motivation. When Alexander George explains the conduct of Woodrow Wilson in terms of psychological compulsions arising from his childhood relations with his father;[9] when William Allen White explains the same conduct in terms of Wilson's fiercely Calvinistic principles;[10] and when someone else explains it in terms of the fact that Wilson found that he gained success by appealing to the people over the heads of the legislators when he was governor of New Jersey and during the days of the New Freedom and that he simply continued to use, with ultimately disastrous results, a tactic which for a long while had served him well [11]—when such writers give their various interpretations, they are in part disagreeing about their immediate subject, but perhaps to a

9. Alexander L. and Juliette L. George, *Woodrow Wilson and Colonel House: A Personality Study* (New York: John Day, 1956).

10. *Woodrow Wilson* (Boston: Houghton Mifflin, 1924).

11. H. C. F. Bell, *Woodrow Wilson and the People* (Garden City, N.Y.: Doubleday, Doran, 1945).

greater degree they are merely applying to it their disagreement about the nature of human motivations.

If I may use my definition still further, the practice of historians in treating certain developments as resulting from prior circumstances or events means that, as Carr has said, the study of history is inescapably the study of causes. Here again, when historians offer alternative explanations of what caused a given event, the nature of causation rather than of the specific event may be the issue on which they disagree. Yet usually, if they debate the point, they will couch their argument in terms of the event and not in terms of a philosophy of causation.

Without attempting to wring all the other possible themes of generalization from my trial definition above, I might point out two other frequent forms of generalization which are suggested. One of these is generalization about the nature of the interplay between, on the one hand, developments and, on the other, the context of culture and institutions within which developments occur. Almost every historian has had occasion to apply assumptions about this interplay. For instance, the character of a culture clearly influences the character of government as an institution, but does the institutional character of the public authority also influence the character of the culture or the personality structure of individuals in the culture? Should a development such as the desegregation of the schools be explained primarily in terms of institutional change—that is, the reversal of judicial rulings between *Plessy* v. *Ferguson* and *Brown* v. *Board of Education*—or should it be explained in cultural terms, such as the changes in the educational and economic status of the Negro and the changes in popular attitudes toward race? The historian's assumptions concerning questions like these are likely to shape his treatment of events fully as much as his scrutiny of the specific data will shape it.

To mention one more class, there are also the evaluative generalizations. Historians sometimes conceal from themselves

the fact that they use such generalizations, and they say that
they abstain from moral judgments of good or evil. Some of
them may indeed succeed in this act of abnegation. But it is
hardly possible to explain why a given program did not accomplish its objectives, why a given policy did or did not
have beneficial results, without in fact making assumptions
about the wisdom of given political tactics or the needs of
a given society. The historian may avoid what Carr calls the
"Good Queen Bess" and the "Bad King John" school of
generalization, but he can hardly make an asesrtion that a
given policy "succeeded" or "failed," that a given leader was
"realistic" or "unrealistic," that a given decision was "effective" or "ineffective" without applying evaluative criteria of
what is beneficial for society. Evaluative generalizations, sol-
emnly exorcised at the front door, will inevitably creep in at
the side entrance, and the historian will be their victim less
often if he fixes them with a steady eye than if he insists they
are not there.

The urgency of the need for a systematic awareness of the
latent generalizations which pervade most of our explicit historical statements is all the greater in view of the ambiguous
relationship between the historian's ideas and his data. He always writes as if he were deriving the ideas from the data
rather than selecting the data in the light of his ideas (which
would be "unhistorical"). But in actual practice, does not the
historian often derive his view of history from his personal
philosophy rather than from his analysis of the evidence? If
he and another historian disagree, is their disagreement always inherent in the evidence or is it often a disagreement
about the generalization which is to be applied to the evidence?
Every historian will recognize, no doubt, that subjective factors are certain to influence his colleagues, and conceivably
even himself. But what we do not always recognize perhaps
is that what appears to be argumentation about a specific historical problem may really be controversy about the nature

of the forces that operate in human society. Insofar as it is the latter, it could not possibly be solved in the terms in which it is being discussed—which is one reason why historical controversies are so seldom resolved.

Two examples will, I believe, reinforce this point. One is that tired bromide: Did the slavery issue cause the Civil War? Historians customarily discuss this in the context of a time-honored sequence of data: the abolition movement, the Compromise of 1850, *Uncle Tom's Cabin*, the Kansas-Nebraska Act, Bleeding Kansas, the Dred Scott Decision, the Lincoln-Douglas debates, etc. But after they have done this, historian A will then conclude that the power of antislavery ideals caused the war, historian B will conclude that the rivalry between agrarian and industrial interests caused a clash that was deterministically inescapable, and historian C will conclude that irrational emotions, springing from unrealistic mental images, were at the bottom of things. The questions arise, therefore, to what extent is any one of these historians deriving his generalizations from the familiar litany of events which he ceremonially recites or to what extent is he bringing them in from some unstated locus of origin—from philosophy, from his unconscious, from his culture, from his daily observation of how human affairs work, or from elsewhere?

Again, in the current historical literature on Populism one historian will explain the Populist impulse in terms of an idealistic reaction against exploitation and gross economic injustices; another will explain it in terms of simple self-interest—the desire of debtors and farmers to gain a better economic position vis-à-vis creditors and industrialists; still another will explain it in terms of the reactions of a social class which felt itself psychologically threatened. Here again, the incongruities lead one to face a question. Is the documented material on Populism the source from which these writers draw their generalizations or is it rather the medium in which they argue their generalizations?

If these examples are valid, their implication is drastic indeed. For they come painfully close to suggesting that until historians recognize their own generalizations they will frequently not even understand what it is intrinsically that they are discussing. This would be even worse than not being aware of the assumptions which they have employed.

In sum, what all this amounts to is that generalization in history is inescapable and that the historian cannot avoid it by making limited statements about limited data. For a microcosm is just as cosmic as a macrocosm. Moreover, relationships between the factors in a microcosm are just as subtle and the generalizations involved in stating these relationships are just as broad as the generalizations concerning the relation between factors in a situation of larger scale.

There is another aspect which makes the conscious recognition of implicit assumptions more urgent than it has been in the past. This is the fact that we now have from the behavioral sciences a far better body of learning with which to criticize historical assumptions than we had in the past. A half-century ago, if a writer made assumptions about the nature of the relationships between the collectivity of individuals who formed a nationality, he would have found very little research by means of which to criticize these assumptions, even if he spelled them out. But today studies by Karl Deutsch of the nature of the relationships involved in the forging of nationality would offer valuable critical tests against which any assumptions could be tried.[12] Similarly, if in the past a writer unconsciously attributed motive to irrational impulses, it would have done him no good to formulate his unconscious assumption, for scholarly knowledge of the workings of the human mind ended at the limits of rationality, but today we

12. Karl W. Deutsch, *Nationalism and Social Communication* (New York: John Wiley and Technology Press of Massachusetts Institute of Technology, 1953); Deutsch *et al.*, *Political Community and the North Atlantic Area* (Princeton: Princeton University Press, 1957).

know enough about the nature of the unconscious to be able to some degree to evaluate our hunches about unconscious motivation. Similarly, an improved knowledge of social structure offers us guide lines for judging the worth of assumptions about the relationships between social classes—if these assumptions are overt and can be examined. In short, the more knowledge we have from any quarter concerning the nature of man and of society, the more imperative it becomes to put our ideas about man and society into a form such that they can be corrected in the light of this knowledge. But only when assumptions are made explicit and are consciously recognized is it possible to refine them, criticize them, and bring related knowledge to bear on them.

While this statement of the need for a better approach to the problem of historical assumptions and generalizations is a personal expression and not a statement from the Committee on Historical Analysis, it is true, nonetheless, that considerations along the same line as these influenced the Committee to settle upon the question of generalization as the most crucial problem to which they could turn their attention. If historical writing is not really a statement of a series of items of data in isolation from one another but is rather a statement of a series of relationships, specified or implied, between the items of data, then formal historical method does not effectively deal with what historical writing deals with, and there is an acute need to bring the two within hailing distance of each other. Therefore, to state again a personal opinion which is shared to a considerable extent by members of the Committee, nothing is more urgent for historians than for them to analyze their practice of generalization, to define the principal kinds of generalization which they engage in, to subject these to critical study, and to seek an organized, conscious view of elements which have remained unorganized and unrecognized though ubiquitous in historical writing.

Obviously, this is more easily said than done; in the span of six years the Committee has not been able to accomplish much more than to reconnoiter the problem and take findings on the present use of generalization and the present views of specialists in various fields concerning the question. Any attempt to make a systematic analysis of particular kinds of generalization—as, for instance, about causation or motivation or of an evaluative nature—was precluded by the fact that practicing historians do not specialize in one kind of generalization or another. They use all kinds in their daily work, and, therefore, no panel of working historians could have been found who were prepared to divide the various kinds of generalization among them and to deal seriatim with each in turn.

This is a difficulty at the practical level. At the theoretical level there is an even more formidable difficulty. For it is perhaps more than conceivable that the process of historical interpretation is simply too intricate to be reduced to any kind of rules or formulas. In the selection of data, it has now come to be accepted as a truism that the historian—or, at least, the modern historian—has an infinity of data from which to select and that his criteria of selection must be sensitive indeed. Yet if the responsibility of selecting from an infinity of data seems forbidding, E. H. Carr has suggested an even more awesome responsibility.[13] As he argues, the historian, in explaining the causes of an event, is faced with an infinity of antecedent circumstances, both remote and immediate, which contributed in some degree to shaping that event. He must also select, therefore, among an infinity of relationships as well as among an infinity of data. This analysis of relationships is considerably more complex than the analysis of data, for in circumstances where the historian is dealing with alternative statements of fact, one alternative is likely to be invalid

13. *Op. cit.*, pp. 138–39.

if the other is valid. Thus, if we are told both that Sergeant Boston Corbett shot John Wilkes Booth dead as he ran out of a barn in Maryland and that Booth escaped and fled to Texas, the acceptance of one statement as valid will automatically dispose of the other as false. But if we say that Booth was able to shoot Lincoln because of his special familiarity with Ford's Theater and that Booth was able to shoot Lincoln because of negligence by Lincoln's guard, both statements have a basic validity, and tests of validity are, therefore, of no value in deciding which statement is more significant.

If the historian has a responsibility not only to work in a context of infinite items of data but also of an infinity of attendant circumstances for each item of data, his only criterion of selection, as Carr observes, must be the significance of the points which he chooses to emphasize. But we have no yardsticks for measuring significance. The evaluation of significance may be a matter of sagacity and applied experience which cannot be taught as method. When we encounter this sagacity in politics, we call it statesmanship, and we do not for a moment suppose that students can be trained in school to be statesmen. When we encounter it in historical studies, we are likely to call it "an awareness of the historical process" (akin to what Finley[14] calls "professionalism"), and we are justified in a skepticism about whether this awareness can be reduced to rules any more than statesmanship can. It is by no means a presumption, therefore, that the use of generalization can be reduced to a science merely by shifting the spotlight of method away from the questions of the validity of data, with which historians are only occasionally concerned, to an analysis of the nature of historical relationships, with which they are constantly concerned.

Whether a systematic analysis and a systematic approach to this problem can ever be developed or not, it would seem

14. Gottschalk, ed., *Generalization in the Writing of History*, pp. 33–34.

that the mere effort to develop them might have therapeutic value. Surely it would temper the recklessness of many historians who are scrupulously objective about their data but subjective about the relationships within the data. It would help to define what is really at issue in many historical controversies where the ostensible point of dispute is only the hook on which the real disagreements are hung. And it would serve the purpose which is served by many other unattainable goals, such as the goal to "know thyself." For even a failing attempt to get there would take the historian far along a road which he needs to travel.

2

THE TASKS OF
RESEARCH IN AMERICAN HISTORY

Such was the title of the session to which David Potter contributed this paper at the Annual Meeting of the American Historical Association held at Philadelphia in December 1963. Other participants were Thomas C. Cochran and C. Vann Woodward, with John Higham serving as chairman. Here again, as in the previous essay, Potter is concerned with the thought processes of historians and especially the difficulties accompanying the shift of emphasis in historical explanation from objective to subjective factors, from rational to non-rational motivation. The paper has not heretofore been published.

I BELIEVE there are essentially two ways of going about defining the "tasks of research" in American history. One way is by taking an inventory of the unworked materials in our libraries, our archives, our manuscript collections. The other is by defining the issues or problems which confront our society. The institutional structure of our profession has consistently impelled us to formulate our tasks in the first of these ways, by taking care to exploit the available sources—the newly opened file of manuscripts, the unresearched topic for which both materials and a model are clearly visible, the freshly discovered trunkful of letters, the foolproof thesis topic. But the dynamic of historical thinking has impelled us to direct our energies in the light of our changing conception of the questions that are important to society. When we make these questions the focus of historical attention, we know that we are doing so at a certain sacrifice of the precision and even the purity of our professional method. Such an approach may involve us with problems which historical method has no ready way of solving, or worse still, to which our traditional method is not applicable. Yet I believe it has been an element of substantive strength, as well as of disciplinary weakness in our profession, that historians have never limited their field, as some social scientists have done, to those problems which their techniques permit them to handle with exactitude. History has never guarded its own disciplinary purity by restricting itself to matters for which it possessed a fully tested methodological and conceptual apparatus of attack. It has never shifted its attention from men to mice because of the attractive way in which mice lend themselves to precise investigation, as men do not. It seems to be a well-established habit of mind among historians to turn their attention to the major questions of society, whether these appear to be technically manageable questions or not.

If this is true, it means that for many historians, the prescription of the tasks of history will vary as their conception of the problems of society varies. This in turn would mean that, whether we wish it or not, part of our assignment is to try to define in what ways our conception of the problems of society is changing. This is itself a historical question, and for the consideration of this question, I venture to offer a historical hypothesis: In the past we have tended to regard the problems or issues of our society as concerned with finding the means for the attainment of a model system whose specifications were generally agreed upon and rarely the subject of controversy. The characteristics of this model society were that it should be highly permissive, mobile, equalitarian, and individualistic. The issues, as we conceived them, revolved around the formulation of political and economic policy which would lead to the attainment of such a model. The goals of emancipation, of cheap land, of universal education, of full employment, and so on and so on, were all deemed important as means to the end of the realization of this social model. Meanwhile, it was assumed that if we could attain permissiveness, equalitarianism, individualism, and high mobility, the optimum society would automatically follow. There was little or no questioning of whether such a model would produce all of the desired social benefits, or what price such a model might cost in terms of stresses and unforeseen side effects. Much of our history therefore has focused upon the political and economic measures by which these goals were to be pursued.

But with the twentieth century two-thirds gone, we have been coming, very gradually and almost unconsciously, to an awareness that our immense success in extending political democracy or economic opportunity and thus in approaching the goals of mobility, of individualism, of permissiveness, of equalitarianism has not produced the society which it was expected to produce. Perhaps it is not too much to suggest that we face a realization somewhat like the one which dawned upon Henry George when he wrote *Progress and Poverty*. He had supposed that increasing economic productivity would lead to a corresponding increase in economic well-being, but by 1879 he confronted the realization that this was simply not true—it did not work that way. We have supposed that increased democracy and a higher standard of living would automatically produce social well-being, but it is now increasingly borne in upon us that this is not entirely true either. Of course, we still have not perfected the political and economic mechanisms. We are still in the midst of a struggle to extend political democracy to Negroes, and we are as yet far from abolishing poverty, though we have abolished the necessity for it. But I doubt if anyone, any longer, really believes that political action or economic policy can solve the problem of ethnic tensions, or that the elimination of our remaining poverty would do as much as is needed to alleviate some of the extremely severe stresses and dislocations in our society. This society, it is now pretty generally recognized, has a heavy incidence of rather acute problems, which no one would have foreseen in the Progressive era: problems of alcoholism, of delinquency, of the abuse of children, of violence, of floating anxiety, of alienation, of disorganization, and of aggressiveness. Will not the questions for historians of the future turn increasingly to matters like these? Insofar as they do—and here is my hypothesis—the tasks of the historian must turn from his traditional concern with questions of the means of attaining our social model to questions about the basic soundness of our social ideals, and about the tenability of the model, even about the nature of the society itself; the development of social organization, of patterns of relatedness between the individual and society; the historical sources of anxiety, and of aggression, and of alienation.

As we do this, of course, some social observers will try to handle the new problems with the old concepts. We will continue to be told, as a whole truth, the unanalyzed part-truth that delinquency is a correlate of economic deprivation; that violence is a heritage of the American frontier; that the peculiar bitterness of American political controversy—a bitterness running through much of our history—is generated by political agitators. But are we not growing increasingly dissatisfied with these answers? Are we not growing more prone to believe that delinquency results from conditions in the formation of personality even more diagnostically than from physical want; that our frontier was a receptacle for the incipient violence in our society as well as an incubator of violence; and that political bitterness will do more to breed agitators than agitators will do to breed political bitterness?

It has been an old and familiar complaint in the criticism of American social history that social history as we knew it —the history written by McMaster, by Oberholtzer, and even by most of the contributors to the Schlesinger and Fox Series —was purely descriptive, and lacking in analytical value. To correct this defect, various organizing devices, such as Dixon R. Fox's concept of "social evolution," were suggested. But none of these ever really took. Perhaps the reason they did not take is obvious. Perhaps we will always treat any material descriptively so long as we do not see that it presents any problems, or issues. In American history, the problems and issues were conceived to reside in the realms of political and economic policy, and our society was not believed to present any problems as such. Where there were no issues, the treatment was bound to be descriptive. Perhaps this was the ultimate smugness of American thought. If anything was wrong in our life, we felt sure it must be because our means were unperfected, never that our ends were open to question. We scarcely conceived the possibility of serious shortcomings in the organic structure or the intrinsic nature of the society itself. But today, we have some reason to believe that there are shortcomings, and that these shortcomings cannot be understood purely in terms of political and economic conditions, or dealt with purely in terms of political and economic policy.

If these observations are sound, I believe it would give us at least a very generalized basis for projecting some tasks of research in American history. In proportion as the American intellectual community changes its concept of the nature of the problems in our life, seeing those problems less in terms of political or economic issues, less in terms of institutional devices and blueprints, and more in terms of social stresses and imbalances, more in terms of psychological needs, personality adjustments, cultural dilemmas—in proportion as these tendencies develop, some historians will define their task as one of exploring the background and the development of these stresses, these imbalances, these adjustments, these dilemmas, these social and cultural phenomena. I would like, then, to suggest some of the implications that may follow if history should indeed tend in the direction of more analytical study of the problems which arise from the way in which our society or our culture has been shaped by our past experience.

One of these implications is that historical study may take on a more deterministic tone. To say this is simply to recognize a further extension of what already prevails. Political history—the study of diplomacy, of legislation, of judicial rulings—tends to minimize the deterministic component in history, because it all deals with policy, and the study of policy always assumes that man can modify his circumstances, control his environment, shape his ends, and perhaps even become the captain of his own fate. Liberals and progressives, who tend to believe that salvation can be achieved through changes made deliberately to improve the institutions, have therefore had a natural affinity for political history, which is often the study of such attempted changes. Even those on the left of center who had determinism doctrinally inculcated in their ideologies—for instance the Marxists with their economic determinism—never dreamed of waiting passively for deterministic forces to work themselves out, but were always very adroit in devising policies to hasten the deterministically inevitable. But social and cultural history tends to emphasize underlying given factors and intractible components in the life of a people, leaving the reader with a sense of being in the grip of blind and uncontrollable forces. Thus, although political history is not philosophically committed to free will, and intellectual and cultural history is not philosophically committed to predestination, it may well be that part of the deterministic thinking which began to show itself noticeably in historical study around the beginning of the century resulted partly from the fact that even then, historians were shifting their attention from political history—the history of policy and of the uses of power—to social and economic history—which is more largely the history of the working of forces in the culture or in the physical environment which lie beyond social control.

A second fundamental implication of the kind of shift in attention which I have suggested is that it will force historians to turn from a type of analysis which explains human motivation and action almost wholly in rational terms to one which takes account increasingly of non-rational (please note, I use "non-rational" rather than "irrational") considerations. A few quick illustrations will convey what I mean. Traditionally, much of our political history has dealt with interest-groups and much of our intellectual history, with ideology. Interest groups, almost by definition, want something specific, know what they want, and know why they want it—that is, know what advantage it will bring them. Their historical conduct is as functional and as rational as that of a man who raises an umbrella when it is raining. Similarly, the history of thought has usually dealt with consciously held ideals or values. Sometimes the stress lay upon the clash of ideals—as in the work of Parrington—sometimes upon the pervasiveness of certain basic ideals—as in the studies of Ralph Gabriel upon democratic thought, and of Louis Hartz upon liberal thought. But in either case the emphasis was upon rational factors— ideas consciously held, conceptually defended, and functionally directed. Thus, although we may have been shifting from a focus on political history, with its strong preoccupation with interest-groups, to a focus on intellectual history, with an equally strong preoccupation with concepts, values, and ideals, the spotlight tended to remain upon factors which lend themselves to analysis in conscious or logical terms. Such factors were deemed to be the fundamental stuff of history.

Yet it must by now be evident that, for a good many years past, American historians have been turning increasingly to the recognition of non-rational factors as keys to the explanation of political, and even of intellectual phenomena. In this connection, certain widely known and clear-cut illustrations will come to mind at once. Richard Hofstadter has applied the concept of "status politics" both to the Progressives of the time of Theodore Roosevelt and Woodrow Wilson on the one hand, and to the adherents of McCarthy and the John Birch Society on the other. David Donald's analysis of the sources of abolitionism suggests that most of the abolitionists may have been troubled by status anxieties and tensions, and that they found the slavery issue a convenient peg on which to hang these psychological troubles.

Numerous other examples would have to be mentioned to suggest the variety of contexts in which non-rational factors have received attention. We have rather consistently used them in explaining Prohibition; and indeed the Prohibition movement, attributed from the beginning to the psychological repressions and frustrations of the "drys," may have been the first major American historical phenomenon to be explained primarily in psychological terms. Again, John Hope Franklin's *The Militant South*, which might alternatively have been entitled *The Violent South*, relies heavily upon psychological factors as well as upon cultural traditions to explain the hair-trigger aggressiveness of the temper of the white South more than a century ago. Again, Lee Benson, in analyzing party affiliation during the Jackson era, relies very little upon party ideology or economic interest to explain why some men became Whigs and others Democrats. Ethnic and religious considerations, which cannot be translated with complete rationality into party ties, seem to him decisive. Likewise, John Higham's treatment of nativism and C. Vann Woodward's treatment of the decline and the souring of Populism after 1896 both take us into realms of human personality which lie outside the orbit of either interests or ideals.

As historians are drawn into these realms, they will find themselves farther and farther away from the disciplinary safeguards which their traditional method gave to them. Historians are, in fact, ill-equipped to deal with the fears, the anxieties, the frustrations, the aggressive impulses of a society. They are ill-prepared to distinguish between real and generative ideas which may shape human purpose and shadow-ideas or rationalizations which merely reflect purpose and seek to clothe it in the garb of respectable or logical ideology. Traditionally, we have regarded such phenomena as matters for the psychologist, important in the personality of the individual person or patient, but not applicable at the more general level of society. Now it appears that, whether reluctantly or not, we must recognize that when given psychological responses or attitudes occur in a sufficiently broad range of the population, they become social phenomena, with a bearing upon the developments in the society, and therefore inescapably relevant for the purposes of the historian.

Because we are ill-equipped to handle the concepts that arise here, we are likely to abuse them in certain respects. Particularly, sound historical analysis is likely to suffer from the fact that when we develop the analysis of non-rational factors as an alternative to the analysis of rational factors in given historical situations, we then, in effect, possess alternative means of dealing with such situations, without adequate criteria for determining which alternative to apply. What I mean by this abstract statement is very simple: The historian will often find that he is dealing with a situation where he has a choice between explaining the behavior of the participants either in terms of ideals or interests on the one hand, or in terms of anxieties and psychological stresses on the other. To choose the one will have the inevitable effect of making the motivation of the participants seem creditable: we tend to sympathize with, or at least to "understand," a rational position even when we do not agree with it. But to choose the other will have the inevitable effect of making the motivation seem discreditable: the irrational fear or antagonism of one group toward another partakes of the nature of paranoia, and we tend to be unsympathetic toward paranoia. To be very concrete, one can place Populism, for instance, in a favorable light by emphasizing the social and economic injustices suffered by the farmers and treating Populism as a logical, realistic reaction to those injustices. One can place it in an unfavorable light by emphasizing the Populist belief in a conspiracy of the forces of evil against the forces of good, and treating it as a manifestation of phantasy. The point is that it

is now possible to arrive at a favorable or an unfavorable conclusion about a given group, not by the direct (and readily
detectable) means of arguing that the given group is right or
wrong, as the case may be, but simply by deciding whether to
apply an analysis in terms of rational motivation or an analysis in terms of non-rational motivation. The possibilities latent
in this option have already been foreshadowed in what seems
to me the alarmingly pregnant suggestion by the authors of
The Radical Right that interest politics tend to prevail in
times of depression, since people become concerned with direct physical needs, while status politics tend to prevail in
times of prosperity, since increased social mobility accentu-
ates the strains upon the status system. Obviously, there is a
measure of truth in this formula. But also, equally obviously,
it forms an invitation to historians to interpret liberal movements in the benign terms of interests or ideals—rational in
either case, and to interpret conservative movements in terms
of status anxieties which are irrational and implicitly malignant.
At least this would be true, if liberal movements flourish more
in periods of depression, as the New Deal certainly did, and
if conservative movements flourish more in times of prosperity, such as the Eisenhower years.

I have tried to point out the tricky implications of this
option between interpretation in rational terms and interpretation in non-rational terms, because I think it is illustrative
of our lack of readiness to move into certain areas of investigation into which the logic of circumstances may force us.
And illustrative, too, of some of the hazards that will confront history as it works with an unfamiliar medium full of
new subtleties and complexities. These features may reinforce
our regret that the larger forces in society are pushing us in
this direction. They may strengthen the tenacity with which
some of us will hold on to a definition of our tasks in terms of
our present disciplinary techniques and archival resources.
But insofar as we regard history as the record of past ex-

perience applied to the issues and the problems of the present, and it is certain that some historians will regard it in this way, the tasks of the historian must change as our conception of the problems and issues of society changes, and we must be prepared for the fact that the historian's work will not lie in those areas where his methods make him feel most at home but in those where society's need for an understanding of its past is most acute. This is not at all to say that the historian should rush ahead as a reckless amateur, without fear and without research. It is rather to say that since he has never been as restricted as other social scientists by his method in his choice of topic, he must, to that extent more than other social scientists, face the fact that his task is always a double one: to move into those areas where the problems of society take him, and to develop methods which will enable him to tackle these unfamiliar assignments with a rigor and a discipline which will carry forward the best traditions of his profession.

3

HISTORY AND THE SOCIAL SCIENCES

History as Social Science, *published in 1971, is a report of the History Panel of the Behavioral and Social Sciences Survey, sponsored jointly by the National Academy of Sciences and the Social Science Research Council. On page 3, editors David S. Landes and Charles Tilly acknowledge that "David Potter (Stanford University) offered vigorous and useful criticism of an intermediate draft." Potter's critique, dated May 1969 and published here for the first time, is a plea for moderation in efforts at drawing history closer to the social sciences. The argument is especially significant because it comes from a historian widely recognized as a champion of interdisciplinary scholarship.*

It seems to me that the Report of the History Panel shows a certain ambiguity on the question whether social scientific history should be encouraged as one variety of history, available along with other varieties oriented in other directions, or whether it should receive a priority as the preferred form of historical study, to be promoted at the expense of other forms of history. To what extent shall the training of graduate students in history or the planning of research programs in history be oriented restrictively to social scientific history?

I recognize, of course, that the Report does not explicitly suggest any such restrictive purpose, and it may seem unwarranted for me to suppose that such a purpose is implied or even that such a result might occur as an unforeseen consequence of the recommendations in the Report. But the Report certainly contemplates the development of a heavy emphasis on social science in historical studies. For instance, the Report states that "In the short run, the likely resistance of influential segments of the historical profession to its [social science history's] growth makes it desirable to earmark certain funds for its promotion." This certainly suggests that the claims of social science in the field of history must be asserted, even if financial weapons have to be employed in order to do so.

Whether the Report does or does not contemplate making the social science approach dominant over other approaches, it is certainly legitimate to consider whether the potential value of the social sciences to history is enough to warrant giving them a central and dominant position in historical studies. Though this question is not raised in direct form in the Report, I would like to offer some suggestions about it.

To begin, let me suggest that the most usual approach to this question is to pose the question whether history is one of the social sciences or one of the humanities, and that this approach is, in fact, not very rewarding. It involves a philosophical discussion of what history ought to be, often giving little attention to what it actually is. Further, it usually runs off into invidious comparison of the merits of the humanities as opposed to the social sciences. It says nothing about the day-to-day work of most historians. An alternative approach would be to ask not what academic flags the historians ought to fly, but what kind of work most historians do, what kinds of questions or problems they try to solve, and what kinds they will probably be dealing with in the future. It is essential to have some idea about this as a preliminary to estimating how much they may rely on the social sciences as the disciplinary tools of their investigation.

It may be reckless to venture any formulation of what pursuits are primary in a field as pluralistic as history, but I suggest that there are two types of phenomena which run most pervasively through historical study and which seem to preoccupy most of the energies of historical scholars.

One of these is the formation and execution of policy. A large proportion of all the work done by historians involves a study of the process by which certain decisions—in legislatures, in courts, in army organizations, in business organizations, in administrative commissions, in mobs, and in endless other groups, were arrived at, and how they were executed. Insofar as most decisions are intended either to bring about a certain result or to avert a result intended by some other party, they involve policy. Historians want to know how and why given organizations choose to follow a given course rather than alternative courses. Usually they also want to evaluate policy: Was a given decision valid in the light of the circumstances? Was it preferable (by whatever criterion of preferability) to possible alternative decisions?

The second type of inquiry concerns the interplay of influence between individuals and groups—especially the influence of ideas. What, for instance, was the impact of the thought of a given person—Marx, Freud, Adam Smith, Darwin, Voltaire—upon society? How did such mass experience as the Great Depression, the Second World War, the Black Death, the Crusades, condition the attitudes of the societies which underwent these experiences? What does the style of a given writer, architect, politician, reformer, publicist, or administrator, reveal about the tendencies prevalent in his society?

Some of these questions might be recognized as humanistic, others as social scientific. But in many cases, the methodological problems of the "social science" question might be much the same as the problems of the "humanistic" question. How, for instance, did Stephen Crane or Frank Norris react to the conditions of industrial capitalism (humanistic); how did Eugene V. Debs or Robert M. La Follette react (social scientific)?

If it is accurate that inquiries of this kind form the principal staple of historical research, a question follows as to what kind of methodological or technical problems such themes involve for the historian, and to what extent the social sciences will provide keys to the solution of such problems.

This latter question—how the social sciences can contribute to more effective treatment of many different problems involving policy or regarding influences and relationships—is too vast and complex to even begin upon it here in any detail. But there seem to be several factors which at least limit the direct applicability of the social sciences. One is the fact that a study of policy involves ultimately a question of judgment rather than a question of science. A policy decision involves the choice of a particular course and the rejection of alternative courses. The historian has the advantage over the person who makes the decision that he knows how the chosen decision resulted, but he knows no more than the person who made the decision about how alternative decisions would have resulted, and, in fact, he does not even know how the chosen decision might have resulted if extraneous events subsequent to that decision had not intervened. No doubt the social sciences can provide great help in refining the analysis of the alternatives between which a choice was ultimately made, but the point here is that social science cannot tell a historian anything much more conclusive in evaluating a given decision than it can tell the participant in the decision. That is, the evaluation cannot be made scientific; it has to remain judgmental.

A second factor is that when the historian deals with ideas and influences, again his problems lie to a great extent outside the range of the social sciences. This is not to deny that social science has an important function. For instance, it would seem vital to the interpretation of motivations. But the direct applicability of social science to a field such as intellectual history seems too tenuous to justify a prescription that the intellectual historian must have social science training.

A third factor, unalterably characteristic of history, is that it deals with heterogeneous elements. For instance, any broad study of the reasons for the voyages of discovery to America and Asia around the end of the fifteenth century will have to take account of (1) scientific developments in cartography, navigation, and shipbuilding, (2) the economic impulses to open up trade with the Indies, (3) the rise of towns and of a merchant class in the towns, (4) the political concentration of power in the new class of monarchs, at the head of nation states which vied with one another for economic power, (5) the obstacles to the continuation of trade through the traditional routes by way of the eastern Mediterranean, and (6) various other factors.

Perhaps the basic problem in dealing with the relationship of such elements as these scientifically is that science works most effectively with congruent or homogeneous components —items which can be factored down to a point where they are interchangeable or at least commensurate. Most of the social sciences attain this homogeneity of data by dealing with only one aspect of human affairs, and an aspect in which the data tend to be congruent. Thus, an economist dealing with the Age of Discovery might brilliantly demonstrate how the circumstances of maritime trade stimulated an impulse to open new routes; or a sociologist might show how changes in the social structure in European populations were increasing social mobility in a way that made the society more open, more adaptable and more responsive to the new opportunities such as the voyages of discovery presented. The historian needs all such analyses, and he should not be entirely dependent on the economist or the sociologist to make them. But after they are made, very often he is still left with the task, again, of *forming a judgment* as to the relationship between all the various factors. The process by which he does this will be directed by applied and trained intelligence, but it will not be a scientific process. The historian remains a generalist and not a specialist, working with heterogeneous and not with homogeneous factors. More and more, as the social sciences have advanced, he has needed access to what they can offer toward the refinement and the solution of his problems. He has suffered increasingly from this lack of access, and will suffer worse if it continues. But even when the access is opened, it is still likely to remain true that the majority of historians will be spending most of their time working on subjects such as those involving specific decisions on questions of policy, or those involving the impact of ideas and influences, or those involving heterogeneous factors, for which the applicability of a social scientific approach still remains, very often, unclear. This will not be because historians are "humanists." It will be because they are generalists and because the topics on which they work compel them to posit relationships between factors which cannot be made commensurate and cannot be reduced to scientific precision. I do not see how there can be any question of the potentially great value of the social sciences to history for the more effective analysis of the questions which historians now study. Nor any question of the value of training, facilities, bibliographical aids, and other items in the recommendations of the Report. Nor of the development of a full-fledged social scientific history for the treatment of such subjects as urbanization, acculturation, collective biography, and social structure.

The only problem that would concern me would be an attempt to exalt social science history at the expense of other kinds of history and to give it such a dominant role in training and research programs that it would drive other kinds of history out of circulation, so to speak.

This contingency, of the domination by social science history, seems to me to arise from some of the recommendations in the Report, for it seems likely that, if the Report were published in its present form, some critics would construe it as an attempt to restructure historical studies on a social science basis. I recognize, of course, that the Report has no such deliberate purpose, and that it disclaims any such purpose. But in the light of the operative proposals, such disclaimers seem somewhat *pro forma*. The proposal for highly organized, long-extended, and handsomely supported seminars is close to the heart of the recommendations, and it is evident that these seminars would be strongly oriented toward social scientific history. They are to be given computer time; they may have members from the social science fields; they are to deal with topics "whose organizing principle is the selection of situations, unrelated in time and space, whose study is relevant to the understanding of some problem of social theory." Now it is self-evident that the establishment of such courses, expensively staffed, equipped with libraries of their own, offering such attractions as secretarial services and publication of the work of the participants, would exercise a tremendous gravitational force in drawing all graduate students in their direction, regardless of the fact that the student would necessarily sacrifice some of his freedom of choice in the selection of a research topic. Again, the Report contains a disclaimer: the graduate student who does not want to join the seminar, in which he would run the risk of serving as "manpower, otherwise unobtainable, to carry out large-scale and long-range research projects"—such a student "whose tastes and subject matter dispose him toward an individual effort" should be assured of "an attractive alternative to the seminar." But the nature of this alternative is not indicated, and skeptical readers are sure to wonder whether the fellowship aid, the lavish facilities, and the prestige of the seminar will really turn out to be matched by the attractive alternative. These matters have a dynamic of their own, regardless of the intentions of those who propose them. What, someone is sure to ask, is all this money being spent for if not to draw historical study closer to the orbit of the social sciences? And to what extent, traditionalists will inquire, does this constitute the use of financial leverage to promote one kind of scholarship at the expense of another?

Personally, I am deeply convinced of the present deficiencies in historical study, and of the value to historians of the social sciences. I am in favor of any step which tends to encourage historians on a voluntary basis to use the social sciences more than they now do. Thus, I would support the proposals to bring the social science literature into the bibliographies used by historians, to hold summer institutes of the kind proposed, to provide financial assistance for historians who seek training in social science, to make historians more familiar with institutions such as the Consortium, and to liberalize the graduate history curriculum in a way which would give students graduate credit for work which they may undertake in the social sciences. I would even be willing to require some work in a subject such as statistics, but I would want to scrutinize this very carefully.

I even regard the proposal for the highly structured and long-extended seminar as most attractive. But I believe that such seminars ought to be post-doctoral, rather than part of the curriculum for the Ph.D. As proposed, the seminar would be, in my opinion, too specialized and too highly structured to meet the broader requirements of graduate training, and I am profoundly doubtful about an arrangement which might seriously diminish the student's freedom in choosing a dissertation subject. The raising of large funds for such seminars might precipitate a battle for the control of the system of graduate training, and while I do not doubt that reform in this system is needed, I believe that it should come from within the profession. A struggle for control might well result in damage to history, without advantage to either faction.

In writing this commentary, I have necessarily placed the emphasis upon my mental reservations and my criticisms. This is, in a sense, unfair to the Report, for I subscribe fully to most of the recommendations, and while I believe that much of the historian's work involves problems outside the orbit of the social sciences, I do not doubt that much also involves problems which lie inside, and that social sciences would do more than anything else to correct the shortcomings of history as it is practiced at the present time.

4

HISTORIANS AND THE PROBLEM
OF LARGE-SCALE COMMUNITY FORMATION

On June 20–22, 1957, about twenty historians and social scientists participated in a conference at the Hoover Institution, Stanford University, entitled "The Historian's Concern with the Formation of Large-Scale Political Communities." In this paper, not previously published, Potter gave special attention to a newly published book, Political Community and the North Atlantic Area *(1957), two of whose eight authors were present at the conference. His treatment of nationalism and the problem of multiple loyalties, with the antebellum South used as an illustration, prefigures the more extensive exploration of these themes in the essay that follows.*

THE PROBLEM of the formation of large-scale political communities is an immense subject in itself, and it might well seem that when the topic at hand is so vast, no preliminary—especially no broader preliminary—should be admitted to the discussion. Yet it may be worthwhile, at least from the standpoint of the historian, to take note of the fact that generalizing about large-scale political communities is only one form of the broader practice of generalizing about groups. For that reason, an awareness of the problems that surround generalizations about any kind of group may be pertinent to the problems of generalizing about large-scale political communities. The questions which arise specifically in connection with political communities of large scale may perhaps be seen in better perspective if they are recognized as arising generically in connection with human groups of almost any kind.

The importance of keeping the over-all problem of group generalization to the forefront seems even more urgent for the historian because as soon as he goes beyond the level of biography, the historian begins to find that it is almost impossible for him to interpret any broad segment of human experience without recognizing certain aggregates of human beings as groups and making generalizations about them on the theory that they can legitimately be differentiated from other human beings who are outside the group. Both the necessities of his medium and his own impulses to reduce his data to an intelligible order seem to impel him to make such generalizations. So powerful, in fact, is the gravitational force which draws him in this direction that he is under a strong temptation to exaggerate the separateness of identity of the given group, or even to postulate a fictitious or imaginary group where none in fact exists in an objective sense.

Accordingly, historians have written at length on a great many kinds of groups. We have histories of sex-groups—for instance, the history of women in colonial America; of age groups, which can be illustrated by studies of the role and status of children at given times; of ethnic groups, for example, John Hope Franklin's history of the Negro in America; of social class groups, for example, Louis Wright's studies of the Virginia gentry in the eighteenth century; of geographic groups, such as one would find in the history which treats of the successive populations of a given area even though these populations have little in common save the place of their residence; of occupational groups, such as a history of textile workers; of interest groups, such as a history of the workers in a given industry, whose specific occupation may vary widely but who have in common a dependence upon the operations of the same economic organization. One can extend the list beyond this to include religious groups—for instance, the history of the Mormons; intellectual groups—I would cite the pragmatists; and even groups of people who have in common mental attitudes which scarcely have enough rational content to justify the term "intellectual," and who might better be designated therefore as psychological groups. In America, the nativism of the Know-nothings or of the Ku Klux Klan would illustrate this category. If this catalogue were protracted further, it might also be shown to include institutional groups—such as a history of the legal profession; and even aesthetic groups—the Pre-Raphaelites, perhaps—or recreational groups, such as the devotees of fox hunting.

I have ventured to spin out this list primarily in order to underscore the fact that no matter what the historian may deal with he almost inevitably becomes involved with the problems of group generalization. But both traditionally and also in his more diversified modern role, the historian has been concerned most of all with political groups. Most often he has concentrated his attention upon the activities of the organization which represented the group—that is, with government in its conduct of affairs of state—rather than upon the group itself. But always there has been a tacit assumption that behind the government stood a population possessing distinctive characteristics and exercising a distinctive influence upon the nature of governmental action. At times, concern with the group itself has been far more direct, and this has been true ever since the time of John Richard Green's and John Bach McMaster's histories of the English people and the American people, respectively. Where the concern has been direct, it has led to specific efforts to demonstrate that the group possesses a true unity, either by ascribing to its members common traits of national or regional character, or by stressing their common adjustment to a distinctive common experience —such as the experience of the frontier in American history.

It is a major anomaly of history as a discipline that although virtually every branch of history, as I have tried to indicate, has dealt with the problem of group generalization in one form or another, the accepted canons of historical method did not in fact lay down any procedural rules or fixed criteria of analysis for handling this problem. Although historical method offered elaborate instructions on the sifting of data and the criticism of sources according to the rules of evidence, it gave the historian not a single star to steer by in the most difficult part of charting his course—that is, in mak-

ing generalizations from the "facts" that had been so painstak-
ingly established. Therefore he was, in fact, left to handle this
essential part of his task on an *ad hoc* basis, by improvisation,
or "common sense." If he was gifted, he found ways to
transcend these problems without exactly solving them. If he
was not, it often happened that his history turned out to be
a set of professionally ascertained "facts," organized and interpreted in the light of subjective ideas and assumptions.
Thus, historians may be in the unenviable position of having
mingled their presentation of professional findings with expressions of purely personal opinion more freely than any
other class of research scholars.

Given these circumstances, it is, perhaps, not strange, that
historians have often shown a distressing lack of sophistication
in their handling of the group concept. For one thing, they
have very often begun by simply assuming the existence of the
group as given and the separateness of its identity as valid,
without taking any of the pains that some other research
worker would devote to the task of establishing the validity
of the group as an objectively delimited body of individuals.
For instance, if a historian writes a history of dentistry in
Oklahoma, very often it is impossible to tell from his mono-
graph whether he feels that dentists in Oklahoma are in fact
distinguishable in any way from dentists in other states, or
whether he has merely found it desirable to limit the area
of his subject for purposes of convenience. All too often, I
am sorry to say, it has been evident that the researcher has
not even asked himself the question whether he is dealing with
a handy-sized segment of a larger group or whether the members of the aggregate with which he is concerned actually possess distinctive attributes which give to them the unitary
character of a true group.

Even when historians have attempted to face up to these
questions, their results will very often be disappointing. Especially in their treatment of political communities they have

been prone to abuse the concepts of national character and of nationality. The national character concept has been mistreated in so many ways that a full discussion would be out of order here, but suffice it to say that intuition, mysticism, and a priori reasoning have had a field day with this concept. Instead of seeking objectively to ascertain national traits by the collection of data, historians have sometimes argued deterministically that since a given factor, such as the frontier, is operative it must produce certain traits and that these traits are therefore qualities of the national character. Or again, they have argued intuitively that since a given trait, such as a bulldog tenacity is well-known to be characteristic of a given people, namely, the English, therefore English individuals who exhibit bulldog tenacity are evincing the national character, and those who do not are not evincing anything. But when they pass from describing the national character to explaining it, it is then that they make the transition from mere intuition to actual mysticism. For it must be said that many historians still write about national character in a way which makes it impossible to tell whether they regard the given character as permanent or as changing, as representing a quality instilled in every individual of the group or as representing a mere statistical tendency to be found in a representatively large proportion of the group, and even whether they believe it to arise from qualities genetically inherent in the group or from adjustments culturally acquired by the group.

If the treatment of national character has been faulty, the discussion of nationality in its relation to the spirit of nationalism has been scarcely less vulnerable. Here historians have very often lapsed into the fallacy of the circular argument, and have explained the formation of nations (or shall I say of large-scale political communities of the national type) by emphasizing the strength of nationalistic impulses among the people. But this amounts, in the last analysis, to explaining a process in terms of a spirit which the process itself has generated. Even in the details of this explanation, the argument is sometimes circular. We find it natural to explain the common nationality of New York and San Francisco by saying that they both lie within the contiguous territory of a single transcontinental republic. Yet in fact New York is closer to Montreal, which we say is not part of a contiguous territory. This means then that contiguity is a concept which we apply after the fact to territory that is already united; it is a geographical fiction which needs to be explained, far more than to serve as an explanation.

Another difficulty lies in the fact that historians of nationality have sometimes written about the nation as if it were the sole group to which individuals belonged and about nationalism as if it were the sole loyalty of the people. Yet the most elementary social analysis will remind us at once that in every society individuals have belonged to a number of groups—the family, the church, the school, the local community, as well as the state—and that each of these groups becomes a focus of loyalty. In fact, the multiplicity of groups increases with the more complex social organization of modern times, and as it does, the multiplicity of loyalties also increases. This means that a given loyalty is seldom an absolute value, but that usually it is a relative value occupying a more or less changeable place in a shifting hierarchy of values. The hierarchical nature of this complex is so basic that it becomes one of the chief responsibilities of statesmen to prevent the clash of loyalties, as between, for instance, church and state or local community and national community. In a parallel sense, it should be the responsibility of historians to recognize that the group is never isolated and the loyalties adhering to it are never absolute. The group is an aggregation which overlaps other aggregations, and it elicits loyalties which are adjusted to and relative to other loyalties. Its own separateness is constantly waxing or waning; the intensity of the loyalties which it evokes is constantly increasing or diminishing. The problem must always be treated in terms of degree. For instance, the story of the American South before the Civil War is not the history of an absolute shift from complete American nationalism to complete Southern nationalism; it is rather the shift from primary American loyalties accompanied by secondary Southern loyalties to primary Southern loyalties accompanied by secondary American loyalties. It is a matter of ebb and flow, not of one totality replacing another. This matter of multiple loyalties is a basic factor in the analysis of groups.

Although the historical understanding of national groups has suffered from the abuse of the national character concept and from the failure to cope with the question of multiple loyalties, perhaps the most serious shortcoming has been somewhat less self-evident and somewhat less easy to explore. This has been what I would call the "constituent ingredient" theory of nationalism—the idea that when certain elements are brought into association, they automatically fuse to generate a spirit of nationalism and thus to set in motion the establishment of a nation. These elements or ingredients—"certain objective bonds" as one historian has called them—usually include common descent, common language, common territory, common religion, common customs and traditions, and they tend to manifest themselves in a common political entity. Now it may be suggested that these enumerated factors have a certain value in dissecting out the various aspects which together make up a sense of community. But to say that this is what common identity consists of, is not at all the same as to say that it explains common identity, which is what many writers apparently have supposed. The real joker in the common-descent-common-language-et-cetera formula is the word "common," which tells us the fact that unity has been achieved but not the explanation of how it has been achieved. In short, the "constituent ingredient" theory tends to conceal the fact that the formation of a nation or of a nationality is a process of the creation of conditions of commonality, and that as a process it cannot be explained by taking a fixed set of ingredients and saying that when these ingredients or most of them are put in at one end of the machine, a nation will come out at the other.

Political Community and the North Atlantic Area, I would like to note, has escaped errors which have been very prevalent in the literature relating to the formation of nations. In the first place, I believe that this book completely avoids the ancient fallacies of circularity in argument. In the second place, it takes a position firmly on the ground that the formation of large-scale political communities is a process and that it must be explained in terms of process rather than of component parts—this feature, by itself, makes the book something of a landmark. In the third place it recognizes very clearly that in the process of group formation there are various degrees of unity or integration. This fact is recognized in part by distinguishing between amalgamated communities, in which a complete merger of states (or peoples, I should suppose) has taken place, and pluralistic communities in which the sense of common identity has become strong enough to make war seem fratricidal or treasonable though a fuller unity has not been achieved. Although the authors do not seem to regard the United States in 1860 as a pluralistic community, the distinction which they make here lends itself very readily to a more refined and more illuminating interpretation of the American Civil War and the subsequent reunion of North and South than can be derived from many of the standard interpretations of that conflict. It may seem astonishing for me to say this of a subject which has been so endlessly worked and re-worked by able historians, but I believe nevertheless that it is true.

The fundamental problem in explaining the Civil War is to account for two things: first, the apparently high degree of fierce and indomitable loyalty with which the Southern people supported a Southern nation, the Confederate States of America; and second, the swiftness and readiness with which they returned to a loyalty to the American nation, so that when the war with Spain came in 1898, they were enlisting in the American army even more heavily than men from other regions. It is easy to explain the first by emphasizing the idea of complete Southern nationalism, or the second by emphasizing the idea of an American nationalism latent in the South throughout the Civil War. But each explanation in a sense undercuts the other and the solution of one part of the problem automatically renders the other part more insoluble.

But using the concepts of an amalgamated and a pluralistic community, as developed in *Political Community*, we have a key to the initial rift between the sections, to the fierceness and determination of the Southern resistance, to the sense of tragedy overhanging the entire war, and to the ultimate ease of reunion.

The initial rift, it might be argued, arose from the growing Northern impulse to regard the union as an amalgamated community and the continuing Southern inclination to regard it as a pluralistic one. Secession was a protest against the amalgamation process. To say this is not inconsistent with an emphasis on the slavery question, for it was slavery which made the South so tenacious in defending pluralism.

The fierceness and bitterness of the Southern resistance was the reaction of men who not only felt that they were the victims of aggression by strangers, but were outraged by a sense of being unjustly subjugated by members of their own community, which was still in a sense a community although a pluralistic one.

The brooding sense of tragedy which haunted the belligerents on both sides also arose from this continued recognition that all were part of a community in the large sense, and therefore that bloodshed within this community was "fratricidal"—the very term used in *Political Community* and an expression often used in the sixties. John C. Reed later wrote a history entitled *The Brothers' War*.

Finally, the ease of reunion by 1898 resulted from the fact that Southern nationalism was never complete. (If it had been it must have lasted far longer.) The South had already moved far toward community in a pluralistic sense before 1861; even the war did not undo much of this progression, and it remained after 1865 only to build a more integral community on the foundations already present. The transition was not wholly from Southern nationalism to American nationalism but from community in the pluralistic sense to a stronger community.

Because of the improved approach which *Political Community* offers for the historical analysis of nationalism, historians can justifiably claim that professional historians working within the medium of history have solved some important problems of their own without appealing to foreign aid. But at the same time when the study offers the concept of process as a means for treating the formation of large-scale communities, it also raises many new questions about the nature of the process—questions on which foreign aid may be needed, and where historians may have to look to the social scientists. For instance, when the study points to varying degrees of unity, various levels of the threshold of integration, and multiplicity of loyalties, it raises questions calling for a more extensive knowledge of the priority and interplay of loyalties in the mind of the individual—questions which necessarily invoke the counsel of the behavioral scientist. By recognizing community formation not as a matter of components, but of values and ways of life, it again leads to a demand for what sociology, psychology, and anthropology can say on these subjects. By its very discriminating attention to the fact that increased intensity of communication does not necessarily lead to increased closeness of community, it calls for analysis of the extent to which a sense of being safeguarded is an essential part of community-formation. (For instance, if I may refer to the American Civil War again, the growing closeness of contact between North and South at a time when the South was not psychologically ready for it, resulted in increased friction rather than increased harmony. The prospect of closer union, without increased protection, seemed menacing to the South.) Or again, by distinguishing between the reactions of elite groups and of the population as a whole, the study introduces questions about the interplay between the initiative of leadership and the response of the group, as well as about the relative incidence and importance of active loyalties at various levels in the social structure. Here again the historian will need to learn all he can from his co-workers in the social sciences. This seems to mean that as history increases the effectiveness of its own analysis, it must also, to some degree, increase its dependence upon related branches of learning. As it extends the diameter of its own mastery, it may very well find that it increases the circumference of the circle along whose rim it comes into conjunction with the social sciences.

5

THE HISTORIAN'S USE
OF NATIONALISM AND VICE VERSA

This is perhaps David Potter's best-known essay. A somewhat abridged version appeared in the American Historical Review, XLVII *(1962), but the complete essay as it is presented here was first published in Alexander V. Riasanovsky and Barnes Riznik, eds.,* Generalizations in Historical Writing *(1963).*

IT IS ONE of the basic characteristics of history that the historian is concerned with human beings but that he does not deal with them primarily as individuals, as does the psychologist or the biographer or the novelist. Instead he deals with them in groups—in religious groups, as when he is concerned with the wars of the sixteenth century; in cultural groups, as when he is treating the broad history of civilizations; in ideological groups, as in the conflict between pragmatists and idealists; in interest groups, such as the landed interest or the moneyed interest; in occupational groups, such as the farmers and the ranchers; or in social groups, such as the gentry and the yeomanry. But most often the historian deals with people in national groups. These national groups usually coincide with a political state; but it would be too restrictive to say that the national group is simply a political group, for very often the historian is not concerned with the political aspects of the history of the group. As a social historian, for instance, he may be interested in the social development of the American people or the English people, and may be quite indifferent to the history of the United States or of Britain as a political entity. Similarly, if he is an intellectual historian, his field of inquiry may be the history of American thought or of British thought—again without any concern for governmental aspects.

Just as the rise of nationalism has been the major political development of modern times, so attention to the national group, rather than to these other groupings, has correspondingly become perhaps the major focus of modern historians. Accordingly, the identity of people in terms of their nationality has grown to transcend all other identities, so that we speak and think constantly in terms of the American people, the Japanese people, the Russian people, and so on. Our attribution of distinctive traits and attitudes, reactions and values, to these groups shows that we do not conceive of them merely in political terms as bodies who happen to be subject to a common political jurisdiction, but rather as aggregations whose common nationality imparts or reflects an integral identity. The idea that the people of the world fall naturally into a series of national groups is one of the dominating presuppositions of our time. For the historian it takes the form of a basic, almost an indispensable, generalization, so that even historians who recognize that exaggerated nationalism is one of the greatest evils of the modern world still are very prone to conceive of the structure of the world in terms of national units.

Because of the constant, pervasive use of this criterion of nationality as the basis for classifying the two and a half billion members of the world's population, the concept of nationality has become a crucial one in modern historical thought, with many far-reaching implications. It is the purpose of this essay, therefore, to explore some of the implications which reside in the historian's concept of nationalism, some of the unrecognized side effects which the concept, with its attendant ideas, has had, and something of the way in which it has affected the treatment of history.

Perhaps the most crucial fact in shaping the historian's use of the idea of nationalism is that he employs it in two quite distinct ways for two different purposes. On the one hand, he uses it in answering a question as to the degree of cohesiveness or group unity which has developed in a given aggregate of people. Here the question is primarily descriptive or observational, and it can be answered in qualified or relative terms, or in terms of degree, with fine distinctions and gradations. Such a question may concern the psychological attitudes of the group, and in fact the prevailing theory of nationalism today emphasizes its psychological character. Thus, for example, Hans Kohn affirms that "nationalism is first and foremost a state of mind, an act of consciousness," and, though he points out that one must also explain the surrounding conditions which produce the state of mind, he accepts as valid, though limited, the statement that a nation is "a group of individuals that feels itself one [and] is ready within limits to sacrifice the individual for the group advantage."[1] Proponents of this psychological view recognize, of course, that a subjective group-feeling is a phenomenon not likely to develop unless there are objective conditions which give rise to it. Conceivably in theory, a group of people might form a nation simply by believing passionately enough that they shared qualities in common, even if this belief were an illusion. But this is only in theory, and in fact nearly all authorities on nationalism have given a great deal of emphasis to the objective or substantive conditions from which the sense of common identity is derived. Such conditions include the sharing of a common language, the occupation of a territorial area which constitutes a natural unit (an island, a river valley, or mountain-girt basin), the adherence to a common religion, and a heritage of common mores and traditions. But these fac-

1. Hans Kohn, *The Idea of Nationalism: A Study of Its Origins and Background* (New York, 1944), 10–20, especially 10, 12.

tors in themselves are not regarded as components of nationality. They are rather prerequisites or raw materials, conducive to the development of the psychological manifestation.

The psychological character of this approach to nationalism deserves emphasis because it carries with it certain important corollaries. It would follow, to begin with, that since nationalism is a form of group loyalty, it is not generically different from other forms of group loyalty. From this it would follow further that nationality is not an absolute condition, but a relative one, for loyalty evolves gradually by imperceptible degrees, both in the individual and in the group; it ebbs and flows; and it is modified by contingencies. If nationalism is a relative manifestation, this fact would also imply that various national groups must vary in the degree of completeness or intensity of their nationality, and further that various elements of the population within the nationality group must vary in the extent to which they share the sense of group identity and the commitment to the group purpose. This, in turn, would mean that loyalty to the nation must exist in the individual not as a unique or exclusive allegiance, but as an attachment concurrent with other forms of group loyalty—to family, to church, to school, and to the individual's native region. Since it exists concurrently, it must also, as has been suggested, partake of the nature of these other forms of loyalty.

All of these corollaries are accepted, explicitly or implicitly, by most writers on nationalism. They are consonant with the theory which writers have found most tenable, and when historians are directly engaged in the specific study of the growth of nationalism, their analysis usually gives due weight to the variable, impalpable, evolutionary, and sometimes partially developed nature of the manifestations of nationalism. In such a context, the historian seldom loses sight of the fact that nationalism is a tendency, an impulse, an attitude of mind rather than an objective, determinate thing.

If the historian had only to deal with the question of the extent to which a group has become national, he would probably never treat it in other terms than these, which are so consistent with his theory and with his general disposition to take a functional rather than a formalistic view of historical phenomena.

But in another—a second—aspect, the historian uses the concept of nationalism in answering a second question which frequently arises in history, as to the validity of a given group's exercising autonomous powers. In human affairs, society has long since agreed to the proposition that when a multiplicity of individuals stand in a certain relation to one another—or to put it more concretely, when they form a community—they incur certain obligations toward one another which they would not have if they were not a community, and that the community has a "right," or enjoys a sanction, to enforce these obligations and to defend itself as a community, if necessary by the use of coercion and violence—which would otherwise be taboo. But the sanction to exercise these powers and the determination of whom they can rightfully be exercised upon—individuals or minority groups—depend entirely upon whether the body seeking to exercise them and the individuals upon whom they are to be exercised form a true community. Thus, the nature of the relation between the individuals involved, rather than the ethical character of the acts performed, actually becomes the standard for judging the rightfulness of the acts. Here the nation occupies a particularly crucial role, for of all human communities it is the one to which this power of regulation, control, coercion, punitive action, and so on, is especially assigned. Therefore in any given case where a body of people contests the exercise of authority by another body over it (and history is full of such cases), the crucial question is fundamentally whether the two are parts of a single community, or, more specifically, a single nation, in which case the exercise is valid; or whether they belong to separate communities, or nations, in which case it is not valid. In such a case, the determination of nationalism ceases to be a merely descriptive matter; it becomes an evaluative matter, for the attribution of nationality sanctions the acts of the group claiming autonomous powers. Further, this determination cannot be made by psychological analysis, which offers only relativistic, qualified, balanced terms, and does not yield yes-or-no, all-or-nothing answers. Such analysis can tell what measure of nationality a group has attained, for that is a question of degree; but it cannot determine whether the group has attained the measure of nationality appropriate to the exercise of national powers, for that is a categorical or classificatory question. The categorical nature of the problem he is dealing with, therefore, tends to draw the historian unconsciously away from his theory. Where his theory tells him that nationalism is a relative thing, existing in partial form, his practice may impel him to treat it as an absolute thing, existing in full or not at all. (For instance, national loyalty may vary enormously, or in subtle degrees, but national citizenship does not vary at all—a man is a citizen or he is an alien.) Where his theory emphasizes the view that national loyalty is a form of group loyalty, and generically similar to other forms of group loyalty, his practice impels him to treat it as a unique form of devotion, potentially antithetical to other forms of loyalty such as regional loyalty. (He even uses a different word for this loyalty—the word "allegiance"). Where his theory recognizes that nationalism is a form of emotion, and that, like other forms of emotion, it will attain varying degrees of intensity in varying segments of the population, his practice is to treat it as a matter of standard, fixed specifications (the citizen is either "loyal" or "disloyal").

Thus, the shift from a descriptive to a classificatory approach is also a shift from a psychological (or functional) approach to an institutional (or formalistic) approach. It is a deceptively easy and, at times, almost imperceptible shift to make, because the nation is, of course, in an extremely real and important sense, an institutional thing. The impulse of nationalism fulfills itself in the formation of the national institutions, and while a nation is truly a body of people who feel themselves to be one, it is also, quite as truly, the organized body of people who share this feeling, together with the organization which the feeling prompts them to set up.

But though these two concepts flow rather naturally into one another, they are in many ways inconsistent with and even antithetical to one another. One treats the nation as an abstraction having no physical reality (only on a political map, which is itself an abstraction, is it possible to see where one nation ends and another begins). But institutionally, the nation assumes all the concreteness which a census of population, an inventory of resources, an army and navy, and all the apparatus of public authority can give to it. In psychological terms, a nation exists only subjectively, as a convergence of men's loyalties; without this convergence there would be no nation. But once the nation has been institutionalized, men tend to regard the institution itself as transcendent—a thing on which the loyalties of men ought to converge simply because it does exist. Again, in theory, the nation survives as a unit because people continue to feel a psychological unity. But in operative terms, its survival may depend upon the power of the state to override divisive impulses and to control an aggregation of people as if they were one, even despite a significant degree of reluctance on the part of some of those who are being thus united.

In short, the institutional view does violence to the historian's theory, for it pulls him in the direction of treating nationality as objective rather than subjective, absolute rather than relative, and total rather than partial. It also impels him to isolate it from and place it in antithesis to other forms of group loyalty, instead of keeping in view the fact that the psychological ingredients of nationalism are the same as for other forms of human identification with large groups. Finally, and most important, it leads him to give a valuative rather than a purely descriptive property to his attribution of nationality.

The political state as we know it today possesses tremendously powerful devices for making the institutional aspects of nationality seem more real than the psychological aspects. With the paraphernalia of symbols (the flag, the crown, the national anthem, the constitution) it evokes the emotional responses of patriotism. By such means as citizenship, territorial boundaries, and sovereignty *vis-à-vis* other political states, it sets up demarcations which separate and even differentiate human beings on one side of an imaginary geographical line from human beings on the other side of this line. Even though it should be situated upon a terrain which lacks any natural geographical unity, it can employ the concept of a "common territory" so persuasively as to create the illusion of commonality for geographically diverse areas, whereas, in the absence of common political jurisdiction, real features of geographical unity will not be recognized as the basis for a commonality. As Karl Deutsch has suggested, there is no reasoning more circular than the argument that Detroit and San Francisco, for instance, are "united" by lying within a "common territory," while Detroit and Toronto are "separated" by not lying in a common territory.[2]

In the same way, although a state may have a population which is varied and lacking in homogeneity, it can bring the concept of a "common citizenship" to bear. By this concept it can create the illusion of an affinity between individuals whose interests may be in conflict, whose cultures may be diverse, and whose values may be antagonistic, while it in-

2. Karl W. Deutsch, *Nationalism and Social Communication: An Inquiry into the Foundations of Nationality* (New York and London, 1953), 4.

hibits the full recognition of features of commonality between individuals who do not share the same citizenship.

To say this is, of course, not to deny that most political states are based upon very real factors of nationality which make for their separateness and identity. The congruence of the nation and the political state is, indeed, very complete in many cases, for political nationality tends to follow cultural boundaries when it is forming and to reinforce the cultural separateness of a national population after it has formed. But the operative importance of formalistic features such as citizenship, jurisdiction, territoriality, and so on, tends to convey an image of nationality which is far more institutional than psychological. And this concept is, of course, far more categorical, more absolute, more unitary in its implications: the individual either is or is not a citizen; the public authority either does or does not have jurisdiction; the disputed area lies either inside or outside of the national boundary. None of these matters is partial, any more than sovereignty itself is partial—and sovereignty, it used to be said, is like virginity in that it cannot be surrendered in part.

The sheer weight and momentum of modern institutional nationalism make it difficult for the historian to resist the institutional concept, especially when this concept is, in certain respects, entirely valid and realistic. He is himself, after all, not only an historian but also a "national" of one or another nation; he is the creature of an age which tends to reify the nation, the inhabitant of a globe which is commonly believed to be composed of one hundred and three "nations" more or less—each with one vote in the U.N., and therefore each, as a nation, interchangeable with each other nation. In theory, he knows that there is a great difference between the nation and the political state, but in a world where all the states claim to be nations and all the nations try to be states, it is difficult for him to remember that they are two things.

When he is offered a complete set of "nations" neat in order, precise in outline, manageable in number, and all alphabetically arranged in the *World Almanac*, it requires a real effort of imagination and even of will on his part to think of the world as composed of inchoate, amorphous congeries of human beings, confused in their groupings, indeterminate in their alignments, and overwhelming in their number.

Nevertheless, historians are now to some extent on guard against mistaking the nation as a people for the nation as a state. Certainly most treatises on nationalism warn them against confusing nationality itself with the forms which the nationalistic impulse has projected.[3] But they are often not on guard against the subtle shift from describing the nationalistic impulse as a socio-psychological phenomenon to using the attribution of nationalism as a valuative device. For it is a paradox not generally recognized that the historian cannot make a simple descriptive observation about the degree of group cohesion among an aggregate of people without inadvertently registering a valuative judgment as to the validity of the powers which this aggregation may assert for itself. If he were applying a standard of ethics, it would be recognized at once as a valuative standard, but since he seemingly applies only a measure of relationships, it is easy to overlook the valuative implications. Yet the concept of the nature of the group may be more crucial than the concept of right and wrong in determining the validity of acts committed in the name of nationality. For even the Declaration of Independence did not proclaim the right of everyone to resist tyranny, but rather the right of "one people to dissolve the political bonds which have connected them with another." The separability of "one people" and "another" was a necessary prerequisite to the dissolution of the bonds. Conversely, a belief that bonds

3. Kohn, *The Idea of Nationalism*, 18–20; Carlton J. H. Hayes, *Essays on Nationalism* (New York, 1928), 4–5.

ought to be dissolved would make it necessary to believe also that the Americans were "one people" and the British "another."

Indeed modern democratic thought, by adopting the view that the ultimate authority lies in the people, has brought us to the point where the nature of the association which constitutes a people takes on almost as mystical a quality as once pertained to the nature of the anointment which a crowned king received from God. For the major premise of democracy, that the majority shall rule, is predicated upon the assumption that there is a body of people forming a single whole of such clearly determinate number that more than half of the number may be recognized as forming a majority. Unless the minority really is identified with and part of such a whole, the decisions of the majority lack any democratic sanction. The majority is arithmetical, but the whole—of which the majority is more than 50 percent—is mystical.

For instance, if the Magyars under Louis Kossuth were a "people," they were morally justified in their "revolution" against the old Austrian Empire in 1848; they were "patriots"; and their uprising was a "war of independence." But if not, they were morally censurable for "rebelling"; they were "traitors"; and their uprising was an "insurrection." If the Croats who, in turn, fought against Kossuth's authority were a "people," then Kossuth was a "tyrant," and his measures against them were "acts of oppression"; but if not, he was merely a resolute leader defending his "nation" against "disruptive elements" that sought to "subvert" it. There is hardly any historical situation for which semantics are more crucial: Indeed, where the concept of nationality is involved, the virtue or the evil of a man's act may not be determined by the character of the act itself, nor even by the motives for which it is executed, but entirely by the status of the group in whose behalf it is undertaken.

In sum, when the historian attributes nationality to any group, he establishes a presumption in favor of any acts involving an exercise of autonomy which the group may commit; when he denies nationality, he establishes a presumption against any exercise of autonomy. The attribution of nationality therefore involves a sanction—a sanction for the exercise of autonomy or self-determination.[4]

Of all the consequences of the shift toward an institutional concept, this insertion of the valuative or sanctioning implication has had, perhaps, the most sweeping consequences. Indeed, the element of sanction is almost the essence of this concept. It carries with it some far-reaching implications, and these implications have had such pervasive effects upon the interpretation of history that it becomes important to examine and recognize them.

To begin with, it is fundamental that once nationality is conceived to imply rights or powers for the national group, and not merely to describe the degree of cohesiveness within that group, the historian will begin to be influenced in his reasoning not only by his observations about the degree of cohesion, but also by his beliefs about the justice or the merits of the group's claim to autonomy. Instead of arguing forward, therefore, from the observation that the evidence indicates a high degree of psychological coherence (nationality), and that consequently the group was justified in acting as a nation, he may be tempted to argue backward, from the conviction that since the group was, in his opinion, justified in exercising national powers, it must have had, psychologically, a high degree of cohesiveness. What appears on its face to be a mere observational or descriptive statement about psychological attitudes may be in fact an indirect form of argumentation about the validity of a set of political claims.

---

4. Rupert Emerson, in *From Empire to Nation: The Rise to Self-Assertion of Asian and African Peoples* (Cambridge, Mass., 1960), 134, speaks of the nation as "the community which legitimizes the state."

In other words, the writer who is trying to rationalize a position need no longer do so with legal or ethical arguments, which are the normal medium of rationalization. Instead, he is likely to rationalize it in terms of cultural and psychological analysis, applying a criterion of relationship rather than a criterion of ethics or of formal sanctions.

On the surface, it often appears today that the nineteenth-century writer on nations who used to argue freely in abstract and formalistic terms—about "compact," "sovereignty," and the like—has been replaced in the twentieth century by a writer who takes a functional approach, tracing the gradual cultural development by which a "people" becomes self-consciously united, and measuring the extent of governmental power in terms of the degree of social need. But to an astonishing degree, the old formalism and the new functionalism come to the same thing. In the past, the ultimate sanction for a government was the possession of sovereignty; today its ultimate sanction is that it acts for a population which constitute a "people" in the special sense which entitles them to self-determination. But the effect, in either case, is to ascribe indirectly a right to the exercise of autonomy.

A second implication of the valuative aspect of nationalism is that it inhibits the historian's recognition of the generic similarity between national loyalty and other forms of group loyalty. It does this because national loyalty, in its valuative sense, must be singular, if not indeed unique. This inhibition cuts off a number of useful insights. It prevents the historian from seeing that in situations where nationalism and sectionalism are both at work they are not necessarily polar or antithetical forces, even though circumstances may cause them to work in opposition to one another. Nationalism, in fact, may be the terminal result of a full development of strong sectional forces, while sectionalism may be an emergent nationalism which has not yet matured.

At a deeper level, this inhibition may blind the historian

to the fact that national loyalty, far from being opposed to
other loyalties, is in fact strengthened by incorporating them.
Harold Guetzkow, in discussing the creation of international
loyalties, makes this point clearly: "The behaviorist leads us
to believe that strong family, local and national loyalties are
helpful in building international loyalties. The analyst assures
us that loyalty is attachable to various objects—an international object as well as a national object. If loyalty is a generalized way of responding, the stronger the loyalty pattern
in a given individual—no matter what its object—the easier
it will be to build loyalties." Guetzkow also quotes the blunter
statement of A. M. Rose that "people can have loyalty to two
[or more] groups or two sets of values, even when these
groups or values are in conflict." [5]

Going a step beyond Guetzkow, Morton Grodzins argues,
in *The Loyal and the Disloyal*, that other loyalties not only
are conducive to strong national loyalty, but are even indispensable to it. "Other loyalties," he says "are . . . the most
important foundation of democratic national loyalty. . . .
The welter of non-national loyalties makes a direct national
loyalty a misnomer. It does not exist. Loyalties are to specific groups, specific goals, specific programs of action. Populations are loyal to the nation as a by-product of satisfactions
achieved within non-national groups, because the nation is
believed to symbolize and sustain these groups. From this
point of view, one is loyal not to nation but to family, business, religion, friends. One fights for the joys of his pinochle
club when he is said to fight for his country." [6]

5. Harold Guetzkow, *Multiple Loyalties* (Princeton, 1955), 37, 39. Also,
Merle Curti, in *The Roots of American Loyalty* (New York, 1948), 47,
says, "Local and regional loyalties did not necessarily conflict with loyalty
to the nation."
6. Morton Grodzins, *The Loyal and the Disloyal: Social Boundaries of
Patriotism and Treason* (Chicago, 1956), 29. See also Morton Grodzins,
"The Basis of National Loyalty," *Bulletin of the Atomic Scientists*, VII
(December, 1951), 356–62.

Historians frequently write about national loyalty as if it were exclusive, and inconsistent with other loyalties, which are described as "competing" or "divided" and which are viewed as detracting from the primary loyalty to the nation. Yet it is self-evident that national loyalty flourishes not by challenging and overpowering all other loyalties, but by subsuming them all in a mutually supportive relation to one another. The strength of the whole is not enhanced by destroying the parts, but is made up of the sum of the parts. The only citizens who are capable of strong national loyalty are those who are capable of strong group loyalty, and such persons are likely to express this capacity in their devotion to their religion, their community, and their families, as well as in their love of country. The nationalism which will utilize this capacity most effectively, therefore, is not the one which overrides and destroys all other objects of loyalty, but the one which draws them all into one transcendent focus. A well-known phrase runs, "for God, for Country, and for Yale"—not "for God, or for Country, or for Yale."

A third implication of the evaluative aspect of nationalism is that it sometimes impels the historian to deny nationality to groups of whom he morally disapproves, even though the group may in every sense fulfill his theoretical criteria of nationality. For instance, if a fascist group should claim a separate nationality, the historian, in theory, need only ask whether the members of the group do in fact feel themselves to be one and whether the regime which they are setting up is established "with the consent of the governed." But in fact he can scarcely accord nationality to a group without also seeming to accord some degree of sanction to the cause for which the group stands—namely the cause of fascism. Since he is reluctant to do this, he tends, as a lawyer would say, to "distinguish" the case and to rationalize a basis for denying the nationalism of the group in question. Most historians, if confronted with the abstract proposition that people who practice wrong cannot be united by deep cultural commonalities, would dismiss it as absurd. Yet the functional implications of the concept of nationalism are such that historians in fact are frequently unwilling to recognize cultural commonalities of this kind in the case of groups whose values they reject.

A fourth warping result of the same evaluative tendency is the belief that nationality must be based upon peculiarly deep-seated cultural affinities among a people, since only such fundamental ties would justify the kind of power and unique autonomy which is ascribed to the national group. No trivial or unworthy grounds for association could justify a group in claiming the kind of immunity from external control, and the power to abuse internal minorities, which are accorded to a nation. Therefore, when the historian is faced with manifestations of nationalism, he will, almost by reflex, begin his analysis of these manifestations by searching for profound common elements in the culture of the group involved. Indeed, there is a standard formula, accepted by all the authorities on the subject, which enjoins him to give his attention to "certain objective bonds [which] delimit a social group, [such as] common descent, language, territory, political entity, customs and tradition, and religion." [7] Accordingly, students of nationalism have emphasized the growth of the vernacular languages in Western Europe; they have ransacked folklore and the popular culture for any features which illustrate a common tradition among the people. Also they have often treated the territorial area which finally eventuated, no matter how fortuitously, from any nationalist movement as the logical

7. Kohn, *The Idea of Nationalism*, 6–10, 13–14. These criteria, so clearly stated by Kohn, are not distinctively his, but are standard criteria among students of nationalism. For a critique of the "illusions concerning the basis of nations and nationalism," however, see Boyd C. Shafer, *Nationalism: Myth and Reality* (New York, 1955), 13–56.

fulfillment of a mystic impulse among the folk to unite a "common territory." The true believer who found it an evidence of divine providence that all our seaports have harbors evinced no greater faith than the historian who defines all the land within a given national jurisdiction as a "common territory" and then uses the assumption that it is a common territory to prove the validity of the national jurisdiction.

This does not mean, of course, that the common cultural factors are not real or, in many cases, of immense importance. Indeed, some of the oldest and most famous nations—England, Japan, and France, among others—lend support to the contention that a population isolated by physical or linguistic or other barriers may develop an extremely clear-cut cultural identity, which may prove by far the most enduring and most cohesive basis of nationality.

But the very preoccupation of historians with classic examples such as these has perhaps led them to overemphasize the cultural component of nationality,[8] and to assume too simple an equation between nationality and culture. There is, of course, no doubt that commonalities in culture have a primary role in generating the spirit of nationalism, but secondarily there is also the reverse effect that movements for political statehood, which are commonly regarded as nationalist movements, tend to claim commonalities of culture as a sanction for their objectives; and if these cultural elements do not exist in reality, the nationalist movement may fabricate them. It is notorious, for instance, that Gaelic was culturally a dying speech in Ireland, and Welsh a dying speech in Wales,

8. Emerson (*From Empire to Nation*, 103) comments that "theoretical approaches to the concepts of nation and nationalism have been dominated by the European experience, even though this European-derived framework fitted the facts in much of the rest of the world in only indifferent fashion at the best."

and that both have received a somewhat artificial rejuvenation because of the zeal of Irish and Welsh nationalists.[9]

In this instance, we are confronted by common cultural factors that are attenuated, yet still very real. But it has seemed increasingly evident in the last quarter of a century that many "nationalist" movements have a minimum of common cultural content and that the impulse which moves them is primarily a negative political reaction against an existing regime (especially a colonial regime). For instance, some of the new nations of Africa appear to consist of territories which, instead of coinciding with any unified culture areas of their own, correspond to the administrative divisions laid down for purposes of bureaucratic convenience by their former colonial masters. It is perhaps the final irony of European colonialism that it is likely to fix the patterns and alignment of the nationalism which replaces it and utterly repudiates it.[10] When a new "nation" is being formed in such

9. Shafer (*Nationalism*, 189) remarks that "within groups not yet nations, linguistic studies were the first signs of a rising national consciousness. They were also consciously made to stimulate it." On the Welsh language, artificially sustained, see Sir Reginald Coupland, *Welsh and Scottish Nationalism: A Study* (London, 1954), 357–66.

10. Emerson (*From Empire to Nation*, 60) observes: "Indeed, the creation of nations themselves is in some instances, as in the Philippines and Ghana, to be attributed primarily to the bringing together of diverse stocks under a single imperial roof. . . . Uncertain as the precise meaning of the term 'national character' may be, it is beyond doubt that the character of the nations now coming into the world has been greatly influenced by the type of colonial regime to which they have been subjected." The heavily negative character of nationalism in modern Africa is suggested by Thomas Hodgkin, in *Nationalism in Colonial Africa* (New York, 1956), 21–23, when he asks, "At what stage is it reasonable to describe a movement of colonial protest or opposition to European authority as 'nationalist' in respect of its aims and character?" and answers, "My own inclination is to use the term nationalist in a broad sense to describe any organization or group that explicitly asserts the rights, claims, and aspirations of a given African society (from the level of the language group to that of Pan-Africa) in opposition to European authority, whatever its institutional form and objectives."

circumstances, it will behoove the leaders to claim for their country all the attributes which have been regarded as giving a sanction to the older and more organic nations. If the highest of all sanctions—a national culture—is lacking, the spokesmen of the "nationalism" in question will be impelled to fabricate or simulate the cultural factors which are needed as proofs of the validity of their nation. Such simulation will, indeed, not be anything new, for the spokesmen of nationalism have always exaggerated the degree of separateness and coherence of the national group, even in the oldest and most fully defined nations, and these nations have always relied upon a certain amount of carefully cultivated mythology to reinforce the unity of their people. Their success in fostering a belief in a common identity has often been an essential part of the process of forging the identity itself; the belief has operated as a kind of self-fulfilling prophecy. If the members of a population are sufficiently persuaded that they have cause to be a unified group, the conviction itself may unify them, and thus may produce the nationalism which it appears to reflect.

But while it is to be expected that nationalist leaders will if necessary contrive a synthetic culture for a particular state, it is all the more vital that the historian should be forever alert to distinguish between a genuine culture generating a genuine nationalism, and a trumped-up nationalism generating the pretense or illusion of a culture. Yet there are certain prevailing traits among historians which limit their capacity to maintain this distinction. For one thing, the historian's conviction that he has a professional duty to ransack all the sources for every scrap of evidence means that he will usually find some data, no matter how tenuous, which can be construed to "prove" the existence of the pretended culture. Further, the historian is not only a historian; he is also a man and a citizen, and his national loyalties as a citizen may sometimes neutralize his impartiality as a historian; it is well known that history has often been a handmaiden of patriotism. Finally, the examples of nationalism which have dominated the historical imagination are deeply rooted, clearly defined, long-sustained nations, and this very preoccupation prompts the historian to think of nationalism as the outgrowth of a cultural group identity of unique depth and pervasiveness—in short, to regard nationalism simply as an aspect of culture. This impulse accords well with his deep-seated moral feeling that no entity ought to enjoy the sanctions which pertain to nationality unless it is based upon a deeply rooted culture.

To repeat, then, the historian has an extremely strong predisposition to equate nationality and culture. This predisposition is so strong that if other important sources of nationalism should exist, recognition of them would be inhibited under our present rationale of nationalism. A question arises, therefore, whether other important sources of nationalism do exist, and, if so, what their nature may be.

There is certainly at least one other important factor besides common culture which may bind an aggregate of individuals together, and this is community of interest, not in the narrow sense of economic advantage only, but in the broad sense of welfare and security through membership in society. It is axiomatic that people tend to give their loyalty to institutions which "protect" them—that is, safeguard their interests—and political allegiance throughout history has been regarded as something given reciprocally in return for protection. Historians have clearly recognized this relationship, and one may add that historians of nationalism have often called attention to it. Thus, when modern nationalism was in its infancy, Voltaire defined the word *patrie* in terms of community of interest. Among modern historians, Hans Kohn affirms that a nationality derives part of its strength from being regarded as "a source of economic well being"; Karl Deutsch states that when he and his collaborators were "studying cases of successful amalgamation" of diverse groups into a single nation, "they found that it was apparently important for each of the participating territories or populations to gain some valued services or opportunities"; Boyd Shafer is particularly explicit in pointing out that for many nationalists "devotion to the national welfare . . . after all was but devotion to their own welfare," that monarch and middle classes at the inception of modern nationalism "found mutual benefit in the joint extension of their mutual interests, which they also could conceive of as *the* national interests," and that these parties were like "stockholders with voting rights in the common enterprise, the nation." One of the clearest affirmations of this idea was made by Harry M. Schulman in a statement to Louis L. Snyder, quoted in Snyder's *The Meaning of Nationalism*. Nationalism, said Schulman, is not a *we*-sentiment, but "a form of homeostasis, the equilibration of opposed vested interests within a series of specialized interdependent functional systems." [11]

But despite the presence of theoretical statements such as these, when historians turn to the examination of nationalism in specific cases, they often seem to neglect the factor of common interest, and to focus their attention very heavily upon common cultural factors. This neglect—curious in any case—has been all the more strange in view of the fact that an emphasis upon the importance of self-interest would fit in well with certain points which the historians customarily stress. One of these is the idea that modern nationalism has risen concurrently with modern democracy. Hans Kohn, for

11. "Quand ceux qui possèdent, comme moi, des champs et des maisons, s'assemblent pour leurs intérêts communs, j'ai ma voix dans cette assemblée; je suis une partie du tout, une partie de la communauté, une partie de la souveraineté, voilà ma patrie." Voltaire, *Dictionnaire Philosophique*, under the entry, "Patrie"; Kohn, *The Idea of Nationalism*, 17; Karl W. Deutsch and others, *Political Community and the North Atlantic Area* (Princeton, 1957), 55; Shafer, *Nationalism*, 100–105, 115; Louis L. Snyder, *The Meaning of Nationalism* (New Brunswick, N.J., 1954), 83. See also Curti, *The Roots of American Loyalty*, Chap. 4, "The Economics of Loyalty," 92–121, 161.

instance, regards this correlation as so close that he denies the existence of any fully developed nationalism prior to the French Revolution.[12] In this connection it is clear that the rise of democracy represents an admission of the masses to certain civic privileges and expectations of property ownership —that is, to a stake in society. The nation state, of course, served as the instrument for the protection of this stake, and the people's spirit of loyalty to the nation was partly their response to that which protected their interests. Until democracy gave them an interest to protect, they were incapable of this response—incapable of nationalism. Hector St. Jean de Crèvecoeur recognized this factor of self-interest very clearly in 1782, when he explained why European immigrants to America proved so quick to develop a loyalty to their new country: "What attachment can a poor European emigrant have for a country where he had nothing? The knowledge of a language, the love of a few kindred as poor as himself, were the only cords that tied him: his country is now that which gives him land, bread, protection, and consequence. *Ubi panis, ibi patria* is the motto of all emigrants." [13]

Another well-recognized aspect of nationalism, into which the factor of self-interest again fits clearly, is the invigorating effect which war has had upon national spirit. Heinrich von Treitschke reduced this to a simple and oft-repeated formula: "Again and again, it has been proved that it is war which turns a people into a nation." Frederick Hertz, who deplored the fact as much as Treitschke rejoiced in it, agreed: "War could be called the greatest instrument of national unification, but for the fact that it also fosters the growth of forces which often imply a new menace to national unity." [14]

12. Kohn, *The Idea of Nationalism*, 3, 10.
13. Hector St. Jean de Crèvecoeur, *Letters from an American Farmer* (London, 1782, in Everyman's Library, New York, 1912), 41–44.
14. Frederick Hertz, *Nationality in History and Politics* (New York, 1944), 37, 218–19. Treitschke is quoted in Shafer, *Nationalism*, 45.

How does war produce this effect? No doubt it does so in a variety of ways and by appealing to a variety of impulses, some of which are irrational. But certainly one of the effects of war is to reorient the pattern of conflicts of interest within any national population. In times of peace, the diversity of interests of various kinds tends to divide the people into antagonistic groups—what James Madison called factions and what we now call pressure groups—and these groups compete for control of public policy. Their relation to one another is primarily one of rivalry. Even in wartime these rivalries will continue; but they tend to become secondary, for war subjects all interests to a common danger and to more vital danger than they ever incur from one another. In the presence of such danger, all interests tend to work together. In this way, war harnesses the motives of self-interest, which ordinarily pull in various directions, and causes them all to pull in the same direction and thus to reinforce the spirit of nationalism.

Despite the importance of democracy as a means of enlarging the community of interest, despite the importance of war as a means of drawing interests which would otherwise be divisive into conjunction, and despite the close correlations which historians have drawn between nationalism on the one hand and democracy and war on the other, these same historians have, for the most part, still failed to follow the logic of their own arguments, and have continued to explain specific nationalistic movements in terms of culture. One has only to read Louis L. Snyder's exhaustive book-length review of the treatments of nationalism by historians, political scientists, economists, social psychologists, psychoanalysts, and psychiatrists to perceive how constantly social scientists of all kinds have relied either upon cultural factors or upon social behavior that results from cultural factors as the master key to nationalism.

This commitment extends far. It controls the thinking of

many historians so completely that whenever a population manifests nationalistic tendencies, the historian, by reflex, reaches for evidence of the growth of cultural bonds as the only conceivable means of explanation. Conversely, whenever deep cleavages appear in a previously nationalized group he hypothesizes the evolution of a separate, new culture as the basis of a new nationalism, and husbands every scrap of evidence, however tenuous, which lends itself to his hypothesis. Although he perhaps recognizes the importance of interests in the abstract, he almost never focuses upon them when analyzing a specific national movement.

To argue that the factor of common interests is an important and somewhat neglected element in nationalism, and that it ought to receive substantial attention, does not mean at all that the concept of interest should replace the concept of culture. The point is rather that nationalism rests on two psychological bases rather than one—feeling of common culture on the one hand and feeling of common interests on the other. It is questionable whether either basis can support a superstructure of nationality without the other. If the historian will recognize this dualism, he will not only possess an effective working concept, but will also free himself from his present compulsion to prove a growth of cultural unity every time he observes an intensification of nationalism and to prove the emergence of a new culture every time a dissident group proclaims its solidarity in nationalistic terms.

Here, then, are a number of propositions about the historian's treatment of nationalism: that he conceives of it abstractly, in sound theoretical terms, regarding it as a form of group loyalty, psychologically similar to other forms of group loyalty, and having the subjective, relativistic, developmental qualities which other forms of group loyalty possess; that the close relation between nationalism and the political state warps the historian's view and causes him to treat it functionally as a monolithic form of loyalty, in antithesis to other forms of group loyalty, instead of recognizing that it is associated with and even derived from those other loyalties; that his use of the concept as a sanction to validate the demands of some groups for autonomy, while denying the similar demands of other groups, leads him into a fallacious correlation between the ethical rightness of a group's policies and the objective separateness of the group's identity; that this valuative use of the concept also impels him to explain the origins of nationalism in terms of deep-seated, long-enduring natural affinities among a people, or in other words to rely too heavily upon cultural factors in his explanation, even where they are tenuous; that this cultural emphasis has, in turn, caused him frequently to overlook factors of self-interest, which have been vital in many historic situations in the integration or in the disintegration of national loyalties.

If these general propositions have any validity, it should be possible to test them by applying them to specific historical situations. Any reader of this essay will perhaps test them in terms of the historical treatment of the nationality or national movement with which he himself is most familiar. For myself, they can most readily be applied in the field of American history. The rest of this essay, therefore, is devoted to a consideration of their applicablity at that point in American history where the question of nationalism is most critical and most complex—namely in the crisis leading to the Civil War.

It is a truism that because of the vast extent of the United States and its great physiographic variety, major areas within the Union have often found their interests in conflict, and the alignment on public issues has followed geographical lines far more often than would occur in a smaller or more homogeneous country. These geographically aligned differentials have, in fact, been a pervasive factor and have presented themselves in many different forms. At times, such as the period of Jacksonian democracy or the Populist revolt, the divisions between East and West have seemed more fundamental than those between North and South, and careful analysis has always shown that these regional differentiations extended beyond a mere dualism. The West, with its frontier attributes, played a distinctive role even during the period when North-South antagonisms were most acute, and indeed the struggle which came to a crisis in 1861 has been seen by Frederick Jackson Turner to consist of a rivalry between the North and the South to draw the West into their respective orbits. Even while North and South were approaching the climactic rivalry of the Civil War, internal conflicts also made themselves felt at a different level, as issues arose between industrial and agricultural areas within the North, or between plantation belts and backwoods districts within the South.

Historians speak of these areas in which distinctive groups are localized or concentrated as sections, and they recognize sectionalism (the tension between such areas) as one of the major themes of American history. In most cases of sectional rivalry, the question of nationalism has not been involved, for the people of one sectional area have not called into question the Union which they share with the rival section, and the loyalties which they give to their own area have not impinged directly upon their national loyalty to the Union. Even when sectional bitterness reached the emotional pitch which it developed in 1896 the rivals sought only to impose their policies upon one another within the Union, not to sever their ties with one another by disrupting the Union.

In the era between 1848 and 1861, however, America's geographically aligned rivalries were drawn into a pattern of intense conflict between the North and the South, and the group loyalties of the people in the South were focused upon a Southern republic in a way which undercut the American nationalism that had previously focused upon the Union. In this case, then, Southernism, instead of working sectionally within a framework of nationalism, tended to take on the character of nationalism itself and to break down the existing pattern of nationalism. Since the Southern movement began as a sectional reaction against this existing pattern, historians frequently evaluate the conflict which developed in terms of sectionalism versus nationalism.

In strict logic the antithesis of sectionalism versus nationalism would not necessarily link one region (the South) with sectionalism, or the other region (the North) with nationalism. On the contrary, it might be argued that nationalistic forces in both the North and the South which placed the welfare of the Union above all regional values were pitted against sectional forces in both regions which gave primary values to regional objectives—such as, for the South, the protection of slavery in the territories or, for the North, the exclusion of slavery from the territories. Viewed in this way, the conflict might be said to involve the triumph of sectionalism over American nationalism within both regions and an ensuing conflict between Northern sectionalism and Southern sectionalism. Alternatively, it might also be argued that Northern group loyalty of the most fundamental kind found a focus in the Union formed in 1787, while Southern group loyalty, also of the deepest sort, found a new focus in a separate Southern republic. Regarded in this way, the conflict might be construed as, in fact, many historians do construe it—as a conflict between Northern (Union) nationalism and Southern (Confederate) nationalism.

Either of these formulations has a certain tenability in theory. In operative terms, however, the forces which saved the American Union were of course centered in the North and those which sought to disrupt it were centered in the South. Consequently it seemed natural afterward, in light of the Union's survival, to link each of the forces at work with one of the rival regions and to speak of nationalism as Northern and sectionalism as Southern.

This attribution, however, at once has the effect of bringing the valuative aspect of the concept of nationalism into
play. It clearly implies a sanction for the Northern position
—the sanction that the "people" involved in the crisis were
the American people, both North and South, since the Union
was the nation, whereas those in the South who "felt themselves to be one" were not one in the ultimate sense, since
the impulse which prompted their unity was sectional rather
than national. Of course, insofar as hindsight furnishes a
legitimate criterion, the conclusion, if not the reason, was
valid, for what the North defended has found fulfillment as
a nation and what the South defended has not. But the questionable feature of this reasoning is that it moves completely
away from the psychological or functional aspects of nationalism toward an analysis that is almost entirely institutional. It
has the effect of prejudging the question which is purportedly
under examination, settling by ascription a point which ought
to be settled by the evaluation of evidence. Instead of testing
the validity of Union and Confederacy as nations by examining the character of the group loyalties attached to them, it
bases a judgment of those group loyalties upon a prior assumption concerning the character, respectively, of the Union
and the Confederacy. By a trick of semantics it makes the
question of group loyalties irrelevant, the assumption being
that no matter what degree of cohesion or intensity these
loyalties may have attained, they are not "national" unless
they attach to a national institution. But the national institution is the result simply of success in fulfilling national impulses, and to say that the Southern impulse was not nationalism because it did not in the long run maintain its attempted
institutional form (the Southern Confederacy) is simply to
say that it was not nationalism because it was not successful.
Here one is reminded of the old riddle, Why is treason never
successful? Answer: Because if it is successful it is not treason.
In fact, the answer has a kind of truth, for treason, as a legal

offense, has to be institutionally defined. But nationalism should not be treated in such institutional terms.

I have already suggested that the element of sanction in the institutional concept sometimes makes it difficult for the historian to attribute nationality to movements of which he morally disapproves, since the attribution itself would imply that the movement has a kind of validity. This factor has certainly influenced the treatment of the question whether the Southern Confederacy was a nation, for the issue between the Union and the Confederacy also became an issue between freedom and slavery. To ascribe nationality to the South is to validate the right of a proslavery movement to autonomy and self-determination. Since few historians in the twentieth century have been willing to do this, their moral position has sometimes run counter to their theory of nationality and has impelled them to shirk the consequences of their own belief that group identity is the basis for autonomy. In other words, once the ethical question of the character of Southern institutions becomes linked with the factual question of the nature of the group loyalties in the South, it becomes very difficult for the historian to deal with the factual question purely on its own merits. If the finding that a majority of Southern citizens wanted a nation of their own is inseparable from the conclusion that the institution of slavery enjoyed a democratic sanction, it is always possible to reverse the reasoning and to argue that since slavery could not have enjoyed a democratic sanction, therefore the Southern people must not have been a "people" in the sense that would entitle them to want a nation of their own.

The position of the strongly antislavery historian on the question of Southern nationality tends to be particularly ironic, for he usually emphasizes more than do most writers the depth of the division between the North and the South. No one stresses more than he the profound authoritarian implications of slavery for the entire intellectual and social life of the South, and the sharpness of the contrast between this society, with its system of legalized caste status, and the free, democratic society of the North. Yet, after making this case, the antislavery historian often takes the view that the Southern assertion of nationality was not justified. Of course, he might simply follow the logic of his moral position and argue that war is justified if waged by one nation to compel another nation to give up slavery. But since he also attaches moral value to the right of self-determination, the recognition of Southern nationality would place him in a moral dilemma. The only way he can have his crusade against slavery and his right of self-determination too is to deny that the principle of self-determination is involved in the case of the crusade against slavery, or in short to deny that the slaveholding belligerent was endowed with such nationality as his own analysis has pretty well demonstrated.

This statement, it might be added, is not intended to deny or question the primacy of moral considerations. It may well be that the abolition of slavery is worth more to mankind than the right of self-determination of peoples, especially since slavery itself denies this right to the slaves. Even if coercion is an evil, it may not be the worst of evils, and a war of subjugation may well be justified by the emancipation of 3,950,000 slaves. It may also be, as Lincoln apparently believed, that the preservation, even by force, of the union which had been formalized by the Constitution of 1787 has a higher value than the purely voluntary self-determination of peoples. All I mean to argue is that a historian should not assert that he regards the right of self-determination as an absolute and then argue that it is not involved in cases where he is unwilling to apply it, or where he thinks some other value has a higher priority.

The equation of Northernism with nationalism and Southernism with sectionalism not only denies by prejudgment, and without actual analysis of group feelings, that the Southern movement could have been national; it also leads to an easy assumption that all Northern support for federal authority must have been nationalistic rather than sectional. But this view tends to obscure the fact that in the North as well as in the South there were deep sectional impulses, and support or nonsupport of the Union was sometimes a matter of sectional tactics rather than of national loyalty. For instance, Northern support for a sectional tariff or for sectional internal improvements, adopted by sectional majorities in the national government, was no less sectional than Southern opposition to them. Northern efforts to put the terminus of a Pacific railroad at Chicago were no less sectional than Southern efforts to put it at New Orleans. Northern determination to keep Negroes (rather than just slaves) out of the territories was no less sectional than Southern determination to carry them there. Even Northern support for Lincoln, who did not so much as run in most of the slave states in 1860, was perhaps just as sectional as Southern support for Breckenridge or for Bell, who did not carry a single free state.

But in the North, sectional forces tended to support a strong Union because it was evident that this Union was becoming one in which the sectional forces of the North would be dominant. Thus the national Union could be made the instrument of these sectional interests. The South, on the other hand, finding itself in a minority position, could not hope to secure national support for sectional objectives, nor even to keep sectional and national interests in coordination with one another, and therefore it was forced to choose between section and nation. If the proslavery elements seemed less nationalistic than the antislavery elements, it was not because one more than the other put peace or national harmony above the question of slavery—for neither of them did—but because the antislavery elements could expect, with their majority status, to employ the national authority for their purposes, while the proslavery forces could not. A Northerner could, and many Northerners did, support the Union for sectional reasons;[15] no Southerner was likely to support it for any other than national reasons.

The historian certainly should make some distinction between the nationalistic motive to support the Union as the embodiment of the "people" as a whole, and the tactical motive to use the authority of the Union for the promotion of sectional interests; but very often both of these impulses are called by the same name, i.e. nationalism.

If the antithesis of Northern nationalism and Southern sectionalism conceals the sectional motivation of much that was done through national means in the North, it also obscures another important reality: namely that a mixture of regional and national loyalties prevailed on both sides. These mixed loyalties did not seem ambiguous or inconsistent in the North because they were not in conflict there, whereas in the South they did conflict and, because they did, were made to seem evidence of what amounted to duplicity—as if devotion to the section in itself demonstrated alienation from the nation and as if nationalism could flourish only as regional loyalties withered away. But in fact, this view is mistaken. To take one concrete example, there was no equivocation on the part of Josiah Quincy of Massachusetts when he declared in 1811 that "the first public love of my heart is the Commonwealth of Massachusetts . . . the love of this Union grows out of this attachment to my native soil." Nor was there ambiguity in Sam Houston of Texas when he asserted that he was a Southerner and a Unionist too, with "a Southern heart, large enough, I trust, to embrace the whole Union if not the whole world"; nor in J. D. B. De Bow when he appealed to his fellow citizens, "as Southerners, as *Americans,*

15. Curti (*The Roots of American Loyalty,* 111) says, "Webster cleverly associated national interest with all the policies which his opponents declared to be sectional in character—tariffs, internal improvements . . . and restriction of the disposal of public lands in the West."

as MEN"; nor in Alexander H. Stephens of Georgia when he said, "I have a patriotism that embraces, I trust, all parts of the Union, . . . yet I must confess my feelings of attachment are most ardent toward that with which all my interests and associations are identified. . . . The South is my home, my fatherland." [16]

If the point here were only that the people of the South became trapped in a conflict of loyalties, it would hardly be worth stating; historians have known it as a truism for a long time. The point is rather that the Northerners and the Southerners were not distinguished from one another by a singularity of loyalty on one side and a multiplicity of loyalties on the other, as though one had been monogamous and the other polygamous. In fact, they both had multiple loyalties, and what distinguished them was that one, being in a majority, was able to keep all its loyalties coordinated, and therefore undivided, while the other, being in a minority, was not able to keep them coordinated, with the result that they did become divided. Multiple loyalties do not inherently produce conflict, and the question whether conflict will develop is entirely separate from the question whether loyalties are multiple.

It would be misleading in the extreme, however, to suggest that the valuative implication of the concept of nationalism has warped only the views of writers whose sympathies lie with the Union. For if it has led some of them to deny that the South was entitled to the sanction of nationality, and to make this denial with little or no reference to psychological realities, it has also led some writers whose sympathies lie

16. Josiah Quincy, in *Annals of Congress*, 11th Cong., 3rd Sess., col. 542 (Jan. 14, 1811); Sam Houston, in *Congressional Globe*, 31st Cong., 1st Sess., Appendix, 102 (Feb. 8, 1850); J. D. B. De Bow in *De Bow's Review*, III (May, 1847), 421, quoted in Robert F. Durden, "J. D. B. De Bow: Convolutions of a Slavery Expansionist," *Journal of Southern History*, XVII (November, 1951), 445; Alexander H. Stephens, in *Congressional Globe*, 28th Cong., 2nd Sess., Appendix, 313–14 (Jan. 25, 1845).

with the South to assert that the Southern claim to nation-
hood was validated by a complete cultural separateness, and
to make this assertion with equally small reference to the
cultural realities.

This is not to deny that there was distinctiveness in the
Southern culture. Southern conservatism, Southern hierarchy,
the cult of chivalry, the unmachined civilization, the folk
society, the rural character of the life, the clan values rather
than the commercial values—all had a deeply significant distinctiveness. But this is not quite the same as *separateness*, and
the efforts of historians to buttress their claim that the South
had a wholly separate culture, self-consciously asserting itself
as a cultural counterpart of political nationalism, have led,
on the whole, to paltry results. Southern writers, like the
nationalistic fabricators of culture mentioned above, issued
periodic manifestoes proclaiming that the South should have
its own literature, but their efforts failed for lack of support
from Southern readers. Southern educators likewise deplored
the infiltration of Yankee ideas in the schools, and when the
crisis was most acute, Southern students departed with great
fanfare from Northern colleges. But Southern education continued to be American education. In the economic area, a
few Southern fire-eaters made a conspicuous point of the
fact that they were wearing homespun, proclaiming the need
for a Southern economic self-sufficiency which was never
realized. But it is crucial that the advocates of a Southern
culture spent much of their time complaining that the South
would not accept their cultural program. Evidence of this
kind is a tenuous basis indeed for arguing that Southern nationalism sprang from a full-bodied Southern culture.[17] If

17. Important studies of cultural aspects of Southern nationalism are:
Jay Hubbell, "Literary Nationalism in the Old South," in *American
Studies in Honor of William K. Boyd*, ed. David Kelly Jackson (Durham,
N.C., 1940), 175–220. John S. Ezell, "A Southern Education for Southrons,"
Journal of Southern History, XVII (August, 1951), 303–27; Merle Curti,

historians had not been captives to the idea that nationality equates with culture, and that where there is separate nationalism there must be culture of equivalent separateness, they would probably have been far quicker to recognize how very thin the historical evidences of a separate Southern culture really are. They would also have been disposed to give more emphasis to the many important cultural features which Southerners shared with other nineteenth-century Americans: the common language which was a transatlantic modification of English, much the same in both the North and the South; the common religion of a people who were overwhelmingly evangelical and Protestant as well as Christian; the common political commitment to democratic institutions; the common system of values which exalted progress, material success, individual self-reliance, and distrust of authority; and the bumptious Americanism which scorned the "decadent monarchies" of the Old World.[18]

But some historians have been compulsively impelled to minimize these factors and to assert the existence of a separate Southern culture, just as others have been compulsively impelled to deny that the Southern movement represented a full nationalism. Just as the antislavery sympathizer finds that

---

The Growth of American Thought (New York, 1943), Chap. 17; Curtis Carroll Davis, *Chronicler of the Cavaliers: A Life of the Virginia Novelist, Dr. William A. Caruthers* (Richmond, 1953); Rollin G. Osterweis, *Romanticism and Nationalism in the Old South* (New Haven, 1949); Avery O. Craven, *The Growth of Southern Nationalism, 1848–1861* (Baton Rouge, 1953). Despite voluminous data, however, these studies lend themselves to the argument that a great effort was being made to create a sense of cultural separateness by self-conscious means, where it scarcely existed objectively. An unpublished paper by Stanley Bailis, written in my graduate seminar at Yale in 1958–59, develops this point very forcibly and effectively.

18. Hans Kohn, *American Nationalism: An Interpretative Essay* (New York, 1957), 106–21, demonstrates far better than most historians of the South the ambivalence in both the cultural affiliations and the loyalties of the people of the South on the eve of the Civil War.

his view of the degree of Southern nationalism cannot be formed on the merits of the question without reference to his conviction that the South had no right to thwart the forces working toward emancipation, so the Southern sympathizer finds that his view of the separateness of Southern culture cannot be formed on the merits of the question without reference to his conviction that the South enjoyed a full national identity, which finds its ultimate sanction in the possession of a full-fledged culture. The attribution of culture is evaluative for the question of nationality, just as the question of nationality, in turn, is evaluative for the justification of the acts of a group claiming a right to exercise autonomy.

To appreciate one important reason for the emphasis of modern historians upon the separateness of the Southern culture, it is necessary only to look at the difference in the way in which the defense of the South has been argued in the more remote and in the more recent past. From the Civil War until 1900, it was notorious that no Southerner seemed capable of writing on any aspect of the Civil War without including a lengthy disquisition on the legal and constitutional right of secession, with copious attention to the exact contractual understandings reached in 1787. But no historian has elaborated such arguments now for more than a generation. Why? Certainly not because the South no longer has defenders. The answer, I think, is that nowadays we do not couch our historical defenses in formalistic or legalistic terms. The sanction for what the South did in 1861 is no longer believed to be what it had agreed to in 1787. The sanction depends rather upon what the Southerners were in 1861—whether they constituted a people in the sense which entitled them to exercise what we now call autonomy or self-determination, rather than what we used to call sovereignty. But insofar as the same conclusion is reached as to whether the South was justified, and insofar as the reasons ostensibly leading to the conclusion may be in fact derived from the conclusion instead of the conclusion being derived from them, the great transformation since the ninteenth century from formalism to functionalism has perhaps not increased the realism of our thinking as much as we sometimes fondly imagine.

The significance of this subtle relation between descriptive observations and their valuative implications is not that it results in specious reasoning, from conclusion to premise instead of from premise to conclusion. It is rather that it tends to reduce the whole analysis to a set of oversimplified antitheses or polarities whose greatest fault is not that they are partisan, but simply that they do not explain anything.

If North and South fought; if one was a "nation" and one was not; if the people of one were "loyal" and those of the other were "disloyal"; or, on the other hand, if they constituted two diverse civilizations, then the investigator is under strong compulsion to reduce the complex forces of the 1850's to simplicity and to come up with antitheses which will fit these dualisms. Hence, we have had a series of sweeping and dramatic contrasts which present North and South in polar terms. Indeed the historiography of the subject is largely a record of how one pair of alternatives has been set up, only to be knocked down and replaced by another.

Thus we were once told that the South was a land of cavaliers, the North, an abode of Puritans; or that the South stood for states' rights, while the North stood for the federal supremacy. Later historians rejected these formulae as fallacious or superficial,[19] but the old yearning for a sharp, clear-cut antithesis still shaped historical thought, and two other, more formidable dualisms were advanced. One of these was pri-

---

19. The "Puritan versus cavalier" thesis began to fade in 1910, when Thomas J. Wertenbaker published *Patrician and Plebeian in Virginia* (Charlottesville, Va., 1910); the formalistic weakness of the concept of states' rights versus nationalism was demonstrated by Arthur M. Schlesinger in "The State Rights Fetish," *New Viewpoints in American History* (New York, 1922), 220-44.

marily an economic argument, brilliantly set forth by Charles A. Beard, that Southern agrarianism and Northern industrialism must necessarily clash because of their dissimilarity. The other was the more broadly social view that North and South were, in fact, "diverse civilizations," and, as such, incapable of maintaining a union with one another.[20]

The quest for an unqualified antithesis still continues. Interpretations now current have turned back to an emphasis, formerly popular in the nineteenth century, upon the basic incompatibility between a slaveholding and a nonslaveholding regime, with all the far-reaching differences in social values and in mode of life which such systems must entail.[21]

These antitheses are in a sense caricatures, perhaps accurate in singling out some distinctive feature, but grossly distorted in the emphasis which they give to it. Because of their vulnerability, revisionist critics have been able to direct damaging criticism at every one of them. The fervently evangelical South, with a large infusion of frontier primitivism and equalitarianism, was by no means cavalier, while the Puritanism which may have dominated New England but had certainly never dominated the North as a whole was already beginning to be diluted by immigration and urbanization at least two decades before the Civil War. Moreover, there were no fully

20. Charles A. and Mary R. Beard, *The Rise of American Civilization* (2 vols.; New York, 1927). One of the authoritative spokesmen of the idea of diverse civilizations was Edward Channing, in his *History of the United States* (6 vols.; New York, 1905–25), VI, 3–4.

21. Arthur M. Schlesinger, Jr., in "The Causes of the Civil War: A Note on Historical Sentimentalism," *Partisan Review*, XVI (October, 1949), 469–81; and Harry V. Jaffa, in *Crisis of the House Divided: An Interpretation of the Issues in the Lincoln-Douglas Debates* (New York, 1959), have done much to reinstate the idea that the conflict was a struggle between freedom and slavery, but Leon F. Litwack, in *North of Slavery: The Negro in the Free States, 1790–1860* (Chicago, 1961), shows that even a genuine sectional division on the slavery question did not necessarily mean any great sectional discrepancy in attitudes toward the Negro. Racism was nationwide.

articulated "planter" and "industrial" civilizations, standing in juxtaposition to one another, for the common conditions of life of plain farmers throughout an overwhelmingly rural republic completely transcended these distinctions. Dirt farmers, South and North, were the backbone of both sections, planter aristocrats and rising industrialists notwithstanding.[22]

Similarly, the political and economic antitheses contain fallacies. Shrewd observers have always perceived the states' rights doctrine to be less a philosophical position than a tactical device, attractive to any minority regardless of latitude, and the doctrine of national supremacy to be one exalted by those who possessed power and wanted to take advantage of it. Scratch a spokesman of state sovereignty and you find, not necessarily a Southerner, but almost invariably a man who sees that he is outnumbered; look beneath the rhetoric which exalts federal supremacy and you discover a motive on the part of a majority group to remove some irksome restriction upon the use of power.

The once-regnant theory that the Civil War was a "clash of economic sections," and that agriculture and industry must inevitably conflict, was hardly less than an assumption that where economies are diversified, they must invariably be antagonistic. There were, in fact, serious antagonisms between the cotton economy and the manufacturing interest, but the trouble with making a theory of them is that it will lead logically to the conclusion that no country can ever achieve real integration economically: although a country without economic diversity would find its integrity as a nation threatened because it is not self-sufficient, if it were to attain economic diversity, it would theoretically find its integrity as a nation threatened because diverse interests had led to internal

22. James G. Randall, in "The Civil War Restudied," *Journal of Southern History*, VI (November, 1940), 439–57, exposed some of the fallacies in the views that agrarian and industrial societies were certain to clash, and that North and South formed diametrically opposed civilizations.

dissensions. The assumption in the first instance is that diverse interests will be complementary; in the second instance, that they will be incompatible. Both are merely assumptions, valid or not according to the individual circumstances; there are many situations in which agricultural areas and industrial areas serve each other as sources of supplies and as markets. Such complementary situations show the fallacy in the a priori supposition that points of dissimilarity are equivalent to points of dissension.

Compared to these other dualisms, the antithesis between slaveholding and nonslaveholding states is at least valid in that there were in fact two groups of states sharply differentiated in the legal status they gave to slavery. This distinction was clear-cut and incontrovertible, as was not the case with the other dualisms that have been mentioned. But even here, the antithesis is less deep than might be supposed, for the distinction was not between one society which accorded equality to the Negro and another which denied it; in fact racism was nationwide, and neither Abraham Lincoln nor any other major leader proposed to place the Negro on the same basis with other citizens. The issue as it stood at that time, unfortunately, was less a question whether the Negro should have status as an equal than a dispute over what form his inferior status should take. For the Negro in America, chattel servitude was sectional but caste inferiority was still national, and thus the slavery issue also failed to present a complete contrast.

Even the seemingly manifest difference between the loyalties of a nationalistic North and a sectionalistic South becomes tenuous when it is examined closely. For copious evidence shows that national as well as local loyalties prevailed in both the North and the South. The North's so-called "nationalism," consisted, as I have already pointed out, partly in its control over federal policy, and in the ability to keep it in alignment with sectional interests, while the South's "sectionalism" was, at least initially, an expression of the lack of such a capacity.

The problem presented by such antitheses as these in the interpretation of history, however, arises not from their oversimplifications or their exaggeration of differences, but from their mistaken attribution of mutual exclusiveness to phenomena which naturally coexist and overlap as national identity and regional identity do. It is false to assume that nationalism is a matter of homogeneity and therefore to conclude that regional diversity—at least when it appears on a North-South axis—is inconsistent with national unity. Once the mistaken assumption of mutual exclusiveness is accepted, the false conclusion follows that sectional distinctiveness can serve as an index of deviation, and by the same token that loyalty to the section can become an index of disloyalty to the Union. Besides mistaking dissimilarity for antagonism, this kind of interpretation has the tendency, where friction exists, to shift attention away from specific disputes between parties and to emphasize their mere lack of resemblance to one another.

The habit of equating diversity with dissension, and of using the word "difference" to mean both at the same time, has taken such deep root in the historiography of the Civil War that it becomes difficult to dissociate the two; nevertheless, history abounds in instances where diversity does not lead to antagonism, where regional identity does not detract from national integrity, and where no one expects them to do so. Outside the United States, for instance, the French, Catholic, peasant culture of the Quebec province presents sharper contrasts to the English, Protestant, pioneer culture of Ontario than North and South ever presented, and strong elements of antagonism have been involved historically; yet there was no "irrepressible conflict" in Canada, and today the diversity is hardly regarded as a serious problem. Within the United States, New Englanders, with their Puritan heritage and their Yankee ways, have kept their distinctiveness, along with a strong affection for their "stern and rockbound coast"; yet these qualities are regarded as reinforcing rather than diminishing the Yankee's Americanism. Even where the South itself is involved, historical interpretation of sectional differences has been too inconsistent to bear scrutiny. From the ratification of the Constitution until the high noon of the New Deal, and to some extent even down to the present, the South has been set apart by its rural society, its staple-crop economy, its tradition of leadership or control by the land-owning interest, its large proportion of Negro population, and its formalized system of caste in race relations. In 1787 these differences were perhaps more pronounced than during the crisis which led to the Civil War, yet historians who assume that such regional dissimilarities made a continuation of peaceful union impossible after 1850 seem completely untroubled by the fact that the very same diversities did not at all prevent the formation of at least a loose union in 1787–88, or the rapid and triumphant growth of American nationalism for nearly forty years thereafter. Since the Civil War, the one-party system of the "solid" South, and the relative poverty of the region, as well as the heritage of bitterness from Civil War and Reconstruction, have made the sectional contrasts in some respects sharper than they were during the antebellum period. Yet these strong sectional factors proved not inconsistent with the swift restoration of American nationalism in the South, which increased steadily at least until 1954.[23] The sectional differences were still there, but in this new context, since they did not lead to war, no one supposed any longer that they must be inherently disruptive. In fact, the readiness with which the South returned to the Union will defy explanation unless it is recognized that Southern loyalties to the Union were never really obliterated but rather were eclipsed by

23. Paul H. Buck, *The Road to Reunion, 1865–1900* (Boston, 1937), traces a swift and easy restoration of harmony between North and South within thirty-five years of Appomattox, which could not possibly have occurred if Southern nationalism had been so deep-seated as, for instance, Polish nationalism was.

other loyalties with which, for a time, they conflicted. It was a dim awareness of this among the participants in the Civil War which gave the conflict its peculiarly tragic tone—its pathos as a "brothers' war."

The historian may feel acutely the need for an explanation of the deep alienation which developed between North and South in the middle of the nineteenth century, but he ought not to allow the urgency of this need to blind him to the fact that he also needs an explanation for the growth of American nationalism between 1800 and 1846 and for the smoothness of the "road to reunion" between 1865 and 1900. No explanation of the sectional strife is really much good if it makes these phenomena of harmony and reconciliation appear impossible. Yet the historian's reliance upon the sharpest conceivable antitheses has led him to explain the schism in terms so deep and total that the subsequent readiness of Southern men, in 1898 and 1917, to enlist in the United States Army and to fight under the American flag would seem quite incredible.

To explain an antagonism which sprang up suddenly, and died down suddenly, the historian does not need to discover, and cannot effectively use, a factor which has been constant over a long period, as the cultural difference between the North and the South has been. He needs to identify a factor which can cause bitter disagreement even among a people who have much basic homogeneity. No factor, I would suggest, will meet this need better than the feeling, widespread in the 1850's in the South, that the South's vital interests were being jeopardized, and that the region was being exposed to the dangers of a slave insurrection, as a result of the hostility of antislavery men in the North. Applied to the sectional crisis, such a view of the sources of friction would make possible the explanation of the Civil War, without making impossible the explanation of the rapid return to union after the war. No cultural explanation will do this.

The cultural factor and the factor of self-interest are, of course, not wholly unrelated, for essential interests are determined partly by cultural values and vice versa. But the fact remains that within an integrated culture acute conflicts of interest may be generated, and between diverse cultures strong community of interests may develop. A body of citizens may exalt the national state as the instrument that unites them with those with whom they have an affinity, but they may also exalt it as the guardian of certain essential interests and social values which they do not necessarily share with the overall society. Despite the emphasis in historical literature upon cultural homogeneity, history itself offers extensive evidence that if a state protects the interests—either real or fancied—of culturally disparate groups in its population, it can command the nationalistic loyalty of such groups without reducing them to a homogeneous body of citizens, and that if it systematically disregards the interests of a group it alienates the group and makes cultural affinities with the majority seem irrelevant.[24] The state, of course, frequently adopts measures adverse to the specific advantage of a given group without seriously endangering the basis of their loyalty, but when it acts against what the group conceives to be its fundamental welfare, there is a question whether loyalty can survive. In fact the members of a group may become alienated even more readily when they feel that they have been victimized by their own kindred rather than by

24. Grodzins (*The Loyal and the Disloyal*, ii) quotes George Washington: "Men . . . may talk of patriotism . . . but whoever builds upon it as the basis for conducting a long and bloody war will find themselves deceived in the end. We must take the passions of men as nature has given them, and those principles as a guide which are generally the rule of Action. I do not mean to exclude altogether the Idea of Patriotism. I know it exists, and I know it has done much in the present Contest. But I will venture to assert, that a great and lasting war can never be supported on this principle alone. It must be aided by a prospect of Interest or some reward."

strangers. In this sense, community of interest many sometimes be a more important condition for nationalism than cultural homogeneity, and conflict of interest may be a greater danger to national union than cultural diversity.

Without laboring this point, it may be worth noting that in situations where conflict occurs, cultural diversity is never the direct cause. This diversity will generate friction only when it has been translated into opposing policies for dealing with a particular question. Therefore even the historian who relies entirely upon cultural explanations to account for a given conflict must reckon with the fact that the disruptive potentials inherent in cultural diversity remain latent until conflicts of interest bring them into play.

Insofar as it is sound to regard the equilibration of interests as a condition necessary to nationalism, it follows that the American Civil War must be interpreted less in terms of antitheses and dissimilarities between North and South, and more in terms of the prolonged sequence of interest conflicts which crystallized along sectional lines. Southerners became progressively more alienated as they became more convinced, first, that the Union was sacrificing their economic welfare by its tariff policy; later, that it was denying them parity in the process of national expansion; and finally, that it was condoning the activities of men who would loose a slave insurrection upon them and expose them to possible butchery.

This does not mean, of course, that anyone need turn to a simple economic interpretation of history, but rather that we should recognize that cultural similarities alone will not provide a basis of affinity between groups who regard each other's policies as endangering their own security. The danger of these conflicts to national unity was fully recognized as early as 1797 and was a major theme in Washington's Farewell Address. Later, control of the national political system became itself a weapon in the warfare between opposing interests, and as it did so, the central government lost much of its potency as a symbol evocative of national loyalties.

Whether slavery did or did not constitute a vital interest for the South is too large a question to be explored here, but there is no doubt that the South believed it did. Also there is no doubt that the emancipation of the slaves was the largest expropriation of property that has ever occurred in the United States—the heaviest blow that any large interest group has ever sustained. The slavery question was a thoroughly tangible matter, and far more than a symbol in a conflict of cultures, but many historians prefer to treat it as if it were no such thing. Southern writers have never wished to believe that the South fought for slavery, while Northern writers have preferred to think in terms of the fulfillment of an ideal of freedom rather than the overthrow of a vast property interest.

By focusing upon conflict of interest as a basic factor it is possible to explain the otherwise stubborn anomaly that the sectional crisis grew in intensity even as the republic grew in homogeneity. Originally, cultural unity was not deemed necessary to the welfare of the Union under the Constitution, and both the Northern and the Southern states fully intended to preserve their respective sectional peculiarities, of which they were acutely aware when they ratified the Constitution. Indeed, they did not ratify it until shrewd calculation had assured each section either that it might hope to gain preponderant weight, or at least that it would be strong enough to maintain the sectional equilibrium in the new system. If the republic had remained static, with the area and population of 1790 more or less permanent, an equilibrium might have been maintained, and the Union might have enjoyed harmony, even without homogeneity. The "house divided," which had in fact been divided from the beginning, might have continued to stand as it had stood for seventy years.

But when growth ensued—with uneven rates of advance for the two sections—the equilibrium was upset. The minority section lost its ability to exercise a joint control in the federal government, and with this control went the power of coordinating national with sectional objectives and thus of maintaining the image of the federal government as the guardian of the essential interests of values of Southern society. The South, therefore, was forced more and more to regard national objectives on the one hand and sectional objectives on the other as the alternatives of a painful choice. Meanwhile, the North did not have to choose between national and sectional objectives because by use of its power it could incorporate sectional goals into the national program. What was good for the North was good for the country, and thus no problem of priority need arise. The potential dilemma of Josiah Quincy's loyalties, which he had stated so clearly, remained a latent dilemma, never developed beyond the verbal level. But Sam Houston and Alexander Stephens lived to see a situation where bigness of heart was not enough and where the Union was so divided that patriotism could no longer embrace it.

If the adjustment of conflicting interests rather than the elimination of cultural differences is in this instance the key to the perpetuation of national unity, and if an equilibrium of power is the condition most favorable to the adjustment of conflicting interests, then the historian has an explanation for the seeming paradox that the crisis of American nationalism came not when regional diversity was greatest, but after many common denominators between the sections had developed and had substantially increased the measure of cultural uniformity. He has also a key to the anomalous fact that from 1787 to 1861 national growth always seemed to endanger national unity: it upset the equation between North and South by introducing new factors of power which potentially jeopardized sectional interests that had previously seemed to be in balance.

If the pattern of loyalties in America between 1820 and 1860 was more intricate than the stark antithesis of nationalism and sectionalism would imply, and if the ultimate conflict between North and South was in part the consequence of the failure of the Union to solve the problems of chronic conflict of interest, even after it had successfully begun to transcend the presumably more difficult obstacles of cultural dissimilarity, the implication is not that a new single-factor analysis should be applied, developing a view which presents the Civil War in the exclusive terms of a conflict between culturally similar groups which both spelled their version of nationalism with the alphabet of self-interest. It is rather to suggest that the valuative elements in the concept of nationalism have influenced too many of the findings of the historian, that the concept has warped his analysis as much as it has assisted it, and that the historical process is far too intricate to be handled in terms of the simple dualisms of culture versus culture, nation versus section, interest versus interest, or Americanism versus Southernism.

6

ABUNDANCE AND THE TURNER THESIS

*This essay constitutes Chapter VII of David Potter's most original book and probably his most famous one—*People of Plenty, *published in 1954. Although it is linked to the book's general argument concerning the influence of economic abundance on the American character, much of the essay can stand alone as a critique of Frederick Jackson Turner's frontier hypothesis.*

No HISTORIAN can overlook the fact that American history has long provided a classic formula for defining and explaining the American character: this is Frederick Jackson Turner's frontier hypothesis. In any appraisal of what history has to contribute, therefore, it is inevitable that we should return ultimately to the Turner theory. And in any evaluation of the factor of abundance, it is vital to establish what relation, if any, existed between the frontier influence specifically and the general influence of economic abundance. Thus I find myself coming around, as all American historians do sooner or later, to that much-debated formulation which the young professor from Wisconsin proposed to the sages of the American Historical Association when they met at Chicago in 1893.

Turner's paper on "The Significance of the Frontier in American History" was not only a turning point in the development of American historical writing; it was also, in the most explicit sense, an explanation of American character, and might, with perfect validity, have been entitled "The Influence of the Frontier on American Character." Passages throughout the essay may be cited to justify this assertion.

For instance, Turner declared that, on the frontier, the "perennial rebirth" of society, the "fluidity of American life, this expansion westward with its new opportunities, its continuous touch with the simplicity of primitive society furnish the forces dominating American character." And, again, "to the frontier, the American intellect owes its striking characteristics." [1]

In any analysis of American character, therefore, Turner and his ideas must be considered with the utmost care. Fortunately, this does not mean that we need undertake any general critique of the entire body of Turner's thought. That is a broad field which has been traversed repeatedly by opposing critics—with Avery O. Craven, Joseph Schafer, and Frederic L. Paxson guarding the essential points of the Turner position and with a number of writers, including Charles A. Beard, Louis Hacker, Fred A. Shannon, James C. Malin, Carlton J. H. Hayes, Murray Kane, Benjamin F. Wright, Jr., and Carter Goodrich in collaboration with Sol Davidson, conducting the assault on specific sectors, while George Wilson Pierson, in a series of articles, has provided a very searching analysis and review of the entire question.[2]

But, in so far as the frontier hypothesis is related to the factor of abundance, it behooves us to take account of it here. Turner himself said, "the Western wilds, from the Alleghenies to the Pacific, constituted the richest free gift that was ever spread out before civilized man. . . . Never again

---

1. All quotations from Turner, except where otherwise noted, are taken from "The Significance of the Frontier in American History," using the revised form which appeared in his *The Frontier in American History* (New York: Henry Holt & Co., 1920).
2. For a bibliography of this literature, with reference not only to the controversial writers, but also to studies of Turner's precursors, his influence, his thought, and his method, by Herman C. Nixon, Everett E. Edwards, Fulmer Mood, and Merle Curti, respectively, see Ray Allen Billington, *Westward Expansion* (New York: Macmillan Co., 1949), pp. 760–61.

can such an opportunity come to the sons of men." [3] And, specifically linking this opportunity with the frontier, he added, "The most significant thing about the American frontier is that it lies at the hither edge of free land."

Of course, it should be recognzied at once that Turner conceived of other factors besides abundance as being present in the frontier condition. To name only two, there was a temporary lowering of civilized standards, and there was a weakening of the power of traditional institutions such as church and school, with a corresponding enhancement of the stature of the individual.

Therefore we are dealing with abundance as one in a complex of factors, and it becomes important to determine, as far as we can, how much of the influence of what Turner called the "frontier" lay in its being on the outskirts of civilization and how much lay in its function as the locus of maximum access to unused resources. The question is a critical one because, if the factor of abundance was really primary, if the most significant thing about the frontier was, as Turner himself asserted, its contiguity to free land, then we ought to recognize the primacy of abundance and speak of the influence of abundance, in whatever form it occurs, and not restrictively in only one of its manifestations—the frontier manifestation. Do we really mean the influence of the frontier, or do we mean the influence of a factor that was especially conspicuous in the frontier situation but that also operated apart from it upon many other parts of American experience? [4] In so far as the latter is what we mean, we might

3. "Contributions of the West to American Democracy," in *The Frontier in American History*, p. 261.
4. "To Turner, however, 'the most significant thing about the American frontier' is not that historically it represents a vast domain of natural resources ready to be transformed into capital through the medium of the productive process, but that it lies geographically at the 'hither edge of free land' " (Murray Kane, "Some Considerations on the Frontier Concept

justifiably regard Turner's famous paper as being, in essence, a study of the significance of economic abundance in American history.

In grappling with this problem, we cannot expect, unfortunately, to secure as much precise guidance as we might wish from an analysis of Turner's own writings. His conception of the frontier was nothing if not a protean one. Sometimes he seems to think of the frontier as a geographical region, as when he says that "the Western wilds from the Alleghenies to the Pacific" were the special area where nature conferred a unique bounty or that a new order of Americanism emerged when "the mountains rose between the pioneer and the seaboard." Sometimes he conceives of a condition, the existence at the edge of settlement of an unused area of free land. In this sense the frontier becomes, as Dixon Ryan Fox said, simply "the edge of the unused." Sometimes, again, he conceives of it as a process: "The peculiarity of American institutions is the fact that they have been compelled to adapt themselves to the changes of an expanding people—to the changes involved in crossing a continent, in winning a wilderness, and in developing at each area of this progress out of the primitive economic and political conditions of the frontier into the complexity of city life." Avery O. Craven has summarized this idea of process very effectively in a paraphrase of the concept as he construes it: "The basic idea . . . was that American history, through most of its course, presents a series of recurring social evolutions in diverse geographical areas as a people advance to colonize a continent. The chief

---

of Frederick Jackson Turner," *Mississippi Valley Historical Review*, XXVII [1940], 389).

"One of the major deficiences of the Turner approach was the failure to see that free raw materials stood in almost exactly the same relation to the opportunity for industrial urbanism as the hither edge of free land did to agriculture" (James C. Malin, "Mobility and History," *Agricultural History*, XVII [1943], 178).

characteristic is expansion; the chief peculiarity of institutions, constant readjustment. . . . Into . . . raw and differing areas men and institutions and ideas poured from older basins, there to return to a more or less primitive state and then to climb slowly back toward complexity. . . . The process was similar in each case, with some common results but always with 'essential differences' due to time and place." [5]

Certainly, then, if Turner did not use the term "frontier" to mean various things at various times, at least he used it in a way that placed heavy stress first on one aspect, then on another, with very little notice to the reader that the cluster of ideas back of the term was being substantially changed. No doubt he was right in the view that a whole complex of factors was associated with the westward advance of settlement and that all these factors ought to be taken into account. But his technique, very frustrating to many critics of the last two decades, was instead of treating the separate constituents as separate constituents, to fuse all and discuss them interchangeably under the rubric "frontier." George Wilson Pierson, who has made a careful analysis of this shifting concept, remarks ruefully that, to Turner, "the West was rough (a geographic factor) and it was empty (a sociological force). Perhaps, then, Turner's greatest achievement was his successful marriage of these two dissimilar forces in the single phrase, *free land.*" [6]

The real key, however, to Turner's thought—both in its strength and in its limitations—will never be grasped if we suppose that this elusiveness of definition was simply the result of a vagueness of mind or an indifference to analysis. It is rather, as Henry Nash Smith has recently argued,

5. "Frederick Jackson Turner," in William T. Hutchinson (ed.), *Marcus W. Jernegan Essays in American Historiography* (Chicago: University of Chicago Press, 1937), p. 254.
6. George Wilson Pierson, "The Frontier and American Institutions," *New England Quarterly*, XV (1942), 252.

the result of Turner's personal predilection for one special social ideal—the ideal of agrarian democracy. As Smith expresses this, "from the time of Franklin down to the end of the frontier period almost a century and a half later, the West had been a constant reminder of the importance of agriculture in American society. It had nourished an agrarian philosophy and an agrarian myth that purported to set forth the character and destinies of the nation. The philosophy and the myth affirmed an admirable set of values, but they ceased very early to be useful in interpreting American society as a whole, because they offered no intellectual apparatus for taking account of the industrial revolution. A system which revolved about a half-mystical conception of nature and held up as an ideal a rudimentary type of agriculture was powerless to confront issues arising from the advance of technology. Agrarian theory encouraged men to ignore the industrial revolution altogether, or to regard it as an unfortunate and anomalous violation of the natural order of things. In the . . . sphere of historical scholarship, for example, the agrarian emphasis of the frontier hypothesis has tended to divert attention from the problems created by industrialization for a half-century during which the United States has become the most powerful industrial nation in the world." Turner's "problem"—the one that he set for himself—was "to find a basis for democracy in some aspect of civilization as he observed it about him in the United States. His determined effort in this direction showed that his mind and his standards of social ethics were subtler and broader than the conceptual system within which the frontier hypothesis had been developed, but he was the prisoner of the assumptions he had taken over from the agrarian tradition." [7]

Applying this dictum specifically to the factor of abundance, one can readily verify Smith's general observations.

7. Henry Nash Smith, *Virgin Land* (Cambridge, Mass.: Harvard University Press, 1950), pp. 258–59.

What happened was that, when abundance operated within an agrarian context—in the form of free land for farmers—Turner seized upon it, but with a tendency to identify the factor with the context, to attribute to the context the results that followed from the operation of the factor, while refusing to recognize the operation of the factor when it occurred outside the selected context.[8]

In this connection it would be misleading to say that Turner refused to admit the existence of nonagrarian frontiers. On the contrary, he mentioned them explicitly and specified also that various frontiers offered various conditions and inducements. In his own words, "the unequal rate of advance compels us to distinguish the frontier into the trader's frontier, the rancher's frontier, or the miner's frontier, and the farmer's frontier."

But, although these dissimilarities forced him grudgingly—"compelled" him, in his own revealing phrase—to give formal recognition to a variety of frontiers, they conspicuously failed to compel him to broaden his concept of the frontier sufficiently to accommodate them. When he came to such matters as the exploitation of salt, coal, oil, and other mineral resources, he would neither separate them out, thus conceding the limitations of his agrarian hypothesis, nor include them actively in his calculations, thus modifying and qualifying the agrarian tenor of his theme.

The arbitrary restrictiveness of this agrarian preoccupation is shown very clearly, it seems to me, in a statement by Carl Becker, who was one of Turner's most brilliant and most faithful followers. Becker said, "The United States has always had, until very recently, more land than it could use and fewer people than it needed." Certainly this premise

8. "Absorption in the Turner philosophy, centering around agriculture, seems to have diverted attention from the significant and all-important fact that there was still opportunity, created by the fluidity of society based on the industrial urbanism" (Malin, *loc. cit.*).

would be difficult to refute. Then he continues: "This is not only the fundamental economic difference between the United States and European countries, but it is a condition which has more influence than any other in determining the course of American history." [9] Today the United States has, perhaps, as large an industrial capacity as the rest of the world, and it was well on the way to such leadership when Becker wrote; yet the factor which he offers as the key to the fundamental economic difference between America and the Old World turns its back upon this major development of our economic life. Clearly, it is not merely the greater endowment of land which has differentiated America's growth from Europe's. It is the greater supply, also, of timber, of iron, of copper, of petroleum, of coal, of hydroelectric power. By some mystic process these may be subsumed under the term "land," but if we should speak of land in this sense, as meaning everything except sea and air, we ought at least to recognize that it is in this form too broad for the agrarians to claim a franchise on it. Indeed, it then becomes more nearly equivalent to physical abundance, or at least potential physical abundance, than to soil.

Because of these anomalies and because of the presence of concealed agrarian dogma in what purports to be an environmental analysis, it becomes important to consider a little more closely what the elements were in the frontier situation as Turner conceived it. I have already suggested that he was by no means schematic in his approach to this question, but I think we may agree in identifying his major points of stress. As I have already observed, he constantly recurred to the factor of plenty in the form of free land. Sometimes he touched this theme as a lyric chord, as when he said, "American democracy was born of no theorist's dream; it was not carried in the *Susan Constant* to Virginia, nor in the *May-*

9. *The United States: An Experiment in Democracy* (New York: Harper & Bros., 1920), p. 143.

flower to Plymouth. It came out of the American forest, and
it gained new strength each time it touched a new frontier.
Not the Constitution, but free land and an abundance of
natural resources open to a fit people, made the democratic
type of society in America for three centuries." [10] Sometimes
he dealt with the same thought in more analytical economic
terms, as when he explained the precise motives that stimulated the westward push: "The farmers [of settled areas]
who lived on soil whose returns were diminished by unro-
tated crops were offered the virgin soil of the frontier at
nominal prices. Their growing families demanded more lands,
and these were dear. The competition of the unexhausted,
cheap, and easily tilled prairie lands compelled the farmer
either to go west and continue the exhaustion of the soil on
a new frontier, or to adopt intensive culture. Thus the census
of 1890 shows, in the Northwest, many counties in which
there is an absolute or a relative decrease of population.
These states have been sending farmers to advance the frontier on the plains and have themselves begun to turn to intensive farming and to manufacture." But, whether in didactic
or in poetic terms, Turner reiterated constantly the factor of
abundance, which he recognized most frequently, but not
invariably, in the form of land.

Another feature of the frontier which Turner consistently
emphasized as important was the fact that it temporarily
emancipated the individual from institutional controls. Often
though he returned to this point, it seems to me that he never
did develop it with real clarity; but there is one formulation
of the idea in his statement that "we have the complex European life sharply precipitated by the wilderness into the simplicity of primitive conditions." This, I take it, means two
things: It means that the system of division of labor, prevalent
in complex societies, breaks down, and the individual is

10. "The West and American Ideals," in *The Frontier in American
History*, p. 293.

obliged to diversify his activities—to produce his own food, to minister to his own soul, to educate his own children, to doctor his own ailments, to provide his own police protection, and to be a true self-sufficing man. It means also that, since he, as an individual, has gone ahead of organized society, leaving it to follow him, he is not overshadowed by the weight of institutions, and his stature as an individual is correspondingly greater.

Another factor that Turner regarded as intrinsic was the way in which the frontier dictated a temporary lowering of the standards of civilization. The pioneers, of course, accepted this regression only because they expected it to pay off in a raising of standards later; but for the first phase, at least, there was an inescapable reduction: "The wilderness masters the colonist. . . . It strips off the garments of civilization and arrays him in the hunting shirt and the moccasin. It puts him in the log cabin of the Cherokee and Iroquois and runs an Indian palisade around him. Before long he has gone to planting Indian corn and plowing with a sharp stick; he shouts the war cry and takes the scalp in orthodox Indian fashion."

It is difficult to be certain whether or not Turner viewed this change with a romantic primitivism that caused him to take pleasure in it; but in any case he certainly regarded it as the most transitory of conditions. Frederic L. Paxson, paraphrasing Turner, expresses the concept well when he says that "as the pioneer trudged ahead of his little procession, along the rugged trails that pierced the mountain gaps, he was only incidentally living in the present. The future filled his mind; a future beginning with the rough shack that must shelter him for his first season; but a future of field after field of fertile land, of houses and livestock, of growing family and the education and religion that it needed." [11]

Along with these factors there was also, as I have sug-

11. *When the West Is Gone* (New York: Henry Holt & Co., 1930), p. 39.

gested previously, the element of successive readjustments, of "perennial rebirth," of constant changes moving in a kind of rhythmic cycle, "the changes involved in crossing a continent, in winning a wilderness, and in developing at each area of this progress out of the primitive economic and political conditions of the frontier into the complexity of city life." Always, of course, this cycle was a democratic one.

Most of the things which the frontier meant to Turner are embraced, I believe, by one or another of these factors. It was the place where free land lay at the edge of settlement; the place where institutions no longer towered over the individual man; the place where European complexity gave way to American simplicity; and the place where democratic growth and change was repeatedly re-enacted as a process and reaffirmed as a principle.

But how did these elements in the pioneer experience impinge upon the American character? What was their influence in shaping the traits of the American people? Here Turner's analysis is somewhat more explicit, and it is, in fact, easier to know what he meant by the "influence of the frontier" than what he meant by the "frontier" itself. First of all, he was confident that the frontier promoted nationalism: the pioneer looked to the national government to adopt the measures he needed—to provide him with internal improvements, to administer the public domain, and still more to accord to the area in which he had settled territorial status and, later, statehood; moreover, the pioneer, on the frontier, mingled with other settlers from other states and even from other countries. Here was the true melting pot, and "on the tide of the Father of Waters, North and South met and mingled into a nation." "It was," he said, "this nationalizing tendency of the West that transformed the democracy of Jefferson into the national republicanism of Monroe and the democracy of Andrew Jackson. The West of the War of 1812, the West of Clay and Benton and Harrison and An-

drew Jackson, shut off by the Middle States and the mountains from the coast sections, had a solidarity of its own with
national tendencies." Second, he was equally confident that
the frontier had fostered democracy: "The most important
effect of the frontier has been in the promotion of democracy
here and in Europe." In this connection Turner often cited
the liberal suffrage provisions with which the frontier states
came into the Union and the reactive effects of these provisions upon the political arrangements in the older states.
Third, he also credited the frontier with stimulating the spirit
of individualism: "Complex society," he felt, "is precipitated
by the wilderness into a kind of primitive organization based
on the family. The tendency is anti-social. It produces antip-
athy to control." And with each family occupying land of
its own, very largely on a self-sufficing basis, there was, in
fact, every reason why the individual should feel a minimum
need to be cared for by society, and therefore a minimum
tolerance for control by society. This was true only on the
farmer's frontier, of course, and Turner himself recognized
that other frontiers might not be individualistic at all. He
himself stated this limitation, saying, "But when the arid lands
and the mineral resources of the Far West were reached, no
conquest was possible by the old individual pioneer methods.
Here expensive irrigation works must be constructed, co-
öperative activity was demanded in utilization of the water
supply, capital beyond the reach of the small farmer was
required. In a word, the physiographic province itself decreed
that the destiny of this new frontier should be social rather
than individual." [12] But, as was characteristic with him, though
he might give lip service to the existence of a variety of
frontiers, it always turned out that the farmer's frontier was
the one he was really talking about, and the others lay somewhere beyond the periphery of his thought. And the farm-

12. "Contributions of the West to American Democracy," in *The Frontier in American History*, p. 258.

er's frontier was unquestionably individualistic. Thus he did not hesitate to rank individualism with his other factors and to declare that the "frontier of settlement . . . carried with it individualism, democracy, and nationalism."

These three were, in a sense, his triad—factors to which he often recurred. But however important they may be and however deeply they may be imbedded in the character, they can hardly be described as "traits of character" or "qualities of mind" in the ordinary sense; and we must therefore go one step further, to ask: How did Turner conceive that the frontier made the pioneer unlike other people? The complete answer, of course, runs through the whole body of his work, but there is a very good summary answer near the end of his famous essay. "To the frontier." he said, "the American intellect owes its striking characteristics. That coarseness and strength combined with acuteness and inquisitiveness; that practical, inventive turn of mind, quick to find expedients; that masterful grasp of material things, lacking in the artistic but powerful to effect great ends; that restless, nervous energy; that dominant individualism, working for good and for evil, and withal that buoyancy and exuberance which comes with freedom—these are traits of the frontier, or traits called out elsewhere because of the existence of the frontier."

Such, then, were the main elements of the frontier hypothesis, as Turner developed it: West of the Alleghenies lay a vast expanse of fertile and unsettled land which became available almost free to those who would cultivate it. Across this area, a frontier or edge of settlement pushed steadily west, and along this frontier individuals who had advanced ahead of society's usual institutional controls accepted a lowering of standards at the time for the sake of progress in the future. Constantly repeating over again a democratic experience, they reinforced the national democratic tradition. All these conditions, of course, influenced the mental traits of those who were directly or indirectly involved in the process, and especially their nationalism, their democracy, and their individualism were stimulated. Certain other qualities—a coarseness, combined with a strength, a practicality and materialism of mind, a restless energy, and a measure of buoyancy or exuberance—were all traceable to this frontier influence.

With this outline of the frontier hypothesis in mind, we can now revert to the question: To what extent was the frontier merely the context in which abundance occurred? To what extent does it explain developments which the concept of abundance alone could not explain?

At times Turner himself seemed almost to equate the frontier with abundance, as, for instance, when he said, "These free lands promoted individualism, economic equality, freedom to rise, democracy." [13] It is probably valid to criticize him for this. But if there was a fallacy in his failure to distinguish between these coinciding factors and his consequent practice of treating qualities which were intrinsically derived from abundance as if they were distinctive to the frontier, it would be the same fallacy in reverse to treat qualities which were intrinsically frontier qualities as if they were attributable to abundance. Bearing this caveat in mind, we can hardly deny that there were a number of influences which were peculiar to the frontier or to abundance in its distinctive frontier form and which did not operate outside the frontier phase. For instance, the pioneer's necessity of submitting to hardships and low living standards as the price of higher standards later must certainly have stimulated his optimism and his belief in progress. Similarly, one can hardly doubt that the mingling of peoples on the frontier and their urgent need for federal legislative measures must have stimulated the growth of nationalism just as Turner said. And again, at an even deeper level, it is hard to doubt that the

13. *Ibid.*, p. 259.

frontier projection of the individual ahead of society and the
self-sufficing way of life on the edge of settlement must have
greatly stimulated American individualism.

But even to say that Turner was right in all these matters is
not to say that he took a comprehensive view of the American
experience. By confining his explanation of Americanism to
the conditions of the pioneer stage of our development, he
placed himself in the position of implying that nothing distinctively American would be left, except as a residue, after
the pioneer stage had been passed. By limiting his recognition
of abundance to its appearance in the form of free land, he
limited his recognition of successive American democratic
readjustments to the successive settlement of new areas of
free land, and thus he cut himself off from a recognition of
the adjustments to technological advance, to urban growth,
and to the higher standard of living, all of which have contributed quite as much as the frontier to the fluidity and
facility for change in American life. Further, by failing to
recognize that the frontier was only one form in which
America offered abundance, he cut himself off from an insight
into the fact that other forms of abundance had superseded
the frontier even before the supply of free land had been
exhausted, with the result that it was not really the end of
free land but rather the substitution of new forms of economic activity which terminated the frontier phase of our
history.

Perhaps it may be in order to say a few words more about
each of these points. In the first place, then, by making the
frontier the one great hopeful factor in our experience,
Turner gave us every cause to feel alarm and pessimism
about the conditions that would follow the disappearance of
the frontier. As he himself expressed it, "since the days when
the fleet of Columbus sailed into the waters of the New
World, America has been another name for opportunity.
. . . He would be a rash prophet who should assert that the

expansive character of American life has now entirely ceased. Movement has been its dominant fact, and, unless this training has no effect upon a people, the American energy will continually demand a wider field for its exercise. But never again will such gifts of free land offer themselves. . . . Now, four centuries from the discovery of America, at the end of a hundred years of life under the Constitution, the frontier has gone, and with its going has closed the first period of American history."

The tone of foreboding in this statement is easily transformed into a defeatist lament or into a conviction that, without the frontier, freedom and opportunity are endangered. To take but one of a good many possible illustrations, Governor Philip La Follette, in his message to the Wisconsin legislature in 1931, observed that "in the days of our pioneer fathers, the free land of the frontier gave this guarantee of freedom and opportunity," but that no such natural safeguard remained in operation after the passing of the frontier.[14]

Some years ago Dixon Ryan Fox pointed out this defeatist corollary of the frontier hypothesis and suggested that broader definition of a frontier which I have already mentioned— namely, "the edge of the unused." This would imply, of course, that science has its frontiers, industry its frontiers, technology its frontiers, and that so long as Americans can advance their standards of living and maintain the fluidity of their lives and their capacity for change along these frontiers,

14. James C. Malin observes that the doctrine of closed space caused "the hysterical conservation movement of the early twentieth century. It remained for the apologists of the New Deal, however, and especially such men as Rexford G. Tugwell and Henry A. Wallace [author of *New Frontiers*], to invoke in extreme form the prestige of the Turner tradition to justify governmental regulation of American life as a substitute for the vanished frontier. . . . In effect it was a repudiation of the America of Turner, accompanied by the application of an unwanted corollary from his own teaching" (*op. cit.*, p. 177).

the disappearance of the agrarian frontier is not at all critical. In terms of abundance, Turner was correct in saying, "Never again will such gifts of free land offer themselves," but his implication that nature would never again offer such bounty is open to challenge, for the frontiers of industry, of invention, and of engineering have continued to bring into play new resources quite as rich as the unbroken sod of the western frontier.

A second point which I believe Turner's agrarian orientation caused him to overlook was the broad variety of factors which have worked to cause unceasing change and development in America and thereby have conditioned the American to a habit of constant adjustment, constant adaptation to new circumstances, and constant readiness to accept or experiment with what is new. It was "to the frontier" that he attributed "that practical inventive turn of mind, quick to find expedients," to it that he credited the fact that Americans were "compelled to adapt themselves to the changes of an expanding people." But clearly it is not "the simplicity of primitive society" which requires new expedients and inventive ability; on the contrary, primitive society was highly repetitive in its patterns and demanded stamina more than talent for innovation; it was an increasingly complex society of rapid technological change, far away from the frontier, which demanded range and flexibility of adjustment. No amount of concentration upon the frontier will give us an awareness of the way in which the American home has been readjusted to the use first of gas and later of electricity; of the way in which American business has been readjusted to the typewriter and the comptometer; of the way in which American communication has been adjusted to the telegraph, the telephone, the radio, and even the motion picture; and of the way in which the American community has been readjusted to the railroad, the streetcar, and the automobile. One has only to compare an old, pre-automobile city, like Boston, with a new, post-automobile city, like Houston, Texas, with its supermarkets, its drive-in restaurants, and its other facilities for automotive living, to appreciate that this is true. Are not these constant changes more important in maintaining the fluidity of American life, in perpetuating the habit of expecting something different, than any number of successive removals to new areas of free land?

A third and final aspect in which the agrarian perspective proved too limiting is in the fact that Turner did not recognize that the attraction of the frontier was simply as the most accessible form of abundance, and therefore he could not conceive that other forms of abundance might replace it as the lodestone to which the needle of American aspirations would point. To him the frontier remained the polar force until it was exhausted; America must turn to second-best resources after this unparalleled opportunity of the frontier had passed. Yet, in fact, what happened was that, as early as the mid-century, if not earlier, American industrial growth, relying upon the use of other forms of abundance than soil fertility, began to compete with the frontier in the opportunities which it offered, and the migration of Americans began to point to the cities rather than to the West.[15] Later, this same industrial growth provided a general standard of living so high that people were no longer willing to abandon it for the sake of what the frontier promised. This can be stated almost in the terms of a formula: The frontier, with its necessity for some reduction of living standards, could attract people from settled areas so long as the existing standards in those areas did not exceed a certain maximum (people would accept a certain unfavorable differential in their cur-

15. Walter P. Webb, *The Great Frontier* (Boston: Houghton Mifflin Co., 1952), p. 374, quotes Carl, in John Steinbeck's "The Red Pony" (1945), "No, no place to go, Jody. Every place is taken. But that's not the worst—no, not the worst. Westering has died out of the people. Westering isn't a hunger any more. It's all done."

rent standards for the sake of potential gain). But when existing city standards exceeded this maximum, when the differential became too great, people would no longer accept it even for all the future rewards that the frontier might promise. To leave a primitive agrarian community and settle in primitive agrarian isolation was one thing, but to leave refrigeration, electric lighting, running water, hospitals, motion pictures, and access to highways was another, and, as these amenities and others like them were introduced, the frontier distinctly lost the universality of its lure. As George W. Pierson says, "When cars, movies, and radios become essentials of the accepted standard of living, subsistence farming is repugnant even to the starving. Measured, therefore, against this concept of a changing fashion or standard of living, it may be suggested that the lure of the land began in Tudor England before there was any available, and ceased in the United States before the available supply gave out." [16] In short, the frontier ceased to operate as a major force in American history not when it disappeared—not when the superintendent of the census abandoned the attempt to map a frontier boundary—but when the primary means of access to abundance passed from the frontier to other focuses in American life.

It is now sixty years since Turner wrote his famous essay. For two-thirds of this period his ideas commanded vast influence and indiscriminate acceptance, and then they encountered a barrage of criticism as severe as it was belated. Some aspects of his thought have received such devastating analysis that no historian today would be likely to make the error of adopting them. For instance, historians today would be wary of the agrarian assumptions in Turner's formulation. But the geographical determinism or environmentalism of Turner still possesses great vitality. The strength of its appeal was demonstrated again in 1952 more strikingly, perhaps, than ever

16. *Op. cit.*, p. 239.

before in this country, with the publication by Walter P. Webb of another and a broader restatement of the frontier hypothesis—not for the United States alone, this time, but for the entire planet.

Webb's *Great Frontier* cuts free of both the restrictive Americanism and the restrictive agrarianism of Turner to propose the thesis that the world frontier, opened up by the age of discovery, was "inherently a vast body of wealth without proprietors," that it precipitated a "sudden, continuing, and ever-increasing flood of wealth" upon the centers of Western civilization, thus inaugurating a period of boom which lasted about four hundred years and during which all the institutions—economic, political, and social—evolved to meet the needs of a world in boom.

In his explicit recognition that the very essence of the frontier was its supply of unappropriated wealth, Webb has clarified a vital factor which remained obscure in Turner, for Turner seemed to sense the point without clearly stating it, and Turner always neglected forms of wealth other than soil fertility. Webb, with his attention to the precious metals and even more with his focus upon the importance of "that form of wealth classed as Things or commodities," everlastingly breaks the link between agrarian thought and the frontier doctrine. Through his clear perception of the part played by abundance, he has demonstrated in thorough and convincing fashion the validity of the precise point which I have attempted to put forward in this analysis.

If it were only a question whether the frontier has significance intrinsically as a locus of wealth, therefore, my comment would be only to echo Professor Webb; but there is another question: whether the *only* significant source of modern wealth is the frontier. Webb seems to contend that it is, for he asserts that "it was the constant distribution on a nominal or free basis of the royal or public domain that kept the boom going and that gave a peculiar dynamic quality to Western civilization for four centuries," [17] and his discussion is pervaded with dark forebodings for the future of a world which no longer commands such a stock of untapped resources.

The theme of American abundance, which is, of course, New World abundance and therefore, in large measure, frontier abundance, is, in many respects, fully in accord with Professor Webb's theme and at first glance might appear identical with it. But, at the point where Webb attributes to the frontier an exclusive function, my argument diverges from his. American abundance has been in part freely supplied by the bounty of nature, but it has also been in part socially created by an advancing technology, and neither of these factors can explain modern society without the other. Abundance, as a horse-breeder might say, is by technology out of environment. Professor Webb has treated the subject as if environment bred abundance by spontaneous generation.

To approach the matter more explicitly, let us consider the basis of our present standard of living, which reflects the supply of goods of all kinds. This standard results not merely from our stock of resources, for primitive peoples with bare subsistence standards have possessed the same resources for as long as fifty thousand years. It results also from our ability to convert these resources into socially useful form—that is, from our productive capacity. Our productive capacity, in turn, depends not only on the raw materials, which are ready to hand, but even more upon our ability to increase, through mechanization, the volume of goods which can be turned out by each worker. If I may allude again to a previously used illustration, an infinite supply of free land would never, by itself, have raised our standard of living very far, for it would never have freed us from the condition in which more than 70 percent of our labor force was required to produce food

17. *Op. cit.*, p. 413.

for our population. But, when technology enabled 11 percent of our labor force to produce food for our population, it freed 60 percent to engage in other activities—that is, to create other goods which would become part of the standard of living.

No doubt it is true that in many societies the level of living will be controlled by the scarcity of resources (e.g., by lack of soil fertility), and certainly there is good reason to feel concern lest such controls should come into play in the future as world population multiplies and world resources are expended. But in most of the societies with which history has had to deal, it was the limited productivity of the worker rather than the absolute lack of resources in the environment which fixed the maximum level for the standard of living. In these societies where technology has been the limiting factor, it would clearly be fallacious to seek the explanation for an increase of wealth solely in the increasing supply of resources, since the society already possessed resources which it was not using.

In practice, however, the forces of technology and environment constantly interact and cannot be isolated. Because they do interact, it might be argued, with some force, that the richness of supply of resources has stimulated the technology—that the spectacle of vast riches waiting to be grasped has inspired men to devise new means for grasping them—and that, in this sense, the great frontier precipitated the new technology. But, without denying either the attractiveness of, or the elements of truth in, such an interpretation, which would buttress the Webb thesis, I think we should recognize that historically the technological revolution seemed to precede the age of discovery. From the time of the Crusades, four centuries before Columbus and Da Gama, western Europe was in transition. The use of gunpowder, the art of printing, improvements in navigation, the revival of commerce, the development of various sciences, and the whole pervasive change known as the Renaissance—all these had paved the way not only for the great geographical discoveries but also for the industrial transformation of Europe. Viewing the matter in this way, it might be argued that what really happened was that an advancing technology opened up a whole new range of potentialities, including the physical resources of the New World, rather than that the epic geographical discoveries called into being a new technology.

Probably it is as fruitless to seek the dynamics of economic change solely in technology as it is to seek them solely in environment. Certainly nothing would be gained by minimizing the environmental factor, and it is not my purpose to assert either that technology can operate without materials or that Webb's Malthusian concern for the future is unjustified. But precisely because the factor of abundance is of capital significance, it is important that it should not become identified with doctrines of geographical determinism. And precisely because Webb's formulation is one of the first fully developed treatments of this factor, it is unfortunate that he should accept geographical determinism as a necessary part of his position. When he rejects what he calls "the Fallacy of New Frontiers," he is not only attacking a glib and overworked slogan, but he is also attacking the belief that science may find new potentialities in physical materials that are currently regarded as valueless—something which science has repeatedly done in the past. When he asserts that "science can do much, but . . . it is not likely soon to find a new world or make the one we have much better than it is," he offers two propositions of very unequal tenor: the prospect of science's finding a new world is indeed remote, but the entire history of science for several centuries would justify our expectation that, if not perverted to the uses of war, it may make our world a great deal better.

If abundance is to be properly understood, it must not be visualized in terms of a storehouse of fixed and universally recognizable assets, reposing on shelves until humanity, by a process of removal, strips all the shelves bare. Rather, abundance resides in a series of physical potentialities, which have never been inventoried at the same value for any two cultures in the past and are not likely to seem of identical worth to different cultures in the future. As recently as twenty years ago, for example, society would not have counted uranium among its important assets. When abundance exercises a function in the history of man, it is not as an absolute factor in nature to which man, as a relative factor, responds. Rather, it is as a physical and cultural factor, involving the interplay between man, himself a geological force, and nature, which holds different meanings for every different human culture and is therefore relative.

In short, abundance is partly a physical and partly a cultural manifestation. For America, from the eighteenth to the twentieth century, the frontier was the focus of abundance, physically because the land there was virgin and culturally because the Anglo-Americans of that time were particularly apt at exploiting the new country.[18] At this lowest threshold of access to abundance, the pioneers found an individualism and a nationalism which they might not have found at other thresholds. But, though physically the frontier remained the site of virgin land, cultural changes gave to the people an aptitude for exploiting new industrial potentialities and thus drew the focus of abundance away from the frontier. But this change of focus itself perpetuated and reinforced the habits of fluidity, of mobility, of change, of the expectation of progress, which have been regarded as distinctive frontier

18. Pierson asks, "What about the Spaniards, who had the run of the whole hemisphere? Did the Mississippi Valley make them democratic, prosperous and numerous? In a word, do not the level of culture and the 'fitness' of a society for the wilderness, matter more than the wilderness? . . . If today a new continent were to rise out of the Pacific Ocean, are we so sure that it would encourage small freeholds, not corporation or governmental monopolies?" (op. cit., p. 253).

traits. The way in which this happened suggests that it was, in reality, abundance in any form, including the frontier form, rather than the frontier in any unique sense, which wrought some of the major results in the American experience. The frontier remained of primary significance precisely as long as it remained the lowest threshold of access to America's abundance; it ceased to be primary when other thresholds were made lower, and not when the edge of unsettled land ceased to exist. American abundance, by contrast, has remained of primary significance both in the frontier phase and in the vast industrial phase which has dominated American life for the past three-quarters of a century. American development and the American character are too complex to be explained by any single factor, but, among the many factors which do have to be taken into account, it is questionable whether any has exerted a more formative or more pervasive influence than the large measure of economic abundance which has been so constantly in evidence.

7

C. VANN WOODWARD

AND THE USES OF HISTORY

"I have lived longer outside of the South than in it," wrote David Potter in 1968, "and hopefully have learned to view it with detachment, though not without fondness. Certainly no longer a Southerner, I am not yet completely denatured." There is no other vision quite like that of the quondam Southerner who has transcended his heritage without cutting all his emotional ties to it, and who has at the same time retained a keen interest in the South as a historical problem. In the case of Potter and of C. Vann Woodward, their Southern connections seem to have been at least partly responsible for the sophisticated perception, the ironical awareness, and the humane personal involvement with which they have viewed not only the South but the past generally. It is therefore appropriate and fortunate that Potter's most extensive study of another scholar should have been this essay on Woodward, whom many would rank first among all historians of the South. It is an essay in which Potter tells us much about Woodward and also perhaps reveals more about himself than in anything else he wrote. The essay appeared originally in Marcus Cunliffe and Robin W. Winks, eds., Pastmasters: Some Essays on American Historians *(1969).*

In 1938, the Macmillan Company published a biography, *Tom Watson, Agrarian Rebel*, by a twenty-nine-year-old assistant professor of Social Science at the University of Florida, Comer Vann Woodward. At the time the book appeared, Woodward had lived for all but one year in the South. The son of Hugh Allison and Bess (Vann) Woodward, he was born in 1908 in the tiny village of Vanndale, Arkansas, some fifty miles from the Mississippi River. Later, he attended high school at Morrilton, a town of 4,000 population at that time, near the center of the state. After two years at a small college in Arkansas, he went to Emory University in Atlanta, where he took his bachelor's degree in 1930. During the next three years he taught English for a year at Georgia Tech, spent a year getting an M.A. at Columbia (1932), went back for another year of teaching at Georgia Tech, and then, in 1934, enrolled at the University of North Carolina at Chapel Hill, where he wrote his study of Watson as a doctoral dissertation. Receiving his Ph.D. in 1937, he married Glenn Boyd McLeod and went to the University of Florida that same year.

Atlanta and Chapel Hill were lively places for a young

Southerner in the years between 1926 and 1937, for they were two of the strategic points where the post-bellum South, running about thirty years behind the calendar, began to move into the twentieth century. For two generations after Appomattox, the compulsive memories of the Lost Cause had held the Southern mind in thrall; myth had grown like ivy over the brick and mortar of Southern historical experience; sentimentality and veneration had inhibited realism.

But by the late twenties the ancient post-Confederate monolith was breaking up. Voices from the outside were coming in. Students at Emory and North Carolina could read in the *American Mercury* H. L. Mencken's monthly excoriations of the South as a Bible Belt and a Sahara of the Bozart (Beaux Arts). Atlanta was the headquarters of the Commission on Interracial Cooperation, founded in 1919, through which Will W. Alexander was working tirelessly to make white Southerners aware of the injustice with which Southern Negroes were obliged to live. Emory had as a debate coach a young but influential graduate student, Glenn Rainey, whose probing questions led a good many Southern youths to reflect for the first time that segregation was perhaps not a necessary part of the order of nature, like sunrise and sunset.[1] Rainey showed the tenor of his social thought by writing an M.A. thesis on the riots in Atlanta in 1906, which exposed racism at its worst. About 1930, Rainey went to an appointment in English at Georgia Tech, where he was so outspoken that at one time, the Georgia legislature, which could not fire him, could at least reduce the annual appropriation of the institution where he taught, by the exact amount of his salary, with his name specified in the bill. Both Rainey and Alexander were, significantly, friends of Woodward's.

1. This comment is based in part on personal knowledge, for I was an undergraduate at Emory, 1928–1932, knew Woodward and Rainey, was coached in debate by Rainey, and was on a debate team with Woodward against the University of Florida.

Alexander, who was very active in securing foundation support for Southern schools and scholars, both white and Negro, was more or less in charge of a program of Southern fellowships offered by the Social Science Research Council, and he spotted Woodward as a suitable recipient for one of these fellowships. After holding the fellowship, Woodward was a frequent visitor at the offices of the Interracial Commission. Similarly, Rainey was responsible for the fact that Woodward was twice appointed to teach English at Georgia Tech. Woodward later warmly acknowledged his intellectual appreciation of Rainey in the introduction to his study of Watson.[2]

The changing temper of the times in Atlanta was also suggested by the fact that it was there that Angelo Herndon, a young Negro Communist who had organized demonstrations by unemployed Negroes, was arrested in 1932 and prosecuted under a statute dating from the Civil War which made it a capital offense to incite "insurrection."

The Herndon case was like the more famous Scottsboro case, which occurred at about the same time, in the sense that the Communist Party attempted to exploit it to propagate Communism rather than to save the accused. Woodward was active in efforts to save Herndon—too active, in fact, to suit Alexander's taste. He became a temporary chairman of a local committee for Herndon's defense and was later left in an awkward position by the party's cynical take-over of the case as a propaganda device.[3]

If Atlanta offered a number of new outlooks upon the South, Chapel Hill offered others still. In fact, the University

2. Woodward, *Tom Watson, Agrarian Rebel* (New York, 1938; reprinted with brief new introduction, 1955), p. ix.
3. Wilma Dykeman and James Stokeley, *Seeds of Southern Change: The Life of Will Alexander* (Chicago, 1962), pp. 155–56. Angelo Herndon, *Let Me Live* (New York, 1937) gives a long and full account of his imprisonment and defense, but does not mention Woodward nor the names of any persons who helped him, other than his lawyers.

of North Carolina, in the years when Woodward was there, was experiencing a remarkable period of creative activity. Within the South, it was excelled in the field of literature by Vanderbilt, where John Crowe Ransom, Allen Tate, Robert Penn Warren, Andrew Lytle, Donald Davidson, and others were joining in an "agrarian" protest against modern industrialism, and were proclaiming, for the first time since the Civil War, that the South, as an agrarian stronghold, had a significant message to offer to the nation. But agrarianism was nostalgic and devoid of a realistic or even a recognizable program. By contrast, North Carolina was the headquarters of a pragmatic school of regionalism, headed by two master sociologists, Rupert B. Vance and Howard W. Odum. Vance and Odum conceived of the South in terms of a regionalism which would no longer isolate Dixie from the national scene, but would enable it to share in the prosperity and the constructive activities of the nation, while preserving its own distinctive qualities and values. Woodward, whose father had become head of the Emory Junior College at Oxford, Georgia, met Odum, whose family also lived in Oxford, and Odum helped arrange a General Education Board fellowship, on which Woodward went to Chapel Hill. It was in 1936, while Woodward was there, that Odum completed the work on his great milestone, *Southern Regions of the United States*. Although Woodward was in history, working under the direction of Howard K. Beale, he was much influenced by Odum and Vance. Also, during these years, on a visit to Nashville, he formed a lasting friendship with Robert Penn Warren.[4]

There are certain similarities and certain differences in the point of view of Beale and in the later point of view of Woodward, and it is instructive to compare the two, for Woodward avoided a certain basic fallacy from which Beale did not es-

4. Woodward, *Watson*, p. ix; Woodward, letter to the author, June 23, 1967.

cape. Though Beale was not a Southerner, this was a fallacy
to which scholars who combined an intellectual commitment
to liberalism with a personal loyalty to the South were peculiarly liable.

Essentially, this fallacy was to regard the South as dominantly "agrarian," as opposed to the North, which was
dominantly "industrial." This simple dualism had been put forward even by Charles A. Beard, a notably hardheaded and
"realistic" historian. It incorporated, of course, a large measure of truth, but in a falsely simplified form it provided
Southerners with a remarkably effective device for sweeping
the awkward questions of slavery and the Negro under the
rug. In a sense, this was an old piece of Southern legerdemain.
The Southern acceptance of Jefferson and Lee (two critics of
slavery) rather than Calhoun and Davis (two apologists of
slavery) as patron saints of the South gave evidence of the
South's psychological need for a self-image would divert
focus from the subordination of the Negro, either as a slave
or as a sharecropper. The work of such Southern historians
as William E. Dodd and Frank L. Owsley reinforced this
self-image at a more intellectual level by treating the South
of Jefferson as normative and the South of Calhoun as an
aberration, and by picturing the ante-bellum South as a yeo-
man society in which slaveholders were not dominant and
slaves were somehow just not a central part of the picture.
The curious effects which could be attained by the employment of this concept became particularly evident when it
was applied to the Reconstruction period. Treated in this
way, the struggles of Reconstruction could be made to appear not as a contest between defenders and opponents of
Negro rights, but as a battle between the landed ("agrarian")
cause and the cause of industrial capitalism, defended by the
Radical Republican hirelings of the new postwar robber
barons. Did not the Radicals conspire to frame a Fourteenth
Amendment which, under the pretense of protecting the

freedmen, would in fact protect corporations from control by the states? So strong was the psychological impulse to identify with the opponents of the robber barons that it lured more than one defender of civil rights as a twentieth-century issue into the anomalous position of defending the Southern whites of the 1860's who enacted the Black Codes and resisted every measure in support of Negro citizenship, Negro enfranchisement, distribution of land to Negroes, and all other measures to improve the lot of freedmen. A supreme bit of irony lay in the fact that Andrew Johnson was re-habilitated as the protagonist who held the Radicals at bay, and Lloyd Paul Stryker, soon to become a dedicated civil-rights zealot, published in 1936 a long and adoring biography of the President who vetoed every piece of civil-rights legislation for Negro welfare between 1866 and 1869.[5]

Howard Beale, a devoted liberal and active member of the American Civil Liberties Union and of an organization for conscientious objectors, accepted this simplified agrarian-industrial dualism, and in 1930 he set the theme for his book *The Critical Year* by picturing the situation after the defeat of the Confederacy in 1865: "An industrialized Northeast, dominated by business principles that were to create the machine-made American of today, faced an agrarian South and West contending for those time-honored principles of frontier individualism and plantation aristocracy which had dominated an America that was passing."[6] Beale's sympathies were all with the South.

Woodward's sympathies were with the South also, and he too was a devoted liberal, but he was too shrewd and too realistic to accept the old dualism. Where previous students had seen only what may be called an "external" fight be-

---

5. Lloyd Paul Stryker, *Andrew Johnson: A Study in Courage* (New York, 1936).
6. Howard K. Beale, *The Critical Year: A Study of Andrew Johnson and Reconstruction* (New York, 1930), p. 1.

tween victorious Northern industrialists and defeated Southern agrarians, Woodward, far more subtly, perceived that
there had always been Whiggish forces in the South, ready
to embrace industrial goals, and that the defeat of the Confederacy had set the stage for these forces to take over.
Therefore the real struggle was internal—within the South—
rather than external. It began at Appomattox and continued
so steadily for the remainder of the century that the traditional historical emphasis upon the end of Reconstruction as
a major breaking point between two eras was largely illusory. In his first published article, Woodward laid his doctrine on the line: "The class that seized power in Georgia
after the overthrow of the Reconstruction regime was neither
the old planter oligarchy nor the small farmer. It was the
rising class of industrial capitalists." [7] For purposes of protective coloration, these industrial capitalists—notably Joseph E.
Brown, John B. Gordon, and Alfred Colquitt—wrapped
themselves in the Confederate flag and offered prayers at the
shrine of the Old Order. But Woodward was not to be
deceived. He recognized that when the agrarian cause discovered a leader in the person of Tom Watson, that leader
found all the forces of the orthodox Southern establishment
arrayed against him.

This point of view had been partially foreshadowed in
previous works—notably in Benjamin B. Kendrick and Alex
M. Arnett, *The South Looks at Its Past* (1935), but most
earlier writers had blurred the point by picturing the struggle
as a conflict between an Old South party of agrarianism and
a New South party of industrialism. But Woodward saw
that the agrarian view had not really been dominant in either
the Old South or the New, and that the conflict was far more
than a rivalry between those who looked to the past and
those who looked to the future.

7. Woodward, "Tom Watson and the Negro in Agrarian Politics," *Journal of Southern History* 4 (1938): 14–15.

Woodward's vision of the so-called Redeemer period between 1877 and the end of the century was a startling one. Previous writers had pictured it as an era of solidarity in the fullest sense. Southern whites were portrayed as standing united in a single party to prevent the recurrence of Negro rule and the other traumas of Reconstruction. Concurrently, all worked together to fulfill the gospel of a New South, in which industry would restore the vigor of a region prostrated by military defeat. But to Woodward it was a period of profound division, with the "wool hat" boys conducting the political equivalent of an unsuccessful guerrilla warfare against the Confederate brigadiers.

Woodward's basic recasting of post-bellum Southern history was accomplished primarily in three books published over a period of thirteen years. First, there was the biography of Watson (1938), second, a study of the Hayes-Tilden election contest of 1876–77, entiled *Reunion and Reaction* (1951), and later in the same year, *Origins of the New South, 1877–1913*. During these years, Woodward had moved from Florida (1937–39) to a visiting appointment at the University of Virginia (1939–40), from Virginia to an Associate Professorship at Scripps (1940–43), from Scripps to three years of service (1943–46) as a lieutenant in the Navy (Office of Naval Intelligence and Naval Office of Public Information), and from there to The Johns Hopkins University. He was to remain at Hopkins for fourteen years and then to move once more to a Sterling Professorship at Yale in 1961.

The historical structure which Woodward erected in these three books has won such wide acceptance today that it will be difficult for many readers to grasp how sweepingly his revision altered the prevailing version of Southern history. Before his life of Watson was published, there was no mature treatment available on the history of the South since Reconstruction. Historically, the whole subject remained in a relatively primitive stage. A number of good monographs existed on limited topics such as, for instance, the history of Populism in a particular state, but the subject as a whole had been only superficially treated in a literature ridden with clichés about the "New South," the "Redeemer governments," the restoration of honest politics through the elimination of the corrupt Negro vote between 1890 and 1908, etc. Woodward detected these banalities with unerring accuracy, demonstrated their flimsiness with trenchant evidence, and put in their place a mature and comprehensive history of the period from 1877 to 1913, based for the first time on extensive research in the primary sources.

Building upon his basic concept of the internal struggle between agrarian and industrial forces, and the defeat of the agrarians, Woodward was able to revise many important features of the then-accepted version of post-bellum Southern history.

First of all, he recognized that the Civil War had not solved the problems of Southern Negroes by emancipation, and that the end of Reconstruction had not solved them by leaving it to Southern whites to set the pattern of race relations in the South. In the New South the rigors of tenancy and of agricultural exploitation had their most brutal impact upon the Negro. Moreover, Woodward avoided the practice of using emphasis upon the agrarian tradition, as it had so often been used, to divert attention from the unlovely realities of the biracial system. Indeed, an agrarian emphasis, instead of diverting attention from the Negro, required an especial focus upon the Negro, for the man who had his roots most firmly in the soil was not the landowner, who might even be an absentee, but the cultivator, who, more likely than not, was a ragged Negro, owning perhaps a mule and a plow but not owning any land whatever. The biography of Watson showed in full detail not only Watson's own ideals of a neo-Jeffersonian agrarian society, but also the complex of legal disabilities, self-perpetuating debt, economic handicaps, and social discriminations which prevented Negro farmers, as well as most whites, from attaining anything like true agrarian status as independent, landowning, diversified farmers who produced for their own use rather than for market.

When this basic approach was applied to specific developments, it exposed an overlay of myth which had completely encrusted many familiar themes, and it led to a remarkable transformation in many images of the past.

To begin with, Woodward's studies demolished the traditional Reconstruction melodrama which depicted all Republicans as spoilsmen and looters, while the Redeemers were separated from them by an impassable gulf and were the saviors of honesty and probity. Others had made this point before, but none quite so effectively as Woodward. He showed clearly that political opportunists like Joseph E. Brown moved readily back and forth across party lines, and that after the carpetbaggers had been driven out, orthodox Democrats used the "New South Gospel" as a cover for lucrative alliances with prominent robber barons. For instance John B. Gordon was not only the most eloquent eulogist of the Confederacy but also one of the most valuable allies of Collis P. Huntington.

A second ironical feature of the post-Reconstruction South which Woodward brought into clear focus was the relationship between the "Bourbons" (though Woodward avoids this ambiguous term) and the Negro vote. Post-Reconstruction myth-makers had created the impression that the Democratic party became the party of white supremacy during the contest with the carpetbaggers in the seventies and that it remained the inveterate foe of Negro participation in politics thereafter. But again Woodward clearly demonstrated that in 1877 leaders of the Southern whites pledged themselves to protect Negro suffrage, and that, after Reconstruction, the Democrats of the Black Belt counties, who were the most rock-ribbed Democrats of all, not only countenanced a continuation of Negro voting, but even controlled a captive Negro vote and employed it flagrantly to defeat the white voters of the hill counties, who were more numerous than those in the Black Belt. This practice became a characteristic phenomenon in the nineties and was used with deadly effect against the Populists. More than once, as Woodward shows, it was the Negro vote which "saved the party of White Supremacy." [8]

Transcending all such points as these, however, is the skill and subtlety with which Woodward has handled the interplay of race and class in the half century after Reconstruction. Very often the truly significant political issues involved interest groups—for instance, the desire of Southern promoters to secure a vast federal grant for a railroad across Texas to California, or the desire of property interests to neutralize the power of agricultural protest organizations—both Negro and white—during the nineties. But these issues between interest groups or social classes were made to appear as race issues, partly in order to conceal the conflict of interest among whites, partly to capitalize on racial antipathies, and partly to divide the white and Negro tenant farmers from one another. For instance, the decision of Southern congressmen not to obstruct the counting of the electoral vote in favor of Hayes was explained to their constituents in terms of a sacrifice made for the sake of inducing Hayes to withdraw federal troops, thus ensuring the overthrow of carpetbag governments in South Carolina, Louisiana, and Florida. But in fact the apparent willingness of Hayes to countenance the Texas and Pacific legislation, and the unwillingness of Tilden, were

8. Almost the only previous writer who had recognized this point even partially was Paul Lewinson, in *Race, Class, and Party: A History of Negro Suffrage and White Politics in the South* (New York, 1932), and his development of the topic was not comparable to Woodward's. Also, for further analysis of the class factor in politics, see Woodward's essay, "The Populist Heritage and the Intellectual," reprinted in Woodward, *The Burden of Southern History* (Baton Rouge, La., 1960; rev. ed., 1968).

decisive in determining the course of many Southern congressmen. Similarly, the disfranchisement of the period 1890–1908 was made to appear simply as a device to eliminate voting by Negroes, on the ground that these votes were ignorant, controllable, and corruptible, and that their elimination was necessary to achieve honest elections. But in fact, the disfranchisement of illiterate voters by a literacy test or of impoverished voters by a poll tax had the effect of eliminating many low-income whites as well as virtually all Negroes. In many Southern states, the franchise was confined, for practical purposes, to less than half of the male citizenry, and to that part in which property ownership was concentrated.

Significant and revealing insights such as these were set by Woodward in a context of skillful and expert historical exposition. This is a quality not easy to explain, or to illustrate by examples, and yet it has been a vital factor in gaining for Woodward the commanding position which he occupies among American historians. The biography of Watson, although his first book, is the best and most revealing biography that has been written of any Southerner living in the period since the Civil War. Moreover, it is one of the foremost psychological studies in American historical literature, even though Woodward abstains completely from offering psychological hypotheses or from applying formal psychological theory. In terms of technique, Woodward is an expert and remarkably versatile historian. For instance, in his *Reunion and Reaction* he has unraveled, from the sources, the story of a secret negotiation between Southern Democrats, interested in the Texas and Pacific railroad project, and Northern Republicans, interested in the election of Hayes to the Presidency. This negotiation had been hidden for more than seven decades, and the parties to it had taken care to avoid leaving any explicit record. Yet by the kind of detective work which historians dream about, but are seldom challenged to employ, Woodward reconstructed virtually every step in the cryptic process by which the participating parties, highly distrustful of one another and acutely apprehensive of disclosure, made indirect approaches to one another, arrived at a scarcely spoken understanding, and ultimately threw dust in the eyes of the spectator public so that the real basis of cooperation was hardly suspected.[9]

In all of this work, Woodward combined a solid command of freshly mined data with a singular talent for interpretation and a capacity for perceiving the meaningful item and for construing his material in broad terms. In fact, it may be said that very few historians have combined his closeness in research with his flair for interpretation, and this combination has been a source of great strength to him. The rare quality of the combination becomes evident when one tries to think of other historians who possess the same dual strength. Often, the man who compares with him in one respect falls short in the other. Richard Hofstadter, for instance, may be his peer in interpreting the Populists, but Hofstadter's data seem sketchy and insubstantial compared with Woodward's. On the other hand, John D. Hicks probably researched the Populist's quite as thoroughly as Woodward has done, but the thoroughness of his investigation did not give him the insights upon society as a whole which Woodward was able to derive from delving into the Southern Populist sources.

From the outset, it was evident that Woodward had ex-

9. For some comments on especial points in *Reunion and Reaction*, see Harry Barnard, *Rutherford B. Hayes and His America* (Indianapolis, 1954), which argues that the factors contributing to the result were more varied than Woodward's account indicates; Joseph Frazier Wall, *Henry Watterson: Reconstructed Rebel* (New York, 1956), pp. 159–67, which denies Woodward's contention that the Southern Democrats were more instrumental than the Northern Democrats in giving up the filibuster against counting the electoral vote; and Thomas B. Alexander, "Persistent Whiggery in the Confederate South, 1860–1877," *Journal of Southern History* 27 (1961): 324–25, which suggests that the Whiggishly inclined bloc of Southern Democrats might have acted as it did even if there had been no Texas and Pacific lobby at work.

ceptional versatility as well as interpretive power. This versatility is perhaps best illustrated by his second book, *The Battle for Leyte Gulf*, which preceded *Reunion and Reaction* and *Origins of the New South* by four years. As a result of his naval service, mentioned above, he had been drawn into an intensive study of the operations which took place in the Philippine seas in October, 1944. Abrupt retooling was demanded of many scholars in the years between 1942 and 1945, but few such conversions were more drastic—or more effective—than this one, which required an historian who had previously dealt only with the South, the Negro, the cotton economy, and the politics of agrarian frustration and discontent, to write expertly of Japanese admirals, naval strategy, the fire power of fighting ships, and the complexities of navigation amid the islands of the Philippine archipelago. The history of naval operations is among the more technical branches of historical study, but Woodward mastered it so thoroughly that he was able to make a clear and vivid narrative of a particularly complex series of naval engagements. Not many books have come out of the Second World War possessing both the narrative and dramatic qualities which appeal to a wide public and the technical virtuosity which wins the respect of professional warriors, but *The Battle for Leyte Gulf* is one of the few which does both.[10]

The Battle for Leyte Gulf is a tour de force which showed what a wide range of things Woodward could do when he put his hand to them. But it is almost purely narrative, and reveals little of his historical philosophy. This philosophy is concerned primarily with the relation of history to society's understanding of itself, and it is most clearly evident in a number of brooding, deeply reflective essays which have very far-ranging implications.

It is perhaps natural that his concern with this broader

10. Review by Captain Paul F. Dugan, U.S.N., in United States Naval Institute, *Proceedings* 73 (1947): 457–58.

problem grew out of his preoccupation with Southern history, especially since Southern history, more than most branches of historical study, seems to point up the anomalous relationships between the past, or our image or legend of the past, and the present, or our image of the present. He first came to grips with this question in a presidential address to the Southern Historical Association in 1953 entitled "The Irony of Southern History." Woodward's title was doubtless suggested by Reinhold Niebuhr's *The Irony of American History* (1952), and it shared Niebuhr's skepticism concerning the American idea of progress as an antidote against evil. But its especial focus was to suggest parallels between the moral dogmatisms of the 1860's and those of the 1950's. In brief, this paper began by arguing that a sense of history involves an awareness of the tragic aspects of life which lie beyond human control. History is incomplete without the dimension of human error and disaster following from error. Human history began, as one might paraphrase it, not with the Garden of Eden and Adamic innocence, but with the loss of innocence and the expulsion from the Garden. But the American experience has lacked this basic historical component, because the American record has been one of uninterrupted and invariable "success." Americans were invincible; there was nothing they could not accomplish; they assumed "that American ideals, values and principles invariably prevail in the end . . . the assumption exposes us to the temptation of believing that we are somehow immune from the forces of history." Hence we have viewed our past in moralistic rather than in historical terms—that is, in terms of categorical choice between right and wrong, rather than in terms of the ambiguities and moral compromises inherent in the human condition. Hence we are especially prone to take dogmatic or absolutist positions—positions which are untempered by a sense of the magnitude of the gap between human aspiration and human attainment. In developing this theme, Woodward drew a parallel between the Southern defense of slavery in the 1840's and 1850's and the American defense of capitalism in the 1940's. The South in the 1840's needed intersectional friends, especially in the West; the United States in the 1940's needed international friends, especially in Western Europe. Both sought to win these friends. Yet the South made the mistake of insisting that the West accept "a system totally unadapted to the conditions and needs of the territories and often offensive to their moral sensibilities." The South also "abandoned its tradition of tolerance" and imposed a rigid demand for orthodoxy on the subject of slavery. The United States might now profit from this experience, Woodward suggested, first, to avoid alienating its potential Western European friends by demanding that they embrace a species of capitalism which many of them regarded with disapproval, and second, to avoid reducing its own vigor by imposing internal controls upon the free discussion of alternatives to the sacrosanct system of capitalism.

But it was not only the South which offered a warning example. There was also a lesson to be learned from the position of the North in the Civil War crisis. For the North had been "overwhelmingly moralistic in its approach." People who subscribe to the moralistic view tend "to appeal to a higher law to justify bloody and revolting means in the name of a noble end." This had happened in the Civil War, and to clinch his argument Woodward quoted Kenneth Stampp: "Yankees went to war animated by the highest ideals of the nineteenth-century middle classes. . . . But what the Yankees achieved—for their generation at least—was a triumph not of middle-class ideals but of middle-class vices. The most striking products of their crusade were the shoddy aristocracy of the North and the ragged children of the South. Among the masses of Americans, there were no victors, only the vanquished." [11]

"The Irony of Southern History" appeared at the height

11. In Woodward, *The Burden of Southern History*, pp. 169, 181, 182, 186, 187 (Vintage edition).

of the McCarthy Era in an early phase of the Cold War. It was, of course, written with reference to these circumstances. In it, Woodward showed more clearly than in any of his previous writings his unusually strong conviction that history should speak to the present. With his subtlety of mind and his disciplined awareness that our image of the past is the product of historians rather than of history, he of course avoided the simplistic ideas that "history repeats itself" or that analogues are ever complete. The context of "The Irony" reminded the reader that slavery was not capitalism, the Western states and territories were not the nations of Europe, and the moral validity of a crusade against slavery was not interchangeable with the moral validity of a crusade against Communism. But if the lessons were not read too literally, he believed that the past had a relevance not only in shaping the present, but in guiding our response to the present. In the case under discussion, the past might serve to remind us that ideological dogmatism could separate a society from its friends and could impair the realism of the society itself; that there was no direct ratio between the degree of moral purpose which went into a crusade and the degree of moral gain which came out, even when the crusade proved "successful"; and that war can have victors without necessarily having winners.

In 1958, Woodward returned to his efforts to relate the unique experience of the South in the past to the generalized experience of American society in the present. In "The Search for Southern Identity," he observed that economically the South, so long a distinctive region, was becoming more and more homogeneous with the rest of the country; the "Bulldozer Revolution" was making it so. With the traditional doctrines of white supremacy discredited, the distinctive Southern feature of segregation was also about to disappear. But when these tangible differentials were obliterated, would there be any distinctive feature left to keep the South from being "submerged under a national steamroller" and rendered "virtually indistinguishable from the other urban-industrial areas of the nation?" Yes, said Woodward, the South would still have its distinctive past experience: this experience included military defeat and subjugation and economic poverty and frustration in a nation which had known only victory and affluence; it included the psychological, subconscious awareness of the guilt of slavery and of discrimination against the Negro in a nation which has known only a complacent and two-dimensional "innocence"; it included the life of an organic society, with strong communal ties and a coherent social order, in a nation which has been structured by rational abstractions operating upon isolated individuals outside of any nexus of concrete personal ties such as one found in the kinship systems of the South.

In this essay, the discourse of the past with the present was brief, but it was pungent. Why did it matter at all whether the Southerner preserved any distinctive identity? And if he did preserve it, why did it matter for him to recognize it? It mattered because "The South . . . remains more American by far than anything else, and has all along. After all, it fell to the lot of one Southerner from Virginia to define America. The definition he wrote in 1776 voiced aspirations that were rooted in his native region before the nation was born. The modern Southerner should be secure enough in his national identity to escape the compulsions of less secure minorities to embrace uncritically all the myths of nationalism. He should be secure enough also not to deny a regional heritage because it is at variance with national myth. It is a heritage that should prove of enduring worth to him as well as to his country." [12]

"The Search for Southern Identity," like "The Irony of Southern History," dealt with the relation of past and pres-

12. *The Burden of Southern History,* pp. 6, 8, 25.

ent, especially in terms of the South and the Southerner. But in "The Age of Reinterpretation," a paper delivered at the meeting of the American Historical Association in 1959, Woodward turned in far more general terms to the problem of the role of the historian as an intermediary between the experience of men of the past and the understanding of men of the future. In this essay, which is widely regarded as his most significant single piece of work and as one of the major contributions to the interpretation of American history, he pointed out, first, the rapidity of change in modern society, and the perspective which this change gives us upon the past. Since 1945, we have entered an age of thermonuclear weapons and of intercontinental missiles, and we have seen the end of the world hegemony of the nations of Western Europe. As these epochal changes occur, they throw much of our past experience into a new light. To begin with they give us a focus, for the first time, upon the fact that for a century and a half the United States enjoyed a unique condition of "free security." During this era of immunity from military or naval threats from other countries, we did not have to use our resources for the maintenance of armament nor the energies of our young men for military service. In terms of economic growth alone, this freedom to direct all our strength into economically productive activities, without diverting it into military preparation, was an inestimable boon, and contributed significantly to the rapid rate of American economic growth in the nineteenth century. Because of its pervasive nature, this security also had some far-reaching side effects. For instance, it got us into the careless practice, in rare occasions of crisis, of going to war first and preparing for it afterward. Another, more important consequence was that it enabled us to get along without real concentrations of political power. Distrustful of power as we had been ever since the time of George III, we happily accepted this opportunity to dispense with it, and set up a governmental system which, through the separation of powers and checks and balances, was subject to long intervals of governmental paralysis, deadlock, or inertia. But our free security enabled us to afford the luxury of a political system that operated only intermittently.

Second, our passage into the nuclear age now enables us to see the history of war in a new light. When war occurs today, we try to keep it a limited war, meaning a nonnuclear war, but all wars before 1945 were nonnuclear wars. As such, they had relevance for one another. The warriors of World War II might still learn from the operations of the Civil War, just as the generals who fought between the Potomac and the James might profit by studying Napoleon's maxims or the military doctrine of Jomini. But changes in man's powers of destruction since 1945 have rendered most of our past military experience obsolete: "We can already see that the vast fleets that concentrated off the Normandy beaches and at Leyte Gulf, or the massed armies that grappled in the Battle of the Bulge or across the Russian Steppes, or for that matter the old-fashioned bomber squadrons that droned back and forth across the English Channel year after year dropping what the air force now contemptuously calls 'iron bombs' were more closely related to a remote past than to a foreseeable future."

Here, as I read it, Woodward is saying that devotees of history frequently seek to justify their study on the ground that there is always a continuity between the past and the present. The study of the past, it is assumed, will reveal the continuity and thus will offer guidance for the present. But, he implies further, this assumption is sometimes wrong. In times of very rapid and fundamental change, the continuity between the past and the present is broken. The task of the historian is not simply to trace the continuity, even when it is tenuous, but to examine the relationship between past and present for the purpose of exposing the discontinuity as much as for emphasizing the continuity. For we could be as dangerously misled by an apparition of continuity which does not really exist as by a failure to recognize continuities which are genuine.

Much of the existing historical literature was written when "free security" was taken for granted and when wars were fought with limited weapons, and that was taken for granted also. It will be a large task to rewrite this history in a way that takes account of our new awareness that these factors were peculiar to a given place and time, and were neither universal nor immutable. But an even greater body of the existing literature was Europe-centered. This literature, also, was most pervasive. Non-Europeans as well as Europeans shared the orientation which saw Europe as the center of the world. "The . . . assumptions of Europocentric history have very largely shaped the interpretation of Asiatic, African, and other non-European history . . . for Europe successfully marketed its historiography abroad, along with its other cultural products, in remote and exotic climates." The recognition, at last, of the restrictiveness of this view creates a need for the rewriting of a very substantial proportion of all of modern history from a new standpoint.

From these three new challenges to the historian Woodward turned back, near the end of his essay, to an evocative and statesman-like affirmation, again, of the role of the historian. The historians of this generation, he asserted, have a peculiar responsibility as intermediaries between a past that could not foresee the future and a future which may not be able to understand the past. For these historians carry with them into the new order a personal experience of the old.

> Americans among them will remember a time when security was assumed to be a natural right, free and unchallengeable. Among them also will be men of many nations who manned the ships and fought the battles of another age of warfare. And nearly all of this generation of historians will have been educated to believe that European culture was

> Civilization and that non-European races, if not natively inferior, were properly under perpetual tutelage. They will be the only generation of historians in history who will be able to interpret the old order to the new order with the advantage and authority derived from firsthand knowledge of the two ages and participation in both.

Here Woodward again affirmed his faith that it is not enough for the historian to understand the past; he must also interpret it to those who live in the present. In the final paragraph of "The Age of Reinterpretation," he made this affirmation even more explicit. The accelerated process of historical change, he said, gives a peculiar urgency to the public demand for answers to questions about the past and its relation to the present and the future.

> If historians evade such questions, people will turn elsewhere for the answers, and modern historians will qualify for the definition that Tolstoi once formulated for academic historians of his own day. He called them deaf men replying to the questions that nobody puts to them. If, on the other hand, they do address themselves seriously to the historical questions for which the new age demands answers, the period might justly come to be known in historiography as the age of reinterpretation.[13]

In this statement, renouncing a traditional concept of restrictions upon the academic historian, Woodward formally enunciated a position which, in operative terms, he had occupied from the beginning of his career. Consistently, his writing had reflected a purpose to identify the true values of the past and to make them meaningful to his contemporaries. In his quest for values, he held to two especially.

One of these was from his own birth and rearing—the value of the Southern heritage. In "The Search for Southern Identity," he had said, "After Faulkner, Wolfe, Warren, and

13. *American Historical Review* 66 (1960): 2, 11, 15, 18, 19.

Welty, no literate Southerner could remain unaware of his heritage or doubt its enduring value." [14] This belief in the enduring values of the South is deep-seated, and when Woodward totally rejects the traditional Southern attitudes on race, he regards it not as a rejection of Southernism but a rejection of a spurious value which has discredited the true Southern position. But he is still capable of resenting even attacks on biracialism when they run over into disparagement of the South as a whole. This fact was evident in his courteous but nonetheless devastating review of Dwight Dumond's indiscriminately worshipful treatment of the abolitionists in a work entitled *Antislavery*.[15] It was evident also in some pointed comments in his essay "From the First Reconstruction to the Second" (1965):

> The South has lately had its "Epitaph" written and its "Mystique" debunked. The implication would seem to be that the South's disputed "distinctiveness" and Southern identity inhere essentially in retrograde racial policies and prejudices. With the gradual disappearance of these, Southerners are expected to lose their identity in a happily homogenized nation. Quite apart from the South's preferences, there are other reasons for skepticism in this matter. The South has long served the nation in ways still in great demand. It has been a moral lightning rod, a deflector of national guilt, a scapegoat for stricken conscience. It has served the country much as the Negro has served the white supremacist—as a floor under self-esteem. This historic role, if nothing else, would spare the region total homogenization, for the national demand for it is greater than ever.[16]

To say that the Southern heritage had enduring value meant that it must not be defined in terms of things that lacked value

14. *The Burden of Southern History*, p. 25.
15. Woodward, "The Antislavery Myth," *The American Scholar* 31 (1962): 318–36.
16. *Harper's*, April, 1965, p. 133.

—such as segregation and the doctrine of white supremacy. Hence Woodward rejected Ulrich Phillips's formulation of "The Central Theme of Southern History," which identified the South in terms of the region's conviction that the South "shall be and remain a white man's country." There is, of course, copious and unedifying evidence that this conviction has been an enduring element in the quality of Southernism, and people who do not like the South are quite ready to make racism a prominent factor in their analysis of Southernism. But precisely because Woodward attached enduring value to some aspects of the Southern tradition, he could not accept their view. The South might have, on one side of its character, a quality of racism, discrimination, and repression, but it also had on the other side, a record of Jeffersonian liberalism. It must be saved from its worse side by an appeal to its better side. Once before the South had made the mistake of giving "priority to the worse side by choosing to identify its whole cause with the one institution [slavery] that was most vulnerable," and it had paid dearly for this folly. This must not happen again:

> . . . if Southernism is allowed to become identified with a last ditch defense of segregation, it will increasingly lose its appeal among the younger generation. Many will be tempted to reject their entire regional identification, even the name "Southern," in order to disassociate themselves from the one discredited aspect.[17]

As a comment on the consequences of identification with a discredited cause, this observation was, no doubt, pragmatic and sagacious, but in terms of historical method, it possessed startling implications. For it clearly implied that the degree of the historian's emphasis upon the identification of the South

17. "The Search for Southern Identity," reprinted in *The Burden of Southern History*, pp. 11, 12.

with slavery and later with segregation should be determined not by the actual extent of the South's commitment to these practices, but by the effect which such an identification would have upon the loyalties of Southerners to the better values of Southernism. The use of history to sanction meritorious values would take a priority over the use of it to portray realistically some of the evils of the past.

To leave the statement at this point would do an injustice to Woodward by picking out one strand of his thought and separating it from the broader fabric of which this strand was a part. This broader context was one of scrupulous adherence to rigorous historical criteria. As much as almost any contemporary American historian, Woodward has approached his material with a dedicated purpose to take the whole record into account, to see all sides of a topic, to qualify and hedge his generalizations, and to avoid the ease of simplification. These traits are strikingly evident, for instance, if one compares his treatment of slavery with the treatments by William E. Dodd and Frank L. Owsley. All three of these men were Southerners; all were committed to a liberal's sympathy with the dirt farmer; and all were embarrassed by the Southern treatment of the Negro. Dodd and Owsley expressed this embarrassment by avoiding the issue—Dodd by arguing that the South would, on its own initiative, have gotten rid of slavery but for the distorting effect of extraneous forces; Owsley by constructing an image of a South populated by "plain folk" (white) or yeomen—a land in which slaveholders were not important and slaves were, somehow, not quite visible.[18] Woodward, by contrast, faced up to the problems of racism, and the latter half of his biography of Watson is a grim record of Negrophobia, blatant discrimination, and lynch law, just as the first half is a record of Watson's effort, in the first phase of his life, to achieve an accord between

18. William E. Dodd, *Statesmen of the Old South* (New York, 1919); Frank L. Owsley, *Plain Folk of the Old South* (Baton Rouge, La., 1949).

Negroes and whites in the Populist movement. ("The People's Party," declared Watson, "says to these two men [the Negro farmer and the White farmer], 'You are made to hate each other because upon that hatred is rested . . . the financial despotism which enslaves you both.' ")[19]

Woodward found an ideal topic in Watson because the early part of Watson's career brought Woodward's second major value, liberalism, into conjunction with his first, the value of the Southern tradition properly understood. The early Watson hated economic exploitation, hated racial antagonism, denounced lynch law, and demanded recognition of the legal rights of Negroes. Woodward, looking for such experience in the past as would be meaningful to the present, found it, almost to perfection, in the career of Watson. That career did not conceal the grim and realistic actuality that segregation and injustice to the Negro dominated the Southern scene in the first two decades of this century, but it did show that *there had been an alternative.* Watson had seen the alternative, though his vision later failed and he lost sight of it. To Woodward, with his conviction that the historian must reconstruct the past accurately and at the same time make it speak to the present, the accuracy of the reconstruction lay in the recognition of Watson's failure and in the ultimate ascendancy of the worst features of his nature. But the message for the present lay in the fact that Watson had for a time seen a vision of a better way. The better way was not illusory; it had been a viable alternative. It failed not because inevitable forces caused it to fail, but because men who might have grasped it did not do so. Other men, in the present, might do so. No deterministic force, in Woodward's belief, foredoomed their effort, for as he has declared, "I am not a determinist of any sort." [20] The first lesson of the

19. Woodward, *Watson*, p. 220.
20. "What Happened to the Civil Rights Movement?" *Harper's*, January, 1967, p. 32.

past to the present is that men have choices and that no iron law of the operation of blind forces prevents men from exercising these choices.

This viewpoint was peculiarly pertinent to Southern attitudes toward segregation, for white Southerners showed a marked tendency to believe that the sharp separation of Negroes and whites was as old as the world, a reflex of basic human nature, and quite beyond the reach of any social policy. Many developments in the 1930's and 1940's led liberals to believe, with increasing conviction, that segregation must be done away with, and that social attitudes toward questions of race must be changed in order that racial relations might change. This conviction was already strong when the decision of the Supreme Court in the case of *Brown* vs. *The Board of Education* was handed down in May, 1954. When the Court spoke, the first reaction throughout the country was to ask how the South would respond. Would it show the old fierce resistance to "outside'" attempts to change the harsh taboos of racial separation, or would it comply with the decision of the Court? Here was a time, indeed, for the past to speak to the present in other than purely traditional terms.

During the following autumn, Woodward delivered the James W. Richard lectures at the University of Virginia. In 1955, while Woodward was Harmsworth Professor of American History at Oxford, they were published under the title of *The Strange Career of Jim Crow*, which quickly became and has remained his most famous book. These lectures really do not compare with his *Watson* or his *Origins of the New South* as major works of history, but they will nevertheless require almost as extensive discussion here because of the misunderstandings and controversy which they engendered and because of the fundamental questions which they raised.

In the first chapter of *The Strange Career*, significantly entitled "Forgotten Alternatives," Woodward sought to develop a point which he had stated clearly, in more condensed form in *Origins of the New South* (pp. 209–212): namely, that the formal structure of legal segregation which the South believed had existed forever had, in fact, not existed in full form until some years after the end of Reconstruction. True, he recognized, separation began soon after the Civil War in the churches, and it began in the schools as soon as former slaves began to go to school. But there was, he believed, scarcely any "evidence of a movement to make segregation universal. . . . More than a decade was to pass after Redemption [the end of Reconstruction] before the first Jim Crow law was to appear upon the law books of a Southern state, and more than two decades before the older states of Virginia, North Carolina, and South Carolina were to adopt such laws." In elaboration of this statement, Woodward proceeded to quote two Northern travelers, one British traveler, two Southern editorials, one Southern white, and one Negro, all seven of whom testified that Negroes and whites in the South mingled, with very little tension and with considerable spontaneity and ease, in public saloons, dining rooms, trains, street cars, theaters, and soda fountains. If this evidence was limited, it was explicit and seemingly quite reliable. With scrupulous care, Woodward also pointed out that there had never been a "golden age of race relations" in the South, and that "the evidence of race conflict and violence, brutality and exploitation in this very period is overwhelming." But the over-all impression, formed by many readers, was that this was a subsidiary point.

Having made this qualification, he then moved on to say that, "before the South capitulated completely to the doctrines of the extreme racists, three alternative philosophies of race relations were put forward": one a conservative or aristocratic philosophy which accepted a responsibility for the paternal care of the Negroes and regarded all lower-class people, either Negro or white, with very much the same condescension; another, a radical philosophy which sought to form a political combination of Negro and white dirt farmers against those who were exploiting them economically; and third, a liberal philosophy which, on principle, advocated equal rights and protection for all citizens. He traced each of these three briefly, and then again entered a disclaimer: he did not wish to exaggerate the degree of interracial harmony. There were Negrophobes and hypocrites in all of these camps. Indeed he concluded:

> My only purpose has been to indicate that things have not always been the same in the South. In a time when the Negroes formed a much larger proportion of the population than they did later, when slavery was a live memory in the minds of both races, and when the memory of the hardships and bitterness of Reconstruction was still fresh, the race policies accepted and pursued in the South were sometimes milder than they became later. The policies of proscription, segregation, and disfranchisement that are often described as the immutable "folkways" of the South, impervious alike to legislative reform and armed intervention, are of a more recent origin. The effort to justify them as a consequence of Reconstruction and a necessity of the times is embarrassed by the fact that they did not originate in those times. And the belief that they are immutable and unchangeable is not supported by history.[21]

Despite all Woodward's care to insert caveats, qualifiers, and disclaimers, *The Strange Career* ran into two difficulties. First was the problem that when the past speaks to the present, it cannot speak to everyone alive in the present, but must speak to particular groups. When Woodward delivered the Richard lectures at Charlottesville, he was speaking to such a group—to Southern whites who needed to learn that segregation had not been included among the Ten Commandments.

21. The quoted passages are from pp. 16, 25, 26, 47, of Woodward, *The Strange Career of Jim Crow* (New York, 1955 edition).

If he had been able to limit his message to the audience for whom it was intended, there would never have been any confusion. The audience knew that segregation and discrimination had been the dominant patterns of the South, and what Woodward told them was that these patterns had not been either absolute or universal or immutable. This was a useful fact for them to learn. But as soon as the lectures were published, they reached a vast audience. Ironically, Woodward's least substantial book was the one that made his public, as distinguished from his professional, reputation. More than any modest man could possibly have anticipated, he found himself addressing a vast, amorphous audience of people, many of whom had formed their impressions of the South from *Gone With the Wind* or *Tobacco Road,* who regarded the region as a never-never land, and who, unlike the people of Charlottesville, were prepared to believe anything. Many of these avid readers wishfully read into Woodward's lectures an idyllic image of a South in which race antagonism did not rear its unlovely head until the twentieth century.

To state this in another way, the historian who seeks to interpret the life of the past to the men of the present usually winds up by giving less of his attention to reconstructing what the past was "really" like, than to identifying the misconceptions of men in the present, and devising ways to correct these misconceptions. But since all sorts of various people entertain all sorts of various misconceptions, the labor of correcting the misconceptions impels the historian to address himself to a focus which is neither unitary nor fixed. What he writes will be relative in any case, but instead of being relative to what happened to a determinate group of people in the past, it becomes relative to what misconceptions are held, at a given moment, by indeterminate groups of people in the present. His task becomes a labor of Hercules. Perhaps the labor it most closely resembles is that of cleaning the Augean stables.

The second difficulty encountered by *The Strange Career* arose from the fact that when an historian has a strong ideological commitment, a tension may be set up between his devotion to the commitment and his devotion to realism for its own sake. In Woodward's own terms, it is ironically conceivable that when a deaf man gives answers to questions which no one is asking, he may be worth listening to precisely because he is more concerned with what he himself sees than with what other people, at the moment, want to know. In any case, Woodward had undertaken the arduous task of finding answers in the Southern past to questions which people were asking in 1954. This undertaking never led him to the obvious fallacies of simpler minds engaged in the same task—the fallacy, for instance, of believing that the South seriously considered abolishing slavery as late as 1830. But it did lead him to an inner struggle in which his historical realism was pitted against his liberal urge to find constructive meanings in the past for the affairs of the present. His realism never lost hold, but his liberal urge constantly impelled him to emphasize viewpoints which his realism constantly impelled him to qualify and dilute.

This inner struggle was, I believe, especially evident in *The Strange Career*. It was evident in the sense that the array of evidence presented, though by no means all on one side, would lead a reader to minimize the importance of segregation in the South in the 1870's, 1880's, and 1890's, far more than the general bulk of other evidence would do.[22] This

22. Barton J. Bernstein calls my attention to the relevance of the Civil Rights Act of 1875 in connection with this question. Evidence concerning this act has been neglected by scholars, but it is very pertinent in two ways: (1) there is palpably a question why the act's supporters deemed it necessary unless discrimination was being practiced; (2) considerable evidence of such discrimination was presented in support of the proposed measure. Of course the discrimination may have been practiced informally, and therefore may not have involved any action by Southern state governments, but the issue of segregation was certainly involved, whether or not in the form of Jim Crow.

fact became apparent subsequently, from a series of intensive analyses of Negro-white relations in the late nineteenth century by a number of investigators working state by state: Charles E. Wynes for Virginia (1961), Frenise A. Logan for North Carolina (1964), and Joel Williamson for South Carolina (1965).

Of these "revisionists," only Wynes discussed Woodward by name, and Wynes was the least disposed of the three to take issue with him. The picture of segregation in Virginia between 1870 and 1900, as Wynes saw it, was mixed. Often the Negro who sought to frequent places of public resort met with rebuffs, but "Occasionally the Negro met no segregation when he entered restaurants, bars, waiting rooms, and other places of public amusement." The Woodward thesis, he thought, was "essentially sound," but most of the time, the Negro did "meet segregation, opposition, or eviction." [23] For North Carolina, Logan emphasized the dominance of segregation somewhat more: "The most effective limitations . . . on the relationship between white and Negro were the unwritten agreements among the whites that any approach to 'social equality' should be resisted at all costs. The matter of social equality was most sharply focused upon when it revolved around the segregation of Negroes on public carriers, in waiting rooms, and in hotels and restaurants." [24] But it was Williamson's conclusions that were most at variance with Woodward's. His evidence seemed to show that "the physical separation of the races was the most revolutionary change in relations between whites and Negroes in South Carolina during Reconstruction." "The pattern of separation was fixed in the minds of the whites almost simultaneously with the emancipation of the Negro. By 1868, the

23. Charles E. Wynes, *Race Relations in Virginia, 1870–1902* (Charlottesville, Va., 1961), pp. 68–110, 144–50, especially pp. 149–50.
24. Frenise A. Logan, *The Negro in North Carolina, 1876–1894* (Chapel Hill, N.C., 1964), pp. 174–88, 209–219, especially p. 215.

physical color line had, for the most part, already crystallized." But the real separation, he continued, was "mental
separation. . . . The rigidity of the physical situation, set as
it was like a mosaic in black and white, itself suggested the
intransigence of spirit which lay behind it . . . the heart-
land of racial exclusiveness remained inviolate; and South
Carolina had become, in reality, two communities—one white
and the other Negro." [25]

More telling, perhaps, than any of these analyses of the
post-bellum period was Richard C. Wade's study in 1964,
Slavery in the Cities. Woodward had regarded it as almost
axiomatic that "segregation would have been impractical under slavery"—that where slavery existed, the circumstances
giving rise to segregation did not exist. But Wade presented
evidence to show that in the towns of the South long before
the Civil War, where the surveillance of the Negroes, characteristic of the slave system, could no longer be maintained,
"the distinction between slave and free Negro was erased;
race became more important than legal status; and a pattern
of segregation emerged inside the broader framework of the
peculiar institution." [26]

In later editions of *The Strange Career* Woodward scrupulously took note of these studies, and in fact he anticipated
them as early as 1957 in a foreword to the first paperback
edition, in which he recognized that segregation was initially
foreshadowed in the cities, even before the end of slavery,
and in which he called attention to a number of early segregation laws (Mississippi and Florida, 1865; Texas, 1866; Ten-
nessee, 1881),[27] which were inconsistent with his earlier state-

25. Joel Williamson, *After Slavery: The Negro in South Carolina During
Reconstruction, 1861–1877* (Chapel Hill, N.C., 1965), pp. 240–99, especially pp. 274, 298–99.
26. Richard C. Wade, *Slavery in the Cities: The South 1820–1860* (New
York, 1964), p. 266 and passim; Woodward, *Strange Career*, p. 14.
27. *Strange Career* (Galaxy edition, 1957), pp. xv–xvi. Other works treating
of the degree of segregation in the post-bellum South, and which Wood-

ment that it was more than a decade after Redemption "before the first Jim Crow law was to appear upon the law books of a Southern state."

If Woodward's dislike of segregation influenced him to minimize its prevalence, some critics have also felt that his desire to demonstrate the historical possibility of close and harmonious working relationships between Negroes and whites led him to overemphasize the importance of the co-operation between Negro and white farmers' alliances in the Populist contests of 1892. Again, this is very much a matter of emphasis. But in any case Woodward had not failed to point out that Watson himself, the chief architect of the cooperation, had recognized that race antagonisms were extremely real, and that the race issue was a great handicap to Southern Populism ("Bryan had *no everlasting and overshadowing Negro question to hamper and handicap his progress. I HAD,*" said Watson).[28]

But there was one other case in which his impulse to find sanction in the past for ideas that he approves in the present may have led him to take a position from which he later felt impelled to withdraw. In 1958, in the *American Scholar* he published an essay, "Equality, the Deferred Commitment." In this paper he discussed the war aims of the Civil War: first, simply the preservation of the Union; later, freedom for the slaves; and finally, near the end, equality for the freedmen. The commitment to this third aim, he recognized, was never as clear-cut as the first two commitments—there was never

---

ward took into account in the original edition of *Strange Career*, include: Vernon L. Wharton, *The Negro in Mississippi, 1865–1890* (Chapel Hill, N.C., 1947), and George B. Tindall, *South Carolina Negroes, 1877–1900* (Columbia, S.C., 1952). The whole question of the origins of segregation has now assumed the dimensions of a full-scale historical controversy, and Joel Williamson has edited a brief volume of selections from Woodward and twelve other writers, including all those cited from note 21 through this note: *The Origins of Segregation* (Boston, 1968).

28. Woodward, *Watson*, p. 220.

an equality proclamation. But though "made piece-meal . . .
and with full implications not spelled out until after the war
. . . it [the commitment] was made." Challenged by Southern aggression against Negro rights after the war, the radical
Republicans "proceeded to make equality as much the law
of the land as freedom." Citing the Fourteenth and Fifteenth
Amendments and the Civil Rights Acts of 1866 and 1875,
Woodward concluded that

> by every device of emphasis, repetition, reenactment, and
> reiteration, the radical lawmakers and Constitution-amenders
> would seem to have nailed down all loose ends, banished all
> ambiguity, and left no doubt whatever about their intention
> to extend Federal protection to Negro equality. So far as it
> was humanly possible to do so by statute and constitutional
> amendment, America would seem to have been fully com-
> mitted to the principle of equality.[29]

Here again, Woodward was seeking to make the past speak
to the present. The past had made a promise to American
Negroes and then defaulted on it. It was the obligation of
the present to honor and fulfill the promise. But some other
scholars hesitated to read the promise of the past in this way
or to agree that the United States had made a firm commitment a century ago to racial equality in the full sense. For
instance, W. R. Brock, in his influential study *An American
Crisis* (1963), wrote: "Racial equality was a hypothesis which
was generally rejected. It was not accepted in the North any
more than it was in the South and even abolitionists were
anxious to disclaim any intention of forcing social contacts
between the races and all shied away from the dread subject
of racial amalgamation."

Brock did not go into much detail about the enactment of
the specific measures which were regarded as embodying the
principle of equality, but also in 1963, in a doctoral disserta-

29. In *The Burden of Southern History*, pp. 75, 77, 78.

tion on radical Republican policy toward the Negro, written at Yale just before Woodward went there, Selden Henry presented a full and close analysis of the many complexities, parliamentary and otherwise, attending the enactment of the principal "equalitarian" measures. Henry made a strong, detailed demonstration that none of these measures involved a clear-cut showdown between the advocates and the opponents of equality for Negroes, and his evidence indicated that opposition to full equality remained in the ascendant throughout Reconstruction.

Woodward, it should be said, had always recognized, even in his "deferred commitment" essay, that there were many crosscurrents in the public attitude toward the freedmen and many mental reservations in the acceptance of equality, but as he considered the problem further, he began to stress the qualifications more than the thesis. By 1965, he was writing, "Even in . . . [the Civil Rights acts, the Reconstruction acts, and the Fourteenth and Fifteenth Amendments]—the very legal foundation for the new order of freedom and equality—can be found the compromises, half-measures, and ambivalences that are in essence concessions to racism." In another year, he made his reversal explicit in an essay in which he cited Henry and declared, "On the issue of Negro equality, the party remained divided, hesitant, and unsure of its purpose. The historic commitment to equality it eventually made was lacking in clarity, ambivalent in purpose, and capable of numerous interpretations." A footnote adds the laconic comment that, "This admittedly represents a change from views earlier expressed on the subject by the author." [30]

30. W. R. Brock, *An American Crisis: Congress and Reconstruction, 1865–1877* (New York, 1963), pp. 285–86; G. Selden Henry, "Radical Republican Policy Toward the Negro During Reconstruction, 1862–1872" (Ph.D. dissertation, Yale, 1963). It is noteworthy that even Woodward's own student James M. MacPherson, *The Struggle for Equality: Abolitionists and the Negro in the Civil War and Reconstruction* (Princeton, N.J., 1964), provides copious evidence of preponderant Northern sentiment against equality for

The urgency of Woodward's desire to find answers in the past which would aid in the quest for solution of the problems of the present must have had some effect upon these views of the past. If it could be shown historically that legalized segregation was relatively a new phenomenon, and that promises of equality were a century old, it might be easier to induce people to abandon segregation and to accord equality to Negroes. Since Woodward himself later modified or even changed his position on both of these matters, it seems reasonable to suppose that the tension between his devotion to liberal goals and his devotion to historical realism distorted his image of the past, at least for a time and to a limited degree.

But, as has already been suggested, Woodward never ignored the complexities. He never failed to point out that he was engaged in weighing conflicting bodies of evidence and that important evidence existed which ran counter to the view he was presenting. Always committed to the historian's task of translating the past to make it intelligible to the present, he was also always scrupulous not to translate too freely. But what he did not reckon with was that many of his readers, with far less disciplined ideological commitments than his, and with painfully limited appreciation of the historical context in which he was writing, did some translating on their own of his translation. The result was that many such readers came away from his writings with the totally fallacious notion that the American people had accepted Negroes as

---

Negroes. At his conclusion, MacPherson states that when the Radical Republicans abandoned the federal enforcement of Negro rights in the South (far short of equality), "The mass of Northern people had never loved the Negro, were tired of 'the everlasting Negro question' and were glad to see the end of it" (p. 431).

Woodward, "Flight from History: the Heritage of the Negro," *Nation*, September 20, 1965, pp. 142–46; Woodward, "Seeds of Failure in Radical Race Policy," in Harold M. Hyman, ed., *New Frontiers of the American Reconstruction* (Urbana, Ill., 1966), p. 130.

equals a hundred years ago and that a utopia of interracial harmony and good will had prevailed until the 1890's.

Woodward has commented unhappily on the strange career which *The Strange Career of Jim Crow* has experienced. In the preface to the second revised edition (1966) he said: "Books that deal with subjects over which current political controversy rages are prone to uses and interpretations beyond the author's intentions or control. The present work has proved no exception and the author has been embarrassed by finding it cited—and misinterpreted—for purposes with which he sympathizes as well as for purposes he deplores." More recently, in *Harper's Magazine*, speaking of himself in the third person, he wrote:

> One historian suggested that the full-blown system of legally enforced segregation was not an immediate sequel of Appomattox, only to find himself cited as authority for the doctrine that Jim Crow was superficially rooted and easily eradicated. And when he called attention to the union of Negroes and whites in Southern Populism, he was interpreted as prophesying millennial developments in politics. It is no news to teachers, of course, that the lessons taught are not always the lessons learned.[31]

If Woodward has been troubled to find his words read in a way which he did not intend, he has clearly been much more troubled to have his hopes for the steady advancement and peaceful success of the Civil Rights movement frustrated. With a liberal's conviction that truth about the past can contribute with certainty to win public backing for voluntary, broadly based social progress, Woodward always intended for history to serve the cause of civil rights without sacrificing its integrity, and for the civil-rights cause to prevail without destroying the more vital values of the Southern tradition.

31. *Strange Career*, 1966 edition, p. vii; "What Happened to the Civil Rights Movement?" (1967), p. 36.

In the first edition of *The Strange Career* he spoke of "the need of the times for whatever light the historian has to shed upon a perplexing and urgent problem." He also asserted that the changes in "the old system of disfranchisement and segregation" were so extensive that they could be termed a "New Reconstruction." His tone, as he himself expressed it, was one of "restrained optimism," and in the 1957 edition he said, "In spite of resistance and recent setbacks, therefore, the preponderant evidence points to the eventual doom of segregation in American life and the triumph of the Second Reconstruction *in the long run.*" [32]

One feature which accentuated the optimistic tenor of *The Strange Career* was that, in it, Woodward did not, in fact, attempt to treat the whole biracial system, in all its historical, economic, and cultural complexities. Instead he dealt quite explicitly with only one feature—namely, the structure of formal, institutional arrangements—mostly in the form of statutes or ordinances—by which the separation of whites and Negroes had been enforced. Indeed it was this structure, strictly speaking, which constituted the "Jim Crow" phenomenon. The Jim Crow structure, of course, did much to maintain the whole system of biracialism, and was so interwoven with the whole system that some optimists mistakenly believed that biracialism could not exist without it. Woodward did not make this error, but he did restrict his focus to one aspect of the system, and to the most vulnerable aspect of all. Once the Brown decision had been made, it was relatively easy to sweep away all the accumulation of public regulations which had imposed legal disabilities and *de jure* segregation upon Negroes. After the court decisions were reinforced by a series of civil-rights acts by Congress in 1957, 1960, and 1964, and by a voting-rights act in 1965, it was

32. The quoted passages are on pp. ix and 124 of the 1955 edition and pp. 153 and 178–79 of the 1957 edition.

possible to say, as Woodward did in the 1966 edition of *The Strange Career*, that "Jim Crow as a legal entity was dead." [33]

But written statutes in books are far easier to change than educational differentials, employment differentials, residential differentials, and other disparities that have already molded the society and irrevocably shaped the lives of millions. Also, formal enactments are easier to get at than covert attitudes and unspoken feelings of apartness. Therefore, even at a time when Jim Crow was dying, racial tensions were becoming in some ways more acute. Because of this, the reader of the 1966 edition of *The Strange Career* was brought abruptly at the end of the book to the disconcerting realization that while his attention had been focused upon the slow demise of formal segregation, the principal issues of interracial antagonism had been shifting elsewhere as the Negro revolution changed course. Only five days after Lyndon Johnson signed the Voting Rights Act, which might be regarded as the final step in the elimination of Jim Crow, the Watts riot broke out in Los Angeles.

Just as the abolition of slavery had ended one stage of the relationship of Negroes and whites in America without solving the problem of that relationship, the abolition of Jim Crow ended another stage, but again without solving the problem of the relationship. Woodward recognized this in three final paragraphs in the 1966 edition, in which he asserted vaguely that "civil rights laws were not enough," and that "broader and more drastic remedies" were needed.[34]

Woodward's impulse to think of the handicaps of American Negroes in terms of formal segregation was, of course, in line with most of the thinking on the subject during the first decade after the Brown decision. Most of the reform activity of that decade was directed toward destroying the barriers

33. P. 189.
34. Pp. 190–91.

of legal separation in schools, buses, waiting rooms, restaurants, etc. So long as this was so, the decline of Jim Crow gave the deceptive appearance of being equivalent to the ending of racial tensions. For a long time no one asked about the cultural, occupational, economic, and other disparities that would be left when formal segregation was swept away, and about the antagonisms that might develop when discrimination and Negro disadvantages were found to remain after all legal inequality had been abolished. Woodward's view was no more restrictive than anyone else's, but his hope, as a Southerner, for a new order, voluntarily instituted, and his faith, as a liberal, in rational, peaceful reform through mediated changes in public policy—these things had given him a perfect affinity for the civil-rights movement, but found him far less compatible with the impulses toward Negro revolution. It is, of course, not yet clear how much of a revolutionary component the Negro movement holds, nor is it clear just how Woodward will respond to some aspects of it. His difficulty in responding showed up rather clearly in 1966 in the brief, hasty, tacked-on passages about the Watts riot. These seemed far less thoughtful than most of his writing, which has consistently been distinguished for its contemplative quality and its interpretive power.

But in January, 1967, in an essay in *Harper's Magazine* entitled "What Happened to the Civil Rights Movement?" he gave a more considered evaluation to the confused status of current Negro-white relationships. This statement offered some striking perspectives, if few answers, and it showed one more phase in Woodward's own quest for the use of history as a means of enabling the past to speak to the present.

From his viewpoint as a liberal,[35] he found the situation

35. The attribution perhaps requires no proving, but Woodward specifically classified himself as "a liberal, even more, a Southern white liberal" in a commentary at a Socialist Scholars Conference in 1966. See *Studies on the Left* 6 (1966): 35.

discouraging. The article was as pessimistic as any that he has published. Beginning with a foreboding reminder of the way in which the First Reconstruction (1865–1877) had lost its idealistic momentum, he sketched the peak of high idealism which the Second Reconstruction (since 1954) had reached in the sit-in movement, the marches on Washington and other cities, and all the singing and the dedication. From this peak, there had been a swift descent with "the triumph of tokenism," the divisions among Negoes, the ghetto riots, and the falling away of white participants in the movement as they shifted their attention to Vietnam, reacted negatively to Negro militancy, or simply became bored with long-sustained idealism, as people so often do. "If we are realists," he said, "we will no longer pretend that the movement for racial justice and Negro rights is sustained by the same foundation of moral assurance, or that it is supported today by the same political coalitions, the same inter-racial accommodations, and such harmony of purpose, commitment and dedication as recently prevailed." Noting "numerous white defections from the commitment to racial justice, the sudden silence in many quarters recently vocal with protest, the mounting appeal to bigotry and the scurry of retreat in Congress," he warned that "it would be the better part of realism to expect things to get worse before they get better." He suggested no specific measures that could make things better.[36]

But even as he discounted the social hopes that have shone implicitly through all of his writing from *Tom Watson* on, even as he recognized the fact that the present, at least at the moment, is not prepared to hear from the past the things which he has spent thirty years trying to show that the past has to say, he reaffirmed the two personal commitments, to historical realism and to liberalism, which he has sometimes had difficulty driving in tandem, but which he has used in

36. "What Happened to the Civil Rights Movement?" Pp. 32, 34, 37.

conjunction as purposefully, as successfully, and with as much evenhanded respect for the integrity of both commitments as any American historian.

His basic historical philosophy from the outset has been that the multiplicity of elements in any situation always offers diverse potentialities, and these diverse potentialities always offer society a choice of alternatives. History can help to show these alternatives. When society sees them, it can escape determinism and exercise choice. In the situation in 1967, Woodward saw many factors reducing the force of the civil-rights movement, but he also saw the presence of the largest body of independent Negro voters in history, and the existence of "a corps of Negro leaders that has not been surpassed in dedication, astuteness, and moral force by the leadership of any other great social movement of the century." The presence of these factors offered an alternative to the threatened deterioration of the civil-rights movement. So long as such elements exist, "there is no realism in accepting the current reaction as irreversible, and no rationality in despair." [37]

This statement was not only a seasoned evaluation, at a crucial transition point in its history, of a movement with which Woodward has been concerned from the beginning. It was also an affirmation, in a new context, of his conception of history as a key which the past gives us for guidance in confronting the problems of the present. But the difficulty with this concept lies in the dilemma: can history retain its integrity as a rigorous and disciplined form of scholarly inquiry even while partaking of public and functional uses in our encounters with current issues? The ideological assertion that it can is not a new conception and does nothing to resolve the dilemma. The resolution can only be meaningful at the operative level, and it is here that Woodward has made

37. *Ibid.,* p. 37.

one of his most distinctive contributions to historiography. Despite what may have been his errors in regard to the absence of formal segregation in the generation after Reconstruction, and the nature of the commitment to equality in the decade after Appomattox, he has been remarkably successful in demonstrating that history can retain its basic scholarly validity even in a context of active presentism. It is not by theoretical logic that he has done this, but by his own treatment of the history of race relations in America.

His greatest significance to historical studies may lie in the fact that he has made himself the foremost practitioner of a concept of history which holds that the experience of the past can find its highest relevance in the guidance which it offers in living with the problems of the present. His work has shown that history can be used in this way, but only in the hands of a scholar of extraordinary maturity, humane understanding, breadth of mind, and capacity to combine tolerance with idealism. And his vicissitudes have shown that, even for a man with these qualities, this may be the most difficult as well as the most rewarding use of history.

8

CONFLICT, CONSENSUS, AND COMITY:
A REVIEW OF RICHARD HOFSTADTER'S
THE PROGRESSIVE HISTORIANS

Nothing that he ever published probably gave Potter more trouble than this review essay, which passed through one rewriting and two extensive revisions before it satisfied the editor of the New York Review of Books. *Confessing that he too had been dissatisfied with the earlier versions, Potter ascribed part of his difficulty to the fact that he found Hofstadter's book "extraordinarily cryptic in relating Turner, Beard, and Parrington to the main idea with which the author is dealing." The essay is presented here as it finally appeared in the* Review *for December 5, 1968, except that the introductory paragraph, deleted by the* Review, *has been restored.*

SINCE 1948, when he published *The American Political Tradition*, Richard Hofstadter has been a leading interpreter of the American historical experience. Winning the highest professional acclaim, he has at the same time reached to the heart of living questions in a way that won for him a large nonprofessional readership. In *The Progressive Historians*, however, although he is still asking what the real issues have been in American history, and how divisive they have actually been, he approaches the problem through an indirect and convoluted medium—a study of the work of three historians, Frederick Jackson Turner, Charles A. Beard, and Vernon Louis Parrington. Many readers previously unfamiliar with this trio may be overwhelmed by Hofstadter's brilliant but lengthy and somewhat esoteric historiographical analyses and may fail to grasp his central conclusions, or even his central theme.

In all of his writing, Hofstadter has sought to define the nature of American society as it has expressed itself politically. His viewpoint has been essentially liberal, with emphasis upon the value of an open society. But he has rejected the optimism and complacency of traditional liberal thought. He has refused to accept the textbook view that American history records a continuous unfolding of the democratic ideal, and he is skeptical even about the commitment of the majority of Americans to such an ideal.

In many of his interpretations, in fact, Hofstadter has been an iconoclast. For instance, he refused to accept Jacksonianism either as coonskin democracy or as incipient nineteenth-century New Dealism; he diagnosed it instead as a movement to admit a new class of entrepreneurs into the economic privileges previously monopolized by the Bank of the United States. He saw Lincoln not as a "Great Emancipator" but as a politician who shrewdly combined the antislavery votes of those who wanted to keep the territories free and the anti-Negro votes of those who wanted to keep the new areas white. He rejected the idea that Progressivism was a pure, liberal reformism, pointing to the "sour" nativistic side of much Progressivism, as shown in Prohibition, the exclusion of the Japanese, and immigration restriction generally. Hofstadter denied the conventional view that the New Deal was merely an extension of Progressive Reform—and therefore "good" because sanctioned by precedents—and argued that in a number of ways, it marked "a drastic new departure . . . in the history of American reformism." For instance, it brought urban, immigrant groups into the stream of American life (though it neglected Negroes), and recognized a new role for the government.

These views, which challenged tradition at many points, are, in their conclusions, not unlike some of the harsh revisionism of the current New Left. But the tone is different, for it is not hostile, nor even astringent. Hofstadter himself perhaps suggests the reason in *The Age of Reform* (1955): "I find that I have been critical of the Populist-Progressive tradition. . . . I say critical, but not hostile, for I am criticizing largely from within." In short, while he saw many aspects of the American past in a realistic, unflattering light, recognizing that it was not what its uncritical admirers had supposed it to be, he cherished it nevertheless. Thus, interpretations which might be regarded as quite damaging were stated with a mellowness that made them seem less drastic than they really were. Perhaps this is an aspect of Hofstadter's largeness of mind and his emotional sympathy for points of view which he reluctantly regards as rationally fallacious.

In his new book, a study of Turner, Beard, and Parrington, one again encounters conclusions damning in themselves but curiously blended with a tone that is almost affectionate. These three men were the giants of American historiography when Hofstadter entered the profession. "I have asked myself why I wrote this book," he writes in his preface, as if he never wondered until after the book was completed. His answer seems subjective. "I started this book out of a personal engagement with the subject, out of some sense of the incompleteness of my reckoning with my intellectual forebears . . . out of the conviction that if I did not write about these men now, the clarification that I hoped for from such a reckoning might never take place. At the point at which I began to have some identity as an historian, it was the work of these men, particularly Beard and Parrington, that interested me as supplying the guiding ideas to the understanding of American history."

Critical but not hostile, Hofstadter here again is an observer of American history "largely from within." He recognizes the personal merits of Turner, Beard, and Parrington, and the stature of their work. He alludes to "the mythic appeal of their ideas which reached outside academic walls and touched readers in the general intellectual public." He remarks that they were among the first academics to recognize that they "must have a reckoning with the world of institutional power," and points out that all three were drawn into "university controversies of varying degrees of acerbity, and each of them left an institution under stress." He shows them to be appealing men, and writes with appreciation of their pioneer achievements in bringing history to terms with an urban, industrial, ethnically diversified society.

But while Hofstadter shows his sympathy for these historians, he shows at the same time an unflinching readiness to examine their shortcomings. There is something admirable but also something ironic in his capacity to hold both perspectives. The irony is underscored by the fact that all three historians are now more or less out-of-date, and Hofstadter's own work went far to out-date them, for his view of Progressivism is vastly different from Parrington's, his view of the nature of the issues in American history is vastly different from Beard's. He himself states that these men are obsolete. On Turner: "the mountain of Turner criticism is his most certain monument"—one way of suggesting that Turner's ideas are now buried and that the barrage of criticism, though long-delayed, was at last overwhelming. On Beard: today, Beard's reputation "stands like an imposing ruin in the landscape of American historiography" . . . his ideas come to us "as a set of lingering resonances." On Parrington: although Hofstadter can still engage his graduate students' minds in Turner and Beard, "I could find no way to interest them in Parrington."

These statements raise questions as to why men of such remarkable talent now seem no longer to be relevant, and if they are not relevant, why Hofstadter has chosen such an intractable subject. Is this long book only an inconclusive chapter in Hofstadter's own intellectual autobiography, or is he addressing himself, as before, to crucial current questions?

He is, I think, speaking, with unnecessary and tantalizing indirectness, to a very large and current question: How does a society handle the kind of controversy which is necessary to all reform and social change, without experiencing a measure of disruption that injures or even destroys the society itself? How can we have consensus without repression or controvery without disruption? In his previous writings, Hofstadter has touched upon another aspect of this problem, for in *The Age of Reform* and later in *The Radical Right*, he developed the view that some controversies are fought over real issues— over conflicting ideals or conflicting interests—but that others derive from psychological anxieties about status rather than from genuine differences on questions of policy. (Prohibition, for instance, may have represented a symbolic attack by rural, Protestant, old-stock Americans against an urban, secular, cosmopolitan society by which they felt threatened.) In his analysis of Progressivism, Hofstadter emphasized the illusory or marginal character of many of the highly dramatized "issues," such as the "titanic" battles between the "people" and the trusts. He stressed the broad agreements of the Progressive period, and other historians have gone further to suggest that the great corporations approved of, or even capitalized upon, measures which the Progressives pictured themselves as winning by crusades against the plutocracy.

While Hofstadter was developing this interpretation, Louis Hartz and Daniel Boorstin were also publishing books which minimized the element of conflict in American history— Hartz arguing that Americans all shared the basic ideology of John Locke, and Boorstin arguing that Americans were highly pragmatic and did not take any ideology seriously enough to be divided by it. In 1959, John Higham, noting the common emphasis on consensus by these and other writers, suggested that a "cult of consensus" was emerging, and he identified Hofstadter as a prominent member of the consensus school.

In writing about Turner, Beard, and Parrington, Hofstadter now addresses himself directly to the question of conflict and consensus, for all three of these were men who read the past as a series of conflicts. Indeed, their optimistic faith in the steady advance of progress was predicated upon a belief that the forces of enlightenment and democracy were waging a constant war against the forces of obscurantism and reaction. Turner constantly stressed the geographical conflict of sections; Beard, the economic conflict of interests; Parrington, the ideological conflict of enlightenment versus reaction. Beard became almost paranoid in suspecting conspiracy on the part of those who opposed "democratic" or "progressive" measures. Parrington had a Manichean view of the world. "The pivotal idea of the Progressive historians," Hofstadter writes, was "economic and political conflict." But he shows they had no criteria for measuring the magnitude and intensity of conflict. Hence they tended to treat every divergence of opinion as if it were a major battle in an epic war. They saw the Constitution as a "counter-revolution" against the Declaration of Independence, the Jacksonian "Revolution" as a coalition of frontiersmen and workingmen against the capitalist elite, the Progressive movement as a crusade against "big business."

Careful historical analysis has qualified, if not discredited, all these simplistic versions of American history. But such exaggerated antitheses were unavoidable in the absence of a broad perspective which would compare political issues in America with those in Europe, and recognize how narrow was the range of disagreement in this country, with its universal acceptance of Lockean liberalism, as compared with the deep divisions in countries which were struggling with a feudal past. In this perspective, Hofstadter concludes that the Progressive historians seemed "comically credulous" to take the conflicts in American politics so seriously.

Instead of opting either for consensus or for conflict, Hofstadter now takes the balanced position that we have had both, and indeed that we have needed both: conflict to activate ideals in an otherwise static situation; consensus to set limits upon the hostilities generated by conflict. This is, to him, far more than an academic matter, of "historians taking sides upon the very question of whether there are sides to take." For historians who put too large an emphasis on consensus will leave the public unprepared for the divisiveness of conflict; historians who see the past as a constant social war will leave us without an awareness of the essential part that underlying agreement has played and of the sheer destructiveness that chronic, unlimited conflict can bring about.

These misapprehensions would be serious in any society. They may now, Hofstadter thinks, be very grave in our present society, which is "in the midst of a dangerous major crisis." He does not specify what this crisis is, but when we remember that he is at Columbia, and when we note the intensity of public bitterness indicated in the daily press, perhaps he does not need to spell out his meaning. In any case, he believes we should be realistic about conflict and consensus, and he has squeezed into the final, too-brief section of his book, an analysis of what he believes realism in this respect requires. First, we must recognize that conflict has been an important feature of our society. Even if the issues with which Turner, Beard, and Parrington were concerned no longer seem authentic and important, we cannot conclude that there were no major issues merely because these three did not discern them. There have been, in Hofstadter's view, very serious issues. These include "the genuinely revolutionary aspects of the American Revolution," the Civil War, and "the racial, ethnic, and religious conflict with which our history is saturated." The real problem is not the question whether issues have existed, but how the important ones can be distinguished from the unimportant ones, or the reconcilable ones from the irreconcilable.

As a step toward such a distinction, Hofstader suggests that conflict may be contained and consensus reached when "those enlisted in society's contending interests have a basic minimal regard for each other: one party or interest seeks the defeat of an opposing interest on matters of policy, but at the same time seeks to avoid crushing the opposition or denying the legitimacy of its existence or values." When this tolerant attitude, which Hofstadter calls "comity," prevails, consensus can be achieved without suppressing dissent, and conflict can operate without becoming disruptive. History, he suggests, can seek to identify the bases of such comity; thus historians can realistically "return to the assessment of conflict in American life without contributing to the disruptive tendencies in American life." Hofstadter ends on a note of aspiration: "In an age when so much of our literature is infused with nihilism, and other social disciplines are driven toward narrow, positivistic inquiry, history may remain the most humanizing of the arts."

Indeed, Hofstadter's concept of comity invites a search for more consensus than the Progressive historians were willing to recognize. Jefferson saying "We are all Republicans; we are all Federalists"; Lincoln invoking "malice toward none and charity for all"; Franklin Roosevelt, holding together his New Deal coalition—all these are examples of the tradition of comity in American life. But comity, as Hofstadter presents it, may be more a measure of the degree of toleration which prevails at any given time than the device for attaining toleration that he seems to think it is. Everyone will agree that some positions held by opponents deserve a "basic minimal regard"; but everyone will also agree that other such positions do not—for instance the Nazi position on the Jews. Does the Soviet action in Czechoslovakia merit comity? Does Mayor Daley merit it? In situations ranging on a scale with imperceptible gradations from high-minded and responsible dissent to vicious and nihilistic destructiveness, how far should comity extend? The question whether comity should be applicable to a given case is itself always a potential issue of conflict. When applied, comity will, of course, have a pacifying effect, but the pacification is the consequence really of the prior agreement that this is a case to which comity is applicable, rather than of the invocation of the principle of comity. I do not think that Hofstadter has taken enough account of this limitation.

Nor has he reckoned with what it is that makes a question a burning issue. Our history is full of issues—Prohibition, Free Silver, the Direct Primary—which galvanized people in one decade and left them cold in the next. But the concept of comity does not tell us why people care so little about public issues at one time and so much at another (certainly this country once had more consensus than it needed and now seems to have less); nor does it tell us why people care so desperately about one issue and not another. Beard and Parrington superimposed upon our history some "issues" which may make them look "comically credulous" today, but historians are not the only victims of belief in fictitious issues; the public also is capable of taking up a spurious issue and waging a conflict over it which is certainly "real," though the issue itself later seems "unreal."

Further, we must reckon with the reason for the decline of the reputation of the Progressive historians. No doubt they exaggerated the depth of the issues, but that is hardly why we now leave them unread. Hofstadter himself gives another reason, which he does not elaborate, when he says, "The new post-war modernism, with its sensationalism, its love of extremes and violence, . . . its interest in madness as a clue to the human . . . its belief that modes of sexuality embody or conceal symbols that are more universally applicable, its sense of outrage, its profound destructive intention [no comity here] . . . seemed in many ways to be a transvaluation of everything that Parrington cared about . . . a generation that has been reading Jean Genet, Henry Miller and William Burroughs sees Parrington . . . as an incomprehensible square."

Here, I think, Hofstadter touches, all too briefly, on the essential reason why Turner, Beard, and Parrington are now usually left unread. They suffer neglect not because of their shortcomings as historians, though Hofstadter is correct in his analysis of these shortcomings, but because their past as they saw it, which seemed so usable when they constructed it half a century ago, no longer seems usable to their readers today. Nor are they really dated by their excessive commitment to the conflict view of history, for with the issues of Vietnam and Black Power we have swung back toward a view which emphasizes conflict. Hofstadter has addressed himself brilliantly and extensively to a number of internal questions about the work of these three historians, but so far as his broader purpose is concerned, these matters are somewhat beside the point. He has slighted the answer to a major question which he himself poses as well as anyone else has done: in what way did the social thought of the early part of the century give vitality to the ideas of these three historians? And more precisely, how have changes in social thought sapped this vitality? The answer is not entirely obvious, as it would have been if they had proclaimed a flat earth shortly before we discovered that the earth is round. Their work still has a certain cogency. Yet their ideas of progress and perfectibility do not really fit our view of the human condition today.

Could Hofstadter have analyzed in a more direct way the specific changes in ideology which have made these three writers, once so perfectly attuned to the prevailing tendencies of social thought, so irrelevant? I think he could have, but he has not quite done so. He might well have developed more adequately his passing implication that the neglect which overtook Turner, Beard, and Parrington resulted not from the specific defects of their history nor from their obsession with conflict but from their being caught in the intellectual riptide which occurs when society is replacing one image of itself with another.

9

ROY F. NICHOLS
AND THE REHABILITATION
OF AMERICAN POLITICAL HISTORY

*This essay, the last that David Potter wrote, appeared origi-
nally in* Pennsylvania History, *January 1971, an issue devoted
entirely to Nichols and his work.*

AMONG AMERICAN HISTORIANS, it would be difficult to find another whose professional interests have been at the same time so omnivorous and so discriminating, so enthusiastic and so analytical, so extensive and at the same time intensive as those of Roy F. Nichols. Usually, each attribute in these pairs is developed at the expense of the other. A man with a gusto for detailed minutiae is likely to neglect the philosophical values of his theme, or *vice versa*. Exuberance is likely to be indiscriminate and a fastidious discrimination inhibits enthusiastic productivity. Many of the great specialists are notoriously oblivious to matters outside the orbit of their specialty, and some of the most eminent generalists have built their overarching hypotheses on sketchy research and mistaken notions of detail.

Anyone knowing only the variety of Nichols' activities might plausibly wonder whether he must not be a dilettante. His interests have ranged from the most abstract levels of theorizing about the use of behavioral concepts in history to insignificant but difficult problems of genealogy—perhaps the least conceptual branch of historical study. His writings have ranged over several centuries of Anglo-American politics, with

extensive forays into the question of the relation of the behavioral sciences to history, into the nature of historical generalization, into the value of local history, and into the establishment of models which would relate political history more
closely to social science and make it less a miscellany of chro-
nology punctuated with anecdote.

But amid all this diversity, it is my belief that the central importance of Nichols' work lies in his rehabilitation of political
history—a rehabilitation accomplished partly through his perception that political history is a far broader subject in its
implications than its traditional practitioners had perceived,
partly through his use of behavioral approaches from the social sciences, and partly through his patient willingness to
work both at the surface level of detailed narrative chronicle,
and also at deeper levels where a questing, probing investigator might grasp the broader meaning of events. No statement characterizes his approach to history better than his own
affirmation that "If the writing of history is to have its greatest
significance and be more than a mere narrative of events, it
ought to attempt to communicate the meaning of what men
have done." [1]

Where an historian has written significantly at the level of
both theory and practice—both conceptualization and application—and where he has linked his work at these two levels
with effectiveness, it is somewhat arbitrary, but perhaps nevertheless necessary, to separate the two levels in discussing his
work. It is also, to some degree, arbitrary to place the consideration of his practice before that of his theory, or *vice versa*.
In the case of Nichols, however, it seems to me that his theory
grew more out of his practice than the reverse. Hence I would
date the beginning of his work in the rehabilitation of American political history from the publication in 1923 of his doctoral dissertation at Columbia, *The Democratic Machine*,

---

1. "The Genealogy of Historical Generalizations," in Louis Gottschalk,
ed., *Generalization in the Writing of History* (Chicago, 1963), p. 142.

1850–1854. This work placed him, at the outset of his career, in a position where his principal theme was political party, party structure, organization, and function. It also placed him in a period where developments were leading to a situation in which party organization proved unable to handle the disruptive forces at work in the society. The democratic process failed; disruption and Civil War followed. In other words, Nichols had entered upon a study of political history in a context which illustrates the most crucial and most universal question of politics. To what extent can society devise mechanisms which will enable its members to live together, to engage in disputes and rivalries (conflict rather than consensus), and to resolve these potentially disruptive divisions without tearing the social fabric and without violence. The art of politics, as Nichols later expressed it was to maintain a "rule of law" and to avoid a "rule of force," to use the pen politically in a way which would make unnecessary any resort to the sword, to substitute "writing" for "fighting." [2] These crisp formulations of the ultimate function of politics did not reach their final phrasing until forty years later, but with *The Democratic Machine,* Nichols was already on his way with a detailed study of the politics of the fifties as a specific theme, which was also a study of the theoretical general problem of the extent and limits of the potentialities of political action as a means of adjusting antagonistic forces without recourse to physical hostilities. During the succeeding forty-four years, Nichols produced a series of volumes which ranged forward and backward over his context, in a progression that moved through the tensions of the fifties, to the Civil War and into the Reconstruction period, and then turned back to examine political origins from the time of Alfred the Great, through English political history and the history of the colonies, to the study of the political organizations of Federalists, Jeffersonians, Jack-

2. *Blueprints for Leviathan: American Style* (New York, 1963), pp. vii–xi, 278.

sonians, and Whigs which preceded the party organizations of the eighteen fifties.

What was to evolve into a grand enterprise reached its second stage with the biography of *Franklin Pierce* in 1931. In 1948, it reached its apex with *The Disruption of American Democracy*, which received the Pulitzer Prize. *The Disruption* carried the story through the failure of the party mechanism to prevent the Civil War. But this was by no means the end of the opus, for his *Blueprints for Leviathan: American Style* (1963) developed some of both the microscopic and the telescopic aspects of his theme. Approximately the first quarter of this book dealt with the broad political background both in England and America, and with the erection of political mechanisms in America up to 1790; the second quarter moved swiftly from there to the crisis of the eighteen fifties and gave the most thorough description ever penned of the passage of the Kansas-Nebraska Act in the House of Representatives. The bulk of the book, thereafter dealt with the breakdown of the political system of the Union in the months immediately preceding the Civil War, the creation of a second political mechanism or Leviathan (the Confederacy), the failure of the Confederate Leviathan (partly because the Southerners themselves were not wholehearted in the support of their new system), and the increased integration and centralization of power in the Leviathan of the Union, as a consequence of the war itself and of the Reconstruction amendments. Having pushed his study forward to the 1870's in *Blueprints for Leviathan*, Nichols then fell back to the period before 1848 for his *Invention of the American Political Parties* in 1967. In this volume, which was the first in chronological sequence and the last in time of composition of a five-volume work, he examined the history of the formation of American political parties, with broad attention to the English and early American background and with extended scrutiny of the Federalist, Jeffersonian, Jacksonian, and Whig political combinations. He concluded that these were not fully institutionalized or fully organized parties, but were more in the nature of *ad hoc* groups, gotten together for the purposes of contesting specific political issues. In his view, the millennium-long evolution of the American political party was not complete until the organizations had developed national central committees and systems of party financing, and these processes became complete in the Democratic Party of 1848. It is clear that when Nichols restricts the term "party" to a political organization with these attributes, he is using the term in a different sense from that employed by Richard McCormick, who regards the Democratic-Republican alignment of the eighteen fifties as the "third" American party system. But as Noble Cunningham has remarked, the question is a definitional one.[3] Nichols does not deny the significance of the earlier organizations, and McCormick would probably not deny the greater institutional completeness of the later structures.

As this essay has already suggested, the most remarkable feature of Nichols' work is the way in which it combines close attention to the details of narrative history with a broad use of the narrative to illustrate theoretical propositions. Many historians who concerned themselves with theory have subordinated their narrative to their intellectual constructs. Thus, while Turner's name is forever linked with the frontier hypothesis, and while Hofstadter's work is essential to anyone who would understand the historiography of the "Progressive Era," one would find Billington far more satisfactory than Turner for the narrative of frontier history, and Mowry or Link than Hofstadter for the narrative of the "Progressive" years. But with Nichols, the narrative has a richness for its own sake, apart from the ideas, so that if one cares only about the antecedents of the Civil War, Nichols will meet one more than half way on that ground, but if one is concerned with

3. In *American Historical Review,* LXXIII (February, 1968), 902.

the theoretical problem of the avoidability of the war, one
finds that Nichols has moved that question away from the riddle of "irresponsibility" and sheer determinism on to a more
practicable level which seeks to measure the limits of what the
instruments of political accommodation are capable of accomplishing in a situation of strife.

As an historian of the Civil War era, Nichols is one of the
great researchers, as well as one of the great interpreters. For
The Disruption of American Democracy, he conducted research in twenty-six states. His bibliography lists 117 manuscript collections, from 48 different depositories, including
eight private libraries. It is easy to imagine the charm with
which he overcame the reluctance of these eight proprietors;
and from the awesome detail of his citations, which sometimes
crowd a score of references into a single footnote, it is easy to
see that these collections were indeed not merely visited, or
looked at, but were thoroughly combed. I abstain from comparable data on his use of newspapers (72 files are listed) and
printed materials, in which he was equally exhaustive.

When Nichols signed the preface to *The Disruption* on
May 31, 1947, the literature of the Civil War bore little resemblance to what it is today. Allan Nevins had signed the preface
to *Ordeal of the Union* over three months earlier, but it was
not until three years later, in *The Emergence of Lincoln*, that
Nevins moved onto the ground which Nichols was traversing
in *The Disruption*. When *The Disruption* came from the press,
the one dominant authority on the era of the Civil War was
James Ford Rhodes. Other major works then extant included
Nicolay and Hay's *Lincoln*, Beveridge's *Lincoln*, the first two
volumes of Randall's *Lincoln*, Channing's sixth volume, Craven's *Coming of the Civil War* and Cole's *The Irrepressible
Conflict*. No professional historian had as yet formally coun-
terattacked the positions of Craven and Randall, and most of
the available biographical studies, now so largely superseded,
were of the vintage of the American Statesman series. Three

of the foremost were Bancroft's *Seward* (1900), Allen Johnson's *Douglas* (1908), and George Fort Milton's *Eve of Conflict* (1934), which was, in fact, a biography of Douglas. Some new works, like Brigance's *Black*, Ranck's *A. G. Brown*, and White's *Rhett* had begun to appear. From these points of departure, *The Disruption* was a major step indeed.

To begin with, Nichols was truly steeped in the milieu of the period. He knew the hangers-on and the back-benchers as well as the leading actors in the drama. This knowledge gave him an insight into the significance of seemingly trivial events whose meaning might have been overlooked by one less thoroughly saturated with the subject. He could hardly have sensed the nuances in the Congress better if he had been a member himself, and he understood the problems posed for the party leaders by such highly personal factors as the corruptibility, the erratic qualities, or the lack of sobriety of individual Congressmen. To illustrate, in exploring the growing rift between Buchanan and Douglas, Nichols notes an occasion when Buchanan addressed a letter to "The Hon. Samuel A. Douglas" —a "lapse of the pen" which could not have been ingratiating to the Little Giant. Or again, in discussing whether secession, even in its final stages, was partly a bluff, he notes that when the Slidells bade good-bye to Washington in February, 1861, Mrs. Slidell left most of her extensive wardrobe behind, very much as she might have done between sessions of Congress. He understands all the details and all the intricacies: I believe his book is the only general account in print which explains how it was possible for Douglas and Lincoln, running against each other in New Jersey on rival statewide tickets, to divide the electoral vote of the state, instead of having it go all one way or all the other.

This total familiarity with a vast mass of detail makes not only for vivid and lively narrative, but also for a grasp of the intrinsic meaning of the events. Thus Nichols was, I believe, the first writer to appreciate fully (in his paper "The Kansas-

Nebraska Act: A Century of Historiography") that while Douglas appeared to be in self-assured command of the Congressional situation at the time of Kansas-Nebraska, he had, in fact, been trapped in a political situation where "a bill ostensibly to organize a territory had been made an instrument of the fundamental political reorganization that the disintegration of the old parties had made inevitable. . . . The great volcano of American politics was in a state of eruption. In the midst of the cataclysm, one sees Douglas crashing and hurtling about, caught like a rock in a gush of lava. When the flow subsided, old landmarks were found to be greatly altered or obliterated." [4]

Again, no one who did not savor detail—apparently random detail—for its own sake, could have portrayed, as Nichols does, the nature of the clique of Senatorial managers who engineered the nomination of Buchanan and, to a great extent controlled administration policy during both the Pierce and the Buchanan administrations. The personalities of James A. Bayard, Judah Benjamin, and especially those two case-hardened exponents of ruthless, backstairs politics—Jesse Bright and John Slidell—these personalities were themselves formative in creating the rigidities which made it impossible by 1860 to make adjustments and concessions which might have held the party together.

Or further, to take one more illustration, Nichols shows his mastery of the factual realities of the secession crisis by the way in which he brushes aside the arguments of some writers that the South over-reacted to the loss of a single Presidential election. As their argument runs, the South was still protected politically by a control of the Senate and also of the Supreme Court. Lincoln would be helpless against the obstructions which these bodies could raise, and the South had only to pa-

4. *Mississippi Valley Historical Review*, XLIII (September, 1956), 187–212, esp. p. 212.

tiently ride out the four short years of his administration. But as Nichols perceptively recognizes, the loss of power in Washington, though galling, was not decisive, and the Southerners knew it. What was decisive was maintaining an intellectual embargo in the South, and behind the barriers of that embargo, first, a degree of solidarity among Southern whites, which would bind the non-slaveholders to the slaveholders in the mystic brotherhood of white supremacy, and second, a degree of isolation for the blacks which would insulate them from insurrectionary propaganda, and thus diminish the nameless danger which transcended all others. The realistic fear in the South was not fear of direct anti-slavery action by Lincoln; it was fear that the embargo would be broken, and that the non-slaveholders would defect or that the slaves would revolt. "If elected," says Nichols, "Lincoln would have the federal patronage at his command. He would be appointing a post-master in every community. Where would he find the men? Not among the aristocracy, not among the fire-eaters, not among the Democrats. Might they not be men of his own humble origin? Already that idea was stirring in the minds of some of the ambitious. . . . Worse still, Lincoln might appoint free Negroes. . . . The new postmasters would not censor the mails, would not burn abolition papers. They would preach to the poor against the rule of the rich and would stir up a class struggle to create a new order in the name of democracy." [5] The peril of Lincoln's election was not that it jeopardized Southern control in national politics, but that it undermined the ascendancy of the planting class in the South—a precarious ascendancy built upon the magic of an unchallenged command, upon the unquestioning loyalty of Southern whites and the unquestioning submission of Southern slaves. But one cleverly aimed question could shatter the magic

5. *The Disruption of American Democracy* (New York, 1948), pp. 352–353.

and the loss of command in national politics made it ever so much easier for someone, white or black, to ask the shattering question.

In short, Nichols' volumes on the period leading to the Civil War represent narrative history at its best. Except for Allan Nevins, who has written on a still broader scale, and Avery Craven, whose scale is uneven (in the sense that he deals with some matters in great detail and with others summarily), there is no modern writer whose account of the road to war can compare with that of Nichols. On analytical points, and on the annals of legislative history and party history, he is, in my opinion, even better than Nevins, which is to say that, on these aspects, he is better than anyone else writing on a general scale.

With the natural gusto and enthusiasm of his temperament, Nichols seems thoroughly to enjoy "Civil War history" for its own sake. From his autobiographical *An Historian's Progress*[6] (an unblushingly "progressive" title, and much less ironical than Henry Adams' "Education"), it appears that he was one of the few professional historians who took spontaneous pleasure in the four long years of the Civil War Centennial—during which he produced many unpublished addresses, a published paper on "Fighting in North Carolina Waters," [7] and an introduction to a new edition of *Battles and Leaders of the Civil War* (1956). All this is to say that if he had confined himself entirely to narrative history, his kind of narrative has enough vitality and imagination, is based upon enough careful delving in the sources, and is of sufficient extent to have established the eminence of his work.

But from the outset he meant to be an analytical historian as well as a narrative one. This purpose has constantly shaped his writing, adding another dimension to his history and requiring a recognition of his historical theory as well as of his historical practice. In fact, with all deference to other narrative his-

6. New York, 1968.
7. *North Carolina Historical Review*, XL (Winter, 1963), 75–84.

torians of the Civil War, Nichols is perhaps the only one who has shown enough interest in theory to make it seem uncertain at times whether his theoretical formulations are primarily a major spin-off from a study, made for its own sake, of the coming of the war; or whether the coming of the war is to him a gigantic case study in the function and malfunction of political mechanisms. Perhaps history is at its finest when it moves between unique events and overarching generalizations so skillfully that one can never be quite certain whether the concrete events are unravelled in order to illustrate the theoretical proposition, or the theoretical proposition is adduced to illuminate the otherwise insignificant detail.[8]

It is difficult, also, to tell how Nichols came by his interest in the theoretical aspects of political history. He, himself, in his *An Historian's Progress* tends to emphasize his specific contacts with men who stimulated his interest in theory. In the Spring of 1931, he participated in a conference with Arthur M. Schlesinger, Dixon R. Fox, R. W. D. Connor, Merle E. Curti, Ralph H. Gabriel, and Samuel F. Bemis which brought in a report recommending that historians should seek to profit by the insights and new methods developed "by the more specialized branches of learning concerned with the study of human behavior." Nichols himself observes that "this conceptualization was one that I have found basic to much of my own thinking and working." Three years later, he was chosen as a delegate of the American Historical Association to the Social Science Research Council, and he remained a member of the Board of the Council for twenty-two years.[9] During these years the behavioral sciences made immense strides. In a chapter entitled "Among the Behavioral Scientists," in *An*

8. "The nature of the conflict can be better understood if it is considered as part of an ancient pattern rather than as an isolated incident, as part of a long contest rather than as a struggle merely of moments in the mid-nineteenth-century United States." *Blueprints for Leviathan*, p. x.
9. *An Historian's Progress*, pp. 116–121.

Historian's Progress, Nichols speaks of his association with
men who very often questioned the worth of history, and who
in fact were far more concerned with problems of conceptualization and generalization than most historians were.[10]
Contact with such men, he says, "gave me a clearer insight
into the significance of history as a mental discipline. Knowledge of history was certainly a phase of behavioral science
and my behavioral conceptualization was guiding me into a
broader humanism." [11]

There is no doubt that Nichols was, indeed, significantly influenced by the viewpoints of the behavioral scientists. He
mentions that these men emphasized "long-term secular trends,
cycles of behavior, recurring patterns of rivalry and adjustment," and indeed one can recognize all of these themes as
threads running through his books on the era preceding the
Civil War. Also, he became vitally concerned with the theoretical side of the writing of history and he was a moving spirit
in an important series of three studies all of which were sponsored by the Social Science Research Council and two of
which were published by it. Its Bulletin 54 (*Theory and Practice in Historical Study* [1946]) and its Bulletin 64 (*Social
Sciences in Historical Study* [1954] were both produced
while he was a member of the Board of the Council, and Louis
Gottschalk's edited volume of essays on *Generalization in the
Writing of History* (1963), contained a paper by Nichols on
"The Genealogy of Historical Generalizations." [12] The thesis
of his paper turned upon the argument that an indispensable
means toward new generalizations is the full understanding by
the writer of past generalizations, and of the emotional or
the cognitive factors which produced such generalizations.

10. *Ibid.,* p. 122.
11. *Ibid.,* p. 132.
12. Nichols was a member of the Council's Committee on Historical
Analysis, which guided the shaping of this volume.

Nichols reviewed the impact of generalizations from the social sciences as contributing to the changes in generalization about the Civil War, and he placed the importance of "new evidence" in a realistic perspective when he observed that, "Under changing circumstances, generalizations are modified not so much because new evidence is discovered as because new minds are at work in a different cultural atmosphere." [13] Certainly the evolution of Afro-American history over the last two decades richly illustrates this axiom.

On the American Civil War, though Nichols had done as much as anyone to illustrate its uniqueness, his controlling impulse was to determine its place in a context of generalization. "The conflict," he said, "was not unique; it was but one of a class of social wars which may occur anywhere in any epoch. . . . At various times in the nineteenth and twentieth centuries . . . there has been the common phenomenon of national unification, generally including a phase of social war, notably in Germany, Italy, and the Dual monarchy. Similar struggles on the field of battle or over the negotiation table have resulted in division as well as unification, in such instances as the separation of Belgium from Holland and of Norway from Sweden and as the breakup of the Ottoman Empire, the Russia of the Tsars, and the Austro-Hungarian monarchy. . . . The American Civil War was perhaps only an example of this type of metanationalistic reaction." [14]

There is no doubt that Nichols' interest in and development of historical theory was sharpened on the whetstone of his association with the behavioral sciences, but I suspect that his own temperament and the challenges of the medium in which he works would have impelled him toward generalization in any case. "By the age of eight," he remarks—and this was some time before he had met any behavioral scientists—"I was

13. "The Genealogy of Historical Generalizations," p. 130.
14. *Ibid.*, p. 139.

deeply interested in the politics of liberalism." [15] At the outset
of his career, in 1923, when he published his doctoral dissertation on *The Democratic Machine* he included a foreword
which looks most unorthodox in a doctoral dissertation, in
which he suggested that politicians are distinguished from
other entrepreneurs by the fact that they deal in power and
not in commodities—they acquire or lose status as their quantum of power increases or diminishes. "The history of the
Democratic Party during the interlude between the sectional
struggles of 1850 and 1854 presents an excellent field for the
study of the *genus* politician. In those days, public opinion
was generally apathetic and the politicians plied their trade
with little interference." [16] During the next four decades,
Nichols was to examine a vast array of individual politicians
with close and eager attention to the details and even the minutiae of their careers, but at the outset, the politician was
already a type as well as an individual. In the words of Ogden
Nash, "Bankers are just like other people only richer." Politicians, also were like other people, only they were working
for different kinds of goals in a different kind of medium.

What I mean to suggest is that while Nichols certainly became interested in historical theory, I believe his interest is
intrinsically more philosophical than it is methodological. I
think also that his historical association with certain personalities such as Stephen A. Douglas, James Buchanan, George
Sanders, John Slidell, August Belmont, and others stimulated
the speculative qualities of his mind even more than his personal association with colleagues on the Social Science Research Council. Most of all, I think the narrowness and conceptual poverty of American political history at the time when
he embarked on his professional career virtually compelled a
man of high talents either to abandon political history or to

15. *An Historian's Progress*, p. 276.
16. *The Democratic Machine, 1850–1854* (New York, 1923), p. 13.

attempt to rehabilitate it as a scholarly study. For by the nine-teen-twenties the great old days of political history ("History is past politics and politics is present history") were long gone. The institutional focus, once regnant at the Johns Hopkins University, had begun to rigidify even before the turn of the century, and had been boldly challenged by Frederick Jackson Turner as early as 1893. In 1927, four years after Nichols published his *Democratic Machine*, intellectual history made a brilliant debut with the first volume of Vernon Parrington's *Main Currents of American Thought*, and in the same year, the first of a thirteen volume series on American social history (the Schlesinger and Fox Series) also appeared. Some of the most imaginative of the younger American historians were turning in these new directions. Meanwhile, political history suffered from conventionality and a willingness to accept superficial treatment of surface events—a tendency which was later irrefutably exposed in Thomas C. Cochran's "The Presidential Synthesis in American Political History." [17] As historians were dividing the terrain of history into fractionized fields, the spokesmen of intellectual, social, economic, and cultural history seemed to claim all the fertile territory, while political history was sharply separated from cultural history, as if the two were antithetical, and politics was left with an arid tract which appeared sterile to many historians. It is no exaggeration to say that political history faced a real crisis in the 1930's and '40's.

Nichols himself sensed the desiccation that seemed to be overtaking American political history. "To me," he writes in his autobiography, "unselective descriptive chronicles were coming to have a minimum of meaning." [18] But far from abandoning political history for this reason, he was deeply convinced that it need not be purely descriptive, need not be in-

17. *American Historical Review*, LIII (July, 1948), 748–759.
18. *An Historian's Progress*, p. 145.

discriminate or random in its recital of facts, and most of all, that it did not exist in isolation from culture and that it was of crucial significance to society.

Political history is the history of the distribution and exercise of power, and as long as power is important, the history which tells where power is vested and how it is used must be important. As Nichols wrote in 1948, in a brilliant defense of political history,

> One of the basic motivations in politics is the desire for power. But how much do we in the United States know of the history of power? Where has it resided from time to time? How has it really been exercised? Here we should find the data regarding the constant struggle between the traditionalist and the reformer often complicated by the not too obvious participation of the interloper. Does power reside in the hands of those who ostensibly are charged with its exercise? With the increasing responsibility of government for matters of technological and military policy and power, how can self-government safeguard traditional rights and liberties and at the same time wield the power necessary to carry out the new responsibilities? Have Americans taken too much for granted the automatic operation of government to protect for them their rights and liberties without being willing to assume the responsibility for looking out for these rights themselves? [19]

If power is historically important, then politics must be important, for politics is the medium within which questions of power are usually worked out. Nichols had grasped this vital point clearly as early as 1922–23, for at that time he wrote a memorandum dealing in part with the relation between conflict on the one hand, and political and party history on the other. Observing first that the basic antagonisms leading to conflict in American society had been to a great extent eco-

19. "Unfinished Business: An Editorial," *Pennsylvania Magazine of History and Biography*, LXX (April, 1948), 114.

nomic in their nature, he went on to observe that these antagonisms had taken the overt form of conflict of section against
section and class against class, but that an analysis of the conflict purely in terms of sectional or class tensions "does not
lead to a profound understanding of the workings of history
unless particular attention is paid to the personnel of these
groups and the machinery used by these sections or classes in
their struggle for control of government. This machinery has
been the party system . . . the keystone of this system has
been the party organization or machine." [20] In short, when
sectional or class antagonism materializes, it materializes in the
form of political conflict.

By this cogent logic, Nichols, at the outset of his career,
made his case for the basic importance of political history, and
even of party history, to the understanding of any society in
which the public participates in the political process. Far from
accepting the separation of political experience from culture,
and even ideology, he perceived that the political system of
any society is perhaps the most significant and revealing aspect
of that society's culture. This point was most ably stated in his
presidential address to the American Historical Association in
1967:

> There are various types of cultural definition, but one in
> particular can be especially useful: namely, I believe, the
> design most indicative of the nature and identity of any so-
> ciety. This is its plan of operation, the force or influence that
> organizes it and keeps within it a semblance of recognizable
> structure and order. In highly complicated societies, this plan
> takes the form of government, the customs of rule, of the
> exercise of authority, of the structure of power. A culture,
> therefore, may be known as a democracy, an empire, a
> totalitarian state. Any such designation is not merely derived
> from constitutional institutions, but it embraces attitudes,
> ideas of community identification, and social as well as po-

20. Quoted in *An Historian's Progress*, pp. 39–40.

litical relationships. The distinguishing characteristic of the society known as the United States of America is the fact that it is a democratic culture dedicated to a self-government in which all are technically involved and in which this interest is demonstrably central to the self-identification of the people. It can be used as the hallmark of the culture.[21]

In short, the allocation and use of power is one of the most vital aspects of any society; this allocation and use is determined and operated by a political process; and the political process is a central feature of the whole system of attitudes, ideology, and modes of action which form the heart of a culture. In the fractionized world of diverse historical "fields," political history can still claim a place as the keystone. But it can only make good this claim if it abandons the random recital of surface events and comes to grips with the fundamental political questions. Among these questions, none is more basic than the question what a political system is intended to do, and whether it functions in such a way as to do what is intended. Like all democratic political systems, the American system was intended, above all, to mediate the rivalries, antagonisms, and conflicts within the society and to resolve them in such a way that conflict would not reach the level of large-scale violence and that the forces of integration would continue to hold the ascendancy over the forces of disintegration or disruption. For seven decades, from 1789 to 1861, the American political system had brilliantly fulfilled these intentions, and then, in 1861, it reached the one point in our history where it failed to do so. Why did the system fail in 1861?

Nichols has devoted five volumes, more or less, to working out his answers to this question, and this essay can hardly undertake a resume of his conclusions, which involve many fac-

21. "History in a Self-Governing Culture," *American Historical Review,* LXXII (January, 1967), 415.

tors. The important point here is that he did not ask merely the specific question, "Why the Civil War?" but also the generic question, "Why did a politically integrative process reverse itself and become, for two decades, a disintegrative process?" and not merely "Why was there acute sectional antagonism?" which is easy, but "Why did this particular antagonism result in a social war?" which is highly difficult.

Without undertaking a full review of Nichols' answers, it may be appropriate at least to indicate some of his leading ideas, and even more to indicate the structure of his ideas, for as he himself remarks, though he had never heard of models or model building, he was "quite unconsciously planning a model." [22] While he was modestly telling his inquiring friends "that I was working on Buchanan," [23] he was in fact working on an analysis of the factors necessary to the success of a democratic political system. His analysis required a consideration of the political system as a whole, and not merely a focus on the personality traits of prominent figures or the dramatic episodes of political conflict. The old style political history, confined to the reenactment of battles in the legislative arena is rather like the old style "drum and trumpet" military history, confined to engagements on the "field of combat"—gallant cavalry charges, heroic rear-guard actions and the like. But as genuine military history must include a consideration of weaponry, recruitment, supply, logistics, *et cetera*, a true political history must include an analysis of the nature of political organization. Thus, Nichols' "model" involved a sweeping examination of the political system of the United States, in func-

22. *An Historian's Progress*, p. 148.
23. I personally can especially appreciate the cryptic understatement that Nichols was "working on Buchanan," for I wrote an M.A. essay on certain aspects of the election of '56, and I too found it a convenient evasion to say that I was working on Buchanan. When I imparted this information to one inquiring lady of my acquaintance, the only response she could muster was to say, "Oh! We used to have a yard-man named Buchanan."

tional rather than in constitutional terms. As he himself states it, he found seven basic features.[24]

First of these features was the fact that by the 1840's politics had become a profession. That is, political activity was conducted by men who made a career of it, in rivalry with other men who also made a career of it and who made it their business to implement successfully (for themselves, that is) the impulses of the part of the society which they represented or sought to represent. Most were "organization men," which made for a kind of politics quite different from what a group of volunteers would have conducted. Second, these professionals survived or perished in a process of popular elections (even senatorial elections were indirectly popular, for state legislators who voted for senators were elected with some reference to the question whom they would support for senator). Survival often depended on the candidate's ability to formulate real or fictitious political issues in terms which would arouse the emotions of the voters. Third, since state and national elections were not coordinated as they are today, elections were far more frequent, and there was never a time when an election campaign was not in progress in at least one of the states.[25] This meant that the excitement and the contrived arousal of the voters was a chronic condition in the political system. No intervals of political tranquility were possible. By the 1850's such chronic excitement "had become dangerous."

Further, the structure of the political system was deeply influenced by its existence within a dualistic context of federalism. The most direct consequence of this federalism appeared in the fact that the political parties themselves were partly national parties and partly state parties. This is Nichols' fourth

---

24. The discussion which follows is based upon *An Historian's Progress*, pp. 148–164; also *The Disruption of American Democracy*, pp. 20–40.
25. "There were [statewide] elections, somewhere, in every month of every year save January, February, and July." *An Historian's Progress*, p. 153.

factor, and, commenting on the autonomous position of each state organization in the major parties, he points out that "by 1850, when there were thirty-one states there were not two parties but sixty-four." The relation of the parties at the state and national levels was almost schizophrenic, for state and national parties were dependent upon one another for success, were constantly under pressure to defer to one another, and yet different state organizations within the same national party might take antithetical positions on public issues, leaving it to the national leaders to improvise frantic, makeshift formulae to hold the national party together. Often national issues were invoked in order to win elections at the state level or *vice versa*. Means at one level could serve ends at another level. Historians, who are prone to focus upon national issues and to disdain state rivalries, have, as a consequence, unconsciously exaggerated the importance of national issues, including the slavery issue, which probably did not preoccupy the minds of voters in the eighteen fifties so exclusively as most twentieth-century readers imagine. It is worth noting in this connection that the very best and most recent research, such as Michael Holt's study of the formation of the Republican Party in Pittsburgh, and the careful quantitative studies by Joel H. Silbey and by Thomas B. Alexander, all bear out the pioneer observations of Nichols that state parties, which, of course influenced policy on the slavery question at the national level, often owed their success within their state to issues unrelated to slavery; and that party cohesion seemed more important on more issues than sectional cohesion (or solidarity on the slavery issue), as measured by voting behavior in the House of Representatives.[26]

26. Holt, *Forging a Majority: The Formation of the Republican Party in Pittsburgh, 1848–1860* (New Haven, 1969); Silbey, *The Shrine of Party: Congressional Voting Behavior, 1841–1852* (Pittsburgh, 1967); Alexander, *Sectional Stress and Party Strength: A Study of Roll-Call Voting Patterns in the United States House of Representatives* (Nashville, 1967).

But not only was a dualistic federalism built into the party system itself. Far more profound and far more complex was a fifth factor, namely that, whether the politicians knew it or not, they were operating a society which was federal, in an even deeper sense than the federalistic political mechanism. This society was a national one in its widely shared commitment to the Protestant ethic and romanticism, and I would add, to individualism; it was held together by its commitment to democracy and to a well-advanced but not yet fully dominant nationalism. But on the other hand, it was weakened by cultural incompatibilities of the New England culture and the Southern culture—incompatibilities which were heightened by the rivalries between these cultures to dominate the new areas of a rapidly expanding republic, and also by the tensions between a growing metropolitanism in the Northeast and a traditionalist parochialism in the South, and most of all by an antislavery sentiment which Southerners bitterly resented as a stigma, a brand of barbarism upon their society and an encouragement to insurrection which might destroy them. As Nichols observes, the politicians at least understood the problems of political federalism and had some sense of how to cope with them, but many did not understand the problem of cultural federalism at all. So little did they understand it that when the crisis came at last, the North could not believe that the South would really secede, and the South could not believe that the North would support a long, deadly, and devastating war to prevent secession. With reference to the complexities and intricacies of the cultural federalism, Nichols makes one of his aptest comments: The Civil War was a brothers' war, as has often been said, but "a brothers' war in which there were more than two brothers."

The sixth factor in Nichols' formulation was the recognition of the non-political elements—such as economic fluctuations, population movements and religious stirrings which impinged significantly upon the political situation, though they were not directly part of it. The seventh was the factor of change which was bringing politics under a new dispensation which was not as reluctant as the old dispensation had been to concentrate and wield political power. The Jeffersonian generation had recognized that minimization of government and adoption of laissez-faire policies were a wonderful protection against clashes between diverse interests in the federal system. But by 1860, there was a growing disposition to let the American Colossus use its power.

Such was the model that Nichols worked out, not even recognizing it himself in its entirety until after he had completed it.[27] Like all models, it is open to criticism, and indeed one of its principal values is that it invites criticism. If a large panel of critics were consulted, I suppose that two criticisms could be anticipated. Some would say that the model does not provide an answer to that perennial riddle: Was the Civil War inevitable? Was the conflict irrepressible? Indeed it does not provide an answer, but to suppose that it ought to is to misapprehend the purpose of a model. The model tells rather at what point the system generated unnecessary friction (in constant elections), at what point it failed (in handling the problems of cultural federalism), and how the antagonisms in the society were either mitigated or intensified as they were translated into political terms. If a model can do this, it has done enough, and answers to riddles ought not to be required of it. Nichols says elsewhere that there "appears to be a continuing process of cultural integration and disintegration." [28] He has looked back over a millennium in the history of England and America for evidence of this cycle. Clearly the events of

27. *An Historian's Progress*, p. 148.
28. *Ibid.*, p. 216. For some thoughtful criticisms of Nichols' approach, as applied in *Blueprints for Leviathan*, see review by Thomas J. Pressly in *Journal of Southern History*, XXX (February, 1964), 94–97.

1845–1877 marked such a cycle. Perhaps this is as much as history can say.[29]

A second criticism might be that the model does not give enough weight to the transcendent importance of the slavery issue as an obstacle to sectional harmony. But critics who would offer this criticism might well remember that the model is a *political* one. One anomaly of the slavery issue is that, while the two sections disagreed deeply about slavery, the two political parties disagreed only marginally in what they were prepared to do about slavery—they had different proposals for the territories, where the issue was perhaps fictitious, but they were both pledged to leave slavery unmolested in the states, where the issue was real. Perhaps this anomaly was part of the politicians' inability to handle cultural federalism.

In any case an extended critique is beyond the scope of this paper. The exact degree of perfection of the model was less important than the fact that a model had been constructed. Nichols had moved into political history when it was in danger of degenerating into a grab bag of isolated events, strung together chronologically, garnished with personalities, and spiced with anecdote. When he left it, it had been revitalized by the recognition that political history must be analyzed as a process, involving fundamental interactions between various factors in the society, and that, as the medium for the functional use of power, politics is as crucial as any process in the society. He had not, of course, done this single-handed. So many historians in the last half-century have contributed to

29. Nothing demonstrates Nichols' basic commitment to history rather than the social sciences more clearly than his repeated attention to analysis over long time-spans. In addition to *Blueprints for Leviathan* and *The Invention of American Political Parties*, see his inaugural lecture at Cambridge University, *The Historical Study of Anglo-American Democracy* (Cambridge, 1949); his "1461–1861: The American Civil War in Perspective," *Journal of Southern History*, XVI (May, 1950), 143–160; and his *The Slow Evolution of American Politics* (Cotton Memorial Papers: University of Texas at El Paso, August 1967).

the revitalization of political history that it would be invidious to name a few of them. But Nichols was certainly one of the earliest and is certainly one of the most important. In his autobiography he modestly depicts himself as a passive witness who had "passed through a cycle of historiography. I had started when the end of political and constitutional interest seemed at hand, and was now [1967] working in an atmosphere of the renaissance of a new, more comprehensive, and more analytic political history." [30] But in fact, Nichols was never for a moment a mere spectator of this change. He was actually as important as any other single figure in bringing about the cycle which he describes himself as having "passed through." It was a crucial cycle in American historiography, and though Nichols' scholarship is important in a number of dimensions, perhaps its greatest importance is in its major contribution to the rehabilitation of American political history.

30. *An Historian's Progress*, p. 239.

II

AMERICAN SOCIETY

10

IS AMERICA A CIVILIZATION?

Shenandoah (*the Washington and Lee University Review*) *published this brief essay in its autumn 1958 issue as part of a symposium that opened with Arnold Toynbee and Max Lerner in disagreement over whether the United States qualified as a separate civilization. Potter, instead of answering the question directly, chose to examine the terminological and classificatory problems that it raised. The resulting analysis constitutes an interesting introduction to the longer and more familiar essay that follows.*

FEW PEOPLE will deny that American society has developed a notable degree of distinctiveness in certain basic ways. For instance, in two centuries of rapid change throughout the world, no country has changed so rapidly as the United States. In this country, technological revolution has paced a social transformation that divorced the American people from much of their past and made them the most mobile, most adaptable, and most rootless people on the planet. Their repudiation of European ideas of hierarchy has led them to institute permissive and voluntaristic rather than coercive or authoritarian, modes of control in their social organization, and it has impelled them to place a uniquely high valuation on the personality of the individual. They have, to a superlative degree, adjusted their values and their way of life to mechanization, so that if the world can show a true machine-age society, it is certainly in the United States. They have created and to some extent become the captives of a standard of living so high that it releases them from the bondage of toil for the necessities of life and thus makes them vulnerable to the bondage of other problems, such as that of personality adjustment. They cherish an ideal of equality but maintain in practice a class structure with invidious differences, and they attempt to reconcile the two by a system which makes the society (as distinguished from the economy) almost uniquely competitive.

Certainly these measures of distinctiveness, and others which every reader can supply for himself, make American society a fit subject for separate study. Certainly, too, they exceed the measures which set most nationality groups apart from one another. But do they warrant us in calling America a civilization? The question is well known to be a debatable one, or at least one which is debated, but does the point of controversy lie in our disagreement about American society, or in our confused use of the term civilization? Is the question substantive or is it semantic?

It is not very hard to see that the term civilization is applied indiscriminately—not to say promiscuously—at a number of different levels. At the highest level, the level at which Arnold Toynbee has used it, it designates one of the few great social systems which, through sixty centuries, have reached a full and more or less separate articulation somewhere on this planet. Most of them have developed in some degree of isolation—either of time or of space—from one another, and the ending of isolation in the modern world makes it reasonably certain that the era of great geographically-centered civilizations is almost past. At another level the term, civilization, often finds application to the cultural differentiations with which diverse nationalities may have varied their expression of one major cultural tradition—thus French civilization, British civilization, German civilization, and perhaps American civilization. Again the term has been used by some writers to emphasize the significance of differences between regions, as when Edward Channing or J. T. Adams asserted that North and South in the United States constituted "diverse civilizations"—asserted this with utter disregard for the broad base of cultural similarities upon which relatively minor regional differences were erected.

The path to clarification is not smoothed by the fact that the term civilization has appealed to some writers as implying a degree of separateness and to others as implying a degree of advancement. Thus advocates of what may be called a cultural Monroe Doctrine like to say that the United States is a civilization in the sense of being set apart, and adverse critics of the condition of American society like to deny that it is a civilization, in the sense of being "civilized,"—both without much regard for any actual criteria of cultural measurement. It is perhaps because of considerations like these that some programs for the study of American society have adopted the deliberately nondescript term American Studies, rather than the more affirmative and more hazardous term American Civilization.

If this were purely a lexical question, I suppose it might be left to the dictionaries, but unfortunately it is symptomatic of a serious general problem in the study of societies, namely that we have no accepted means for holding in proper balance with one another the points of similarity which mark the continuity between given societies and the points of dissimilarity which mark their separateness. At one end of the scale, Boyd C. Shafer reminds us that human beings everywhere have a great many qualities in common; at the other end, Carl Carmer finds it plausible to say of the state of Alabama that "the Congo is not more different from Massachusetts or Kansas or California"; and there is nothing in our way of handling these matters to remind us of the one point of view when the other is about to run away with us.

Other branches of study are, I am afraid, well in advance of the study of human society in this matter. The linguists certainly have a clearer concept of the difference between a culture and a sub-culture. In fact historians tend to equate culture with nationality, attributing a distinct national character to each country which has achieved separate sovereignty, and treating these national characters as if they were more or less equally distinctive in their identity. This ignores the profound separateness with which the national culture of some countries such as Japan has developed, and the superficiality in the national variation between cultures of other countries, such as the three countries of Scandinavia or some of the republics of Central and South America. The linguists have certainly done better in dealing with the romance languages collectively than the historians have done in dealing with Mediterranean society collectively; yet there are many elements, such as the Roman law, which run through the institutions of the Mediterranean area as much as any linguistic thread runs through the speech of that area.

Students of the life sciences, zoology and botany, have succeeded best of all, for they are now in the second century of their practice of giving to every body of identical individuals —whether algae or anthropoids—a double name, including one generic name, which the body may share with other related bodies and one specific name which distinguishes it from all other bodies that are not identical. This binomial practice does not prevent students of plant and animal life from disagreeing about similarities and differences; it does not prevent some of them (known as splitters) from exaggerating the differences, nor others (known as lumpers) from exaggerating the similarities, but it does, by the juxtaposition of generic and specific names, challenge every worker to keep in mind the similarities while he is elaborating the differences or to consider the differences while he is searching for the similarities. The binominal system could, of course, never be transferred out of zoology into history, but it is a pity that no balancing question intrudes itself upon the historical investigator to temper his comparisons when on the one hand he sweepingly proclaims the universality of human nature, or on the other, asserts that American society is based upon a rejection of European values.

When he writes that Dixie and New England were as distinct in 1860 as the contrasts of agrarianism and industrialism could make them, he needs to be reminded how much evangelical morality, mercenary commercialism, frontier equalitarianism, democratic competitiveness, and jingoistic Americanism there was in both societies. When he views American society as derivative, he needs to remember how different was the environment to which European ways were transplanted, how rapid and how sweeping was the adaptation. When, on the other hand, he fancies that American life sprang from the forest primeval, someone should jog his elbow and remind him that he cannot open his mouth without Greek words, Latin words, Germanic words, and Anglo-Saxon words coming out. He cannot put pen to paper without reproducing the alphabet of the Phoenicians and the numerical system of the Arabs. He is a newcomer here, and he gets his ideas of religion from ancient Palestine, his ideas of morality from the Old Testament prophets, his ideas of justice from ancient Rome, and his notions of liberty from ancient Greece. Who, then, is the American, this new man?

He is a man with a society in its origins derivative, in its character very extensively adapted. The application of the term civilization implicitly denies the derivation; the withholding of the term denies the adaptation. What we need is not a verdict, awarding or enjoining the term, but a capacity to distinguish and even to designate readily the major levels of cultural differentiation, ranging from the separate universe of the Mayas to the local peculiarities of any regional or provincial society. Some terms, such as culture and sub-culture already exist, but they have not been effectively ranked to apply at commonly understood levels. So long as this deficiency in our scale of ideas and our store of words continues, civilization is likely to remain a subjective term, implicitly boasting a degree of excellence or a degree of independence, rather than an objective one indicating the ratio which prevails in American society between the distinctively American characteristics and the characteristics shared with Western culture.

11

THE QUEST FOR
THE NATIONAL CHARACTER

This essay was written especially for The Reconstruction of American History *(1962), a collection of historiographical studies edited by John Higham. But "national character" is a subject without clear bounds, and Potter wisely made no effort to survey all the literature relevant to the theme. Instead, he concentrated upon what he considered to be the two principal "composite images" that had emerged—one stressing the American's individualism and the other, his conformism. Thus the essay became in considerable part an effort to accommodate the conflicting views of Turner and Tocqueville on the extent to which the nineteenth-century American could be regarded as an individualist.*

UNLIKE MOST NATIONALITY GROUPS in the world today, the people of the United States are not ethnically rooted in the land where they live. The French have remote Gallic antecedents; the Germans, Teutonic; the English, Anglo-Saxon; the Italians, Roman; the Irish, Celtic; but the only people in America who can claim ancient American origins are a remnant of Red Indians. In any deep dimension of time, all other Americans are immigrants. They began as Europeans (or in the case of 10 percent of the population, as Africans), and if they became Americans it was only, somehow, after a relatively recent passage westbound across the Atlantic.

It is, perhaps, this recency of arrival which has given to Americans a somewhat compulsive preoccupation with the question of their Americanism. No people can really qualify as a nation in the true sense unless they are united by important qualities or values in common. If they share the same ethnic, or linguistic, or religious, or political heritage, the foundations of nationality can hardly be questioned. But when their ethnic, religious, linguistic, and political heritage is mixed, as in the case of the American people, nationality can hardly exist at all unless it takes the form of a common ad-

justment to conditions of a new land, a common commitment
to shared values, a common esteem for certain qualities of
character, or a common set of adaptive traits and attitudes.
It is partly for this reason that Americans, although committed to the principle of freedom of thought, have nevertheless placed such heavy emphasis upon the obligation to accept certain undefined tenets of "Americanism." It is for this
same reason, also, that Americans have insisted upon their
distinctiveness from the Old World from which they are derived. More than two centuries ago Hector St. John de
Crèvecœur asked a famous question, "What then is the American, this new man?" He simply assumed, without arguing the
point, that the American is a new man, and he only inquired
wherein the American is different. A countless array of
writers, including not only careful historians and social scientists but also professional patriots, hit-and-run travellers,
itinerant lecturers, intuitive-minded amateurs of all sorts, have
been repeating Crèvecœur's question and seeking to answer
it ever since.

A thick volume would hardly suffice even to summarize
the diverse interpretations which these various writers have
advanced in describing or explaining the American character.
Almost every trait, good or bad, has been attributed to the
American people by someone,[1] and almost every explanation,
from Darwinian selection to toilet-training, has been advanced to account for the attributed qualities. But it is probably safe to say that at bottom there have been only two
primary ways of explaining the American, and that almost
all of the innumerable interpretations which have been formulated can be grouped around or at least oriented to these two

---

1. Lee Coleman, "What is American: a Study of Alleged American Traits,"
in *Social Forces*, XIX (1941), surveyed a large body of the literature on
the American character and concluded that "almost every conceivable
value or trait has at one time or another been imputed to American culture
by authoritative observers."

basic explanations, which serve as polar points for all the literature.

The most disconcerting fact about these two composite images of the American is that they are strikingly dissimilar and seemingly about as inconsistent with one another as two interpretations of the same phenomenon could possibly be. One depicts the American primarily as an individualist and an idealist, while the other makes him out as a conformist and a materialist. Both images have been developed with great detail and elaborate explanation in extensive bodies of literature, and both are worth a close scrutiny.

For those who have seen the American primarily as an individualist, the story of his evolution as a distinctive type dates back possibly to the actual moment of his decision to migrate from Europe to the New World, for this was a process in which the daring and venturesome were more prone to risk life in a new country while the timid and the conventional were more disposed to remain at home. If the selective factors in the migration had the effect of screening out men of low initiative, the conditions of life in the North American wilderness, it is argued, must have further heightened the exercise of individual resourcefulness, for they constantly confronted the settler with circumstances in which he could rely upon no one but himself, and where the capacity to improvise a solution for a problem was not infrequently necessary to survival.

In many ways the colonial American exemplified attitudes that were individualistic. Although he made his first settlements by the removal of whole communities which were transplanted bodily—complete with all their ecclesiastical and legal institutions—he turned increasingly, in the later process of settlement, to a more and more individualistic mode of pioneering, in which one separate family would take up title to a separate, perhaps an isolated, tract of land, and would move to this land long in advance of any general settlement, leaving churches and courts and schools far behind. His religion, whether Calvinistic Puritanism or emotional revivalism, made him individually responsible for his own salvation, without the intervention of ecclesiastical intermediaries between himself and his God. His economy, which was based very heavily upon subsistence farming, with very little division of labor, also impelled him to cope with a diversity of problems and to depend upon no one but himself.

With all of these conditions at work, the tendency to place a premium upon individual self-reliance was no doubt well developed long before the cult of the American as an individualist crystallized in a conceptual form. But it did crystallize, and it took on almost its classic formulation in the thought of Thomas Jefferson.

It may seem paradoxical to regard Jefferson as a delineator of American national character, for in direct terms he did not attempt to describe the American character at all. But he did conceive that one particular kind of society was necessary to the fulfillment of American ideals, and further that one particular kind of person, namely the independent farmer, was a necessary component in the optimum society. He believed that the principles of liberty and equality, which he cherished so deeply, could not exist in a hierarchical society, such as that of Europe, nor, indeed, in any society where economic and social circumstances enabled one set of men to dominate and exploit the rest. An urban society or a commercial society, with its concentration of financial power into a few hands and its imposition of dependence through a wage system, scarcely lent itself better than an aristocracy to his basic values. In fact, only a society of small husbandmen who tilled their own soil and found sustenance in their own produce could achieve the combination of independence and equalitarianism which he envisioned for the ideal society. Thus, although Jefferson did not write a description of the national character, he erected a model for it, and the model ultimately had more influence than a description could ever have exercised. The model American was a plain, straightforward agrarian democrat, an individualist in his desire for freedom for himself, and an idealist in his desire for equality for all men.

Jefferson's image of the American as a man of independence, both in his values and in his mode of life, has had immense appeal to Americans ever since. They found this image best exemplified in the man of the frontier, for he, as a pioneer, seemed to illustrate the qualities of independence and self-reliance in their most pronounced and most dramatic form. Thus in a tradition of something like folklore, half-legendary figures like Davy Crockett have symbolized America as well as symbolizing the frontier. In literature, ever since J. Fenimore Cooper's Leatherstocking tales, the frontier scout, at home under the open sky, free from the trammels of an organized and stratified society, has been cherished as an incarnation of American qualities.[2] In American politics the voters showed such a marked preference for men who had been born in log cabins that many an ambitious candidate pretended to pioneer origins which were in fact fictitious.

The pioneer is, of course, not necessarily an agrarian (he may be a hunter, a trapper, a cowboy, a prospector for gold), and the agrarian is not necessarily a pioneer (he may be a European peasant tilling his ancestral acres), but the American frontier was basically an agricultural frontier, and the pioneer was usually a farmer. Thus it was possible to make an equation between the pioneer and the agrarian, and since the pioneer evinced the agrarian traits in their most picturesque and most appealing form there was a strong psychological impulse to concentrate the diffused agrarian ideal into a sharp frontier focus. This is, in part, what Frederick

2. Henry Nash Smith, *Virgin Land: the American West as Symbol and Myth* (1950), brilliantly analyzes the effect which the image of the Western pioneer has had upon the American imagination.

Jackson Turner did in 1893 when he wrote "The Significance of the Frontier in American History." In this famous essay Turner offered an explanation of what has been distinctive in American history, but it is not as widely realized as it might be that he also penned a major contribution to the literature of national character. Thus Turner affirmed categorically that "The American intellect owes its striking characteristics to the frontier. That coarseness and strength, combined with acuteness and acquisitiveness; that practical inventive turn of mind, quick to find expedients; that masterful grasp of material things, lacking in the artistic but powerful to effect great ends; that restless, nervous energy; that dominant individualism, working for good and for evil; and withal, that buoyancy and exuberance which comes with freedom— these are traits of the frontier, or traits called out elsewhere because of the existence of the frontier." [3]

A significant but somewhat unnoticed aspect of Turner's treatment is the fact that, in his quest to discover the traits of the American character, he relied for proof not upon descriptive evidence that given traits actually prevailed, but upon the argument that given conditions in the environment would necessarily cause the development of certain traits. Thus the cheapness of land on the frontier would make for universal land-holding which in turn would make for equalitarianism in the society. The absence of division of labor on the frontier would force each man to do most things for himself, and this would breed self-reliance. The pitting of the individual man against the elemental forces of the wilderness and of nature would further reinforce this self-reliance. Similarly, the fact that a man had moved out in advance of society's institutions and its stratified structure would mean that he could find independence, without being overshadowed by the

3. Frederick J. Turner, *The Frontier in American History* (Henry Holt and Co., 1920), p. 37.

institutions, and could enjoy an equality unknown to stratified society. All of this argument was made without any sustained effort to measure exactly how much recognizable equalitarianism and individualism and self-reliance actually were in evidence either on the American frontier or in American society. There is little reason to doubt that most of his arguments were valid or that most of the traits which he emphasized did actually prevail, but it is nevertheless ironical that Turner's interpretation, which exercised such vast influence upon historians, was not based upon the historian's kind of proof, which is from evidence, but upon an argument from logic which so often fails to work out in historical experience.

But no matter how he arrived at it, Turner's picture reaffirmed some by-now-familiar beliefs about the American character. The American was equalitarian, stoutly maintaining the practices of both social and political democracy; he had a spirit of freedom reflected in his buoyance and exuberance; he was individualistic—hence "practical and inventive," "quick to find expedients," "restless, nervous, acquisitive." Turner was too much a scholar to let his evident fondness for the frontiersman run away with him entirely, and he took pains to point out that this development was not without its sordid aspects. There was a marked primitivism about the frontier, and with it, to some extent, a regression from civilized standards. The buoyant and exuberant frontiersman sometimes emulated his Indian neighbors in taking the scalps of his adversaries. Coarse qualities sometimes proved to have more survival value than gentle ones. But on the whole this regression was brief, and certainly a rough-and-ready society had its compensating advantages. Turner admired his frontiersman, and thus Turner's American, like Jefferson's American, was partly a realistic portrait from life and partly an idealized model from social philosophy. Also, though one of these figures was an agrarian and the other was a frontiersman, both were very much the same man—democratic, freedom-loving, self-reliant, and individualistic.

An essay like this is hardly the place to prove either the validity or the invalidity of the Jeffersonian and Turnerian conception of the American character. The attempt to do so would involve a review of the entire range of American historical experience, and in the course of such a review the proponents of this conception could point to a vast body of evidence in support of their interpretation. They could argue, with much force, that Americans have consistently been zealous to defend individualism by defending the rights and the welfare of the individual, and that our whole history is a protracted record of our government's recognizing its responsibility to an ever broader range of people—to men without property, to men held in slavery, to women, to small enterprises threatened by monopoly, to children laboring in factories, to industrial workers, to the ill, to the elderly, and to the unemployed. This record, it can further be argued, is also a record of the practical idealism of the American people, unceasingly at work.

But without attempting a verdict on the historical validity of this image of the American as individualist and idealist, it is important to bear in mind that this image has been partly a portrait, but also partly a model. In so far as it is a portrait —a likeness by an observer reporting on Americans whom he knew—it can be regarded as authentic testimony on the American character. But in so far as it is a model—an idealization of what is best in Americanism, and of what Americans should strive to be, it will only be misleading if used as evidence of what ordinary Americans are like in their everyday lives. It is also important to recognize that the Jefferson-Turner image posited several traits as distinctively American, and that they are not all necessarily of equal validity. Particularly, Jefferson and Turner both believed that love of equality and love of liberty go together. For Jefferson the very fact, stated in the Declaration of Independence, that "all men are created equal," carried with it the corollary that they are all therefore "entitled to [and would be eager for] life, liberty, and the pursuit of happiness." From this premise it is easy to slide imperceptibly into the position of holding that equalitarianism and individualism are inseparably linked, or even that they are somehow the same thing. This is, indeed, almost an officially sanctioned ambiguity in the American creed. But it requires only a little thoughtful reflection to recognize that equalitarianism and individualism do not necessarily go together. Alexis de Tocqueville understood this fact more than a century ago, and out of his recognition he framed an analysis which is not only the most brilliant single account of the American character, but is also the only major alternative to the Jefferson-Turner image.

After travelling the length and breadth of the United States for ten months at the height of Andrew Jackson's ascendancy, Tocqueville felt no doubt of the depth of the commitment of Americans to democracy. Throughout two volumes which ranged over every aspect of American life, he consistently emphasized democracy as a pervasive factor. But the democracy which he wrote about was far removed from Thomas Jefferson's dream.

"Liberty," he observed of the Americans, "is not the chief object of their desires; equality is their idol. They make rapid and sudden efforts to obtain liberty, and if they miss their aim resign themselves to their disappointment; but nothing can satisfy them without equality, and they would rather perish than lose it." [4]

This emphasis upon equality was not, in itself, inconsistent with the most orthodox Jeffersonian ideas, and indeed Tocqueville took care to recognize that under certain circum-

4. Alexis de Tocqueville, *Democracy in America*, edited by Phillips Bradley (Alfred A. Knopf, 1946), I, 53–4.

stances equality and freedom might "meet and blend." But such circumstances would be rare, and the usual effects of equality would be to encourage conformity and discourage individualism, to regiment opinion and to inhibit dissent. Tocqueville justified this seemingly paradoxical conclusion by arguing that:

> When the inhabitant of a democratic country compares himself individually with all those about him, he feels with pride that he is the equal of any one of them; but when he comes to survey the totality of his fellows, and to place himself in contrast with so huge a body, he is instantly overwhelmed by the sense of his own insignificance and weakness. The same equality that renders him independent of each of his fellow citizens, taken severally, exposes him alone and unprotected to the influence of the greater number. The public, therefore, among a democratic people, has a singular power, which aristocratic nations cannot conceive; for it does not persuade others to its beliefs, but it imposes them and makes them permeate the thinking of everyone by a sort of enormous pressure of the mind of all upon the individual intelligence.[5]

At the time when Tocqueville wrote, he expressed admiration for the American people in many ways, and when he criticized adversely his tone was abstract, bland, and free of the petulance and the personalities that characterized some critics, like Mrs. Trollope and Charles Dickens. Consequently, Tocqueville was relatively well received in the United States, and we have largely forgotten what a severe verdict his observations implied. But, in fact, he pictured the American character as the very embodiment of conformity, of conformity so extreme that not only individualism but even freedom was endangered. Because of the enormous weight with which the opinion of the majority pressed upon the individual, Tocqueville said, the person in the minority "not

5. *Ibid.*, II, 94; II, 10.

only mistrusts his strength, but even doubts of his right; and he is very near acknowledging that he is in the wrong when the greater number of his countrymen assert that he is so. The majority do not need to force him; they convince him." "The principle of equality," as a consequence, had the effect of "prohibiting him from thinking at all," and "freedom of opinion does not exist in America." Instead of reinforcing liberty, therefore, equality constituted a danger to liberty. It caused the majority "to despise and undervalue the rights of private persons," and led on to the pessimistic conclusion that "Despotism appears . . . peculiarly to be dreaded in democratic times." [6]

Tocqueville was perhaps the originator of the criticism of the American as conformist, but he also voiced another criticism which has had many echoes, but which did not originate with him. This was the condemnation of the American as a materialist. As early as 1805 Richard Parkinson had observed that "all men there [in America] make it [money] their pursuit," and in 1823 William Faux had asserted that "two selfish gods, pleasure and gain, enslave the Americans." In the interval between the publication of the first and second parts of Tocqueville's study, Washington Irving coined his classic phrase concerning "the almighty dollar, that great object of universal devotion throughout the land." [7] But it remained for Tocqueville, himself, to link materialism with equality, as he had already linked conformity.

> "Of all passions," he said, "which originate in or are fostered by equality, there is one which it renders peculiarly intense, and which it also infuses into the heart of every man: I mean the love of well-being. The taste for well-being is the

6. *Ibid.*, II, 261; II, 11; I, 265; II, 326; II, 322.
7. Richard Parkinson, *A Tour in America in 1798–1800* (2 vols., 1805), II, 652; William Faux, *Memorable Days in America* (1823), p. 417; Washington Irving, "The Creole Village," in *The Knickerbocker Magazine*, November 1836.

> prominent and indelible feature of democratic times. . . .
> The effort to satisfy even the least wants of the body and to
> provide the little conveniences of life is uppermost in every
> mind."

He described this craving for physical comforts as a "pas-
sion," and affirmed that "I know of no country, indeed, where
the love of money has taken stronger hold on the affections
of men." [8]

For more than a century we have lived with the contrasting images of the American character which Thomas Jefferson and Alexis de Tocqueville visualized. Both of these images
presented the American as an equalitarian and therefore as a
democrat, but one was an agrarian democrat while the other
was a majoritarian democrat; one an independent individualist, the other a mass-dominated conformist; one an idealist,
the other a materialist. Through many decades of self-scrutiny
Americans have been seeing one or the other of these images
whenever they looked into the mirror of self-analysis.

The discrepancy between the two images is so great that
it must bring the searcher for the American character up
with a jerk, and must force him to grapple with the question
whether these seemingly antithetical versions of the American
can be reconciled in any way. Can the old familiar formula
for embracing opposite reports—that the situation presents a
paradox—be stretched to encompass both Tocqueville and
Jefferson? Or is there so grave a flaw somewhere that one
must question the whole idea of national character and call
to mind all the warnings that thoughtful men have uttered
against the very concept that national groups can be distinguished from one another in terms of collective group traits.

Certainly there is a sound enough basis for doubting the
validity of generalizations about national character. To begin
with, many of these generalizations have been derived not

8. Tocqueville, *Democracy in America*, II, 26; II, 128; II, 129; I, 51.

from any dispassionate observation or any quest for truth, but from superheated patriotism which sought only to glorify one national group by invidious comparison with other national groups, or from a pseudoscientific racism which claimed innately superior qualities for favored ethnic groups. Further, the explanations which were offered to account for the ascribed traits were as suspect as the ascriptions themselves. No one today will accept the notions which once prevailed that such qualities as the capacity for self-government are inherited in the genes, nor will anyone credit the notion that national character is a unique quality which manifests itself mystically in all the inhabitants of a given country. Between the chauvinistic purposes for which the concept of national character was used, and the irrationality with which it was supported, it fell during the 1930's into a disrepute from which it has by no means fully recovered.

Some thinkers of a skeptical turn of mind had rejected the idea of national character even at a time when most historians accepted it without question. Thus, for instance, John Stuart Mill as early as 1849 observed that "of all vulgar modes of escaping from the consideration of the effect of social and moral influences on the human mind, the most vulgar is that of attributing diversities of character to inherent natural differences." Sir John Seely said, "no explanation is so vague, so cheap, and so difficult to verify." [9]

But it was particularly at the time of the rise of Fascism and Naziism, when the vicious aspects of extreme nationalism and of racism became glaringly conspicuous, that historians in general began to repudiate the idea of national character and to disavow it as an intellectual concept, even though they sometimes continued to employ it as a working device in their treatment of the peoples with whose history they were

9. Mill, *The Principles of Political Economy* (1849), I, 390; Seely, quoted by Boyd C. Shafer, "Men Are More Alike," *American Historical Review*, LVII (1952), 606.

concerned. To historians whose skepticism had been aroused, the conflicting nature of the images of the American as an individualistic democrat or as a conformist democrat would have seemed simply to illustrate further the already demonstrated flimsiness and fallacious quality of all generalizations about national character.

But to deny that the inhabitants of one country may, as a group, evince a given trait in higher degree than the inhabitants of some other country amounts almost to a denial that the culture of one people can be different from the culture of another people. To escape the pitfalls of racism in this way is to fly from one error into the embrace of another, and students of culture—primarily anthropologists, rather than historians—perceived that rejection of the idea that a group could be distinctive, along with the idea that the distinction was eternal and immutable in the genes, involved the ancient logical fallacy of throwing out the baby along with the bath. Accordingly, the study of national character came under the special sponsorship of cultural anthropology, and in the 'forties a number of outstanding workers in this field tackled the problem of national character, including the American character, with a methodological precision and objectivity that had never been applied to the subject before. After their investigations, they felt no doubt that national character was a reality—an observable and demonstrable reality. One of them, Margaret Mead, declared that "In every culture, in Samoa, in Germany, in Iceland, in Bali, and in the United States of America, we will find consistencies and regularities in the way in which new born babies grow up and assume the attitudes and behavior patterns of their elders—and this we may call 'character formation.' We will find that Samoans may be said to have a Samoan character structure and Americans an American character structure." [10] Another, the late Clyde Kluckhohn, wrote:

"The statistical prediction can safely be made that a hundred Americans, for example, will display certain defined characteristics more frequently than will a hundred Englishmen comparably distributed as to age, sex, social class, and vocation." [11]

If these new students were correct, it meant that there was some kind of identifiable American character. It might conform to the Jeffersonian image; it might conform to the Tocquevillian image; it might conform in part to both; or it might conform to neither. But in any event discouraged investigators were enjoined against giving up the quest with the conclusion that there is no American character. It has been said that a philosopher is a blind man in a dark room looking for a black cat that isn't there; the student of national character might also, at times, resemble a blind man in a dark room, looking for a black cat, but the cultural anthropologists exhorted him to persevere in spite of the problems of visibility, for the cat was indubitably there.

Still confronted with the conflicting images of the agrarian democrat and the majoritarian democrat, the investigator might avoid an outright rejection of either by taking the position that the American character has changed, and that each of these images was at one time valid and realistic, but that in the twentieth century the qualities of conformity and materialism have grown increasingly prominent, while the qualities of individualism and idealism have diminished. This interpretation of a changing American character has had a number of adherents in the last two decades, for it accords well with the observation that the conditions of the American

10. Margaret Mead, *And Keep Your Powder Dry* (William Morrow and Co., 1942), p. 21. Miss Mead also says, "The way in which people behave is all of a piece, their virtues and their sins, the way they slap the baby, handle their court cases, and bury their dead."
11. Clyde Kluckhohn and Henry A. Murray, *Personality in Nature, Society, and Culture* (Alfred A. Knopf, 1949), p. 36.

culture have changed. As they do so, of course the qualities of a character that is derived from the culture might be expected to change correspondingly. Thus, Henry S. Commager, in his *The American Mind* (1950), portrayed in two contrasting chapters "the nineteenth-century American" and "the twentieth-century American." Similarly, David Riesman, in *The Lonely Crowd* (1950), significantly sub-titled *A Study of the Changing American Character*, pictured two types of Americans, first an "inner-directed man," whose values were deeply internalized and who adhered to these values tenaciously, regardless of the opinions of his peers (clearly an individualist), and second an "other-directed man," who subordinated his own internal values to the changing expectations directed toward him by changing peer groups (in short, a conformist).

Although he viewed his inner-directed man as having been superseded historically by his other-directed man, Riesman did not attempt to explain in historical terms the reason for the change. He made a rather limited effort to relate his stages of character formation to stages of population growth, but he has since then not used population phase as a key. Meanwhile, it is fairly clear, from Riesman's own context, as well as from history in general, that there were changes in the culture which would have accounted for the transition in character. Most nineteenth-century Americans were self-employed; most were engaged in agriculture; most produced a part of their own food and clothing. These facts meant that their well-being did not depend on the good will or the services of their associates, but upon their resourcefulness in wrestling with the elemental forces of Nature. Even their physical isolation from their fellows added something to the independence of their natures. But most twentieth-century Americans work for wages or salaries, many of them in very large employee groups; most are engaged in office or factory work; most are highly specialized, and are reliant upon many others to supply their needs in an economy with an advanced division of labor. Men now do depend upon the good will and the services of their fellows. This means that what they achieve depends less upon stamina and hardihood than upon their capacity to get along with other people and to fit smoothly into a co-operative relationship. In short, the culture now places a premium upon the qualities which will enable the individual to function effectively as a member of a large organizational group. The strategic importance of this institutional factor has been well recognized by William H. Whyte, Jr., in his significantly titled book *The Organization Man* (1956)—for the conformity of Whyte's bureaucratized individual results from the fact that he lives under an imperative to succeed in a situation where promotion and even survival depend upon effective interaction with others in an hierarchical structure.

Thus, by an argument from logic (always a treacherous substitute for direct observation in historical study), one can make a strong case that the nineteenth-century American should have been (and therefore must have been) an individualist, while the twentieth-century American should be (and therefore is) a conformist. But this formula crashes headlong into the obdurate fact that no Americans have ever been more classically conformist than Tocqueville's Jacksonian democrats—hardy specimens of the frontier breed, far back in the nineteenth century, long before the age of corporate images, peer groups, marginal differentiation, and status frustration. In short, Tocqueville's nineteenth-century American, whether frontiersman or no, was to some extent an other-directed man. Carl N. Degler has pointed out this identity in a very cogent essay, in which he demonstrates very forcibly that most of our easy assumptions about the immense contrast between the nineteenth-century American and the twentieth-century American are vulnerable indeed.[12]

This conclusion should, perhaps, have been evident from the outset, in view of the fact that it was Tocqueville who, in the nineteenth century, gave us the image which we now frequently identify as the twentieth-century American. But in any case, the fact that he did so means that we can hardly resolve the dilemma of our individualist democrat and our majoritarian democrat by assuming that both are historically valid but that one replaced the other. The problem of determining what use we can make of either of these images, in view of the fact that each casts doubt upon the other, still remains. Is it possible to uncover common factors in these apparently contradictory images, and thus to make use of them both in our quest for a definition of the national character? For no matter whether either of these versions of the American is realistic as a type or image, there is no doubt that both of them reflect fundamental aspects of the American experience.

There is no purpose, at this point in this essay, to execute a neat, pre-arranged sleight-of-hand by which the individualist democrat and the conformist democrat will cast off their disguises and will reveal themselves as identical twin Yankee Doodle Dandies, both born on the Fourth of July. On the contrary, intractable, irresolvable discrepancies exist between the two figures, and it will probably never be possible to go very far in the direction of accepting the one without treating the other as a fictitious image, to be rejected as reflecting an anti-democratic bias and as at odds with the evidence from actual observation of the behavior of *Homo americanus* in his native haunts. At the same time, however, it is both necessary to probe for the common factors, and legitimate to observe that there is one common factor conspicuous in the

---

12. Carl N. Degler, "The Sociologist as Historian: Riesman's *The Lonely Crowd*," *American Quarterly*, XV (1963), 483–497.

extreme—namely the emphasis on equality, so dear both to Jefferson's American and to Tocqueville's. One of these figures, it will be recalled, has held no truth to be more self-evident than that all men are created equal, while the other has made equality his "idol," far more jealously guarded than his liberty.

If the commitment to equality is so dominant a feature in both of these representations of the American, it will perhaps serve as a key to various facets of the national character, even to contradictory aspects of this character. In a society as complex as that of the United States, in fact, it may be that the common factors underlying the various manifestations are all that our quest should seek. For it is evident that American life and American energy have expressed themselves in a great diversity of ways, and any effort to define the American as if nearly two hundred million persons all corresponded to a single type would certainly reduce complex data to a blunt, crude, and oversimplified form. To detect what qualities Americans share in their diversity may be far more revealing than to superimpose the stereotype of a fictitious uniformity. If this is true, it means that our quest must be to discover the varied and dissimilar ways in which the commitment to equality expresses itself—the different forms which it takes in different individuals—rather than to regard it as an undifferentiated component which shows in all individuals in the same way. Figuratively, one might say that in seeking for what is common, one should think of the metal from which Americans are forged, no matter into how many shapes this metal may be cast, rather than thinking of a die with which they all are stamped into an identical shape. If the problem is viewed in this way, it will be readily apparent that Tocqueville made a pregnant statement when he observed that the idea of equality was "the fundamental fact from which all others seem to be derived."

The term "equality" is a loose-fitting garment and it has

meant very different things at very different times. It is very frequently used to imply parity or uniformity. The grenadiers in the King of Prussia's guard were equal in that they were all, uniformly, over six feet six inches tall. Particularly, it can mean, and often does mean in some social philosophies, uniformity of material welfare—of income, of medical care, etc. But people are clearly not uniform in strength or intelligence or beauty, and one must ask, therefore, what kind of uniformity Americans believed in. Did they believe in an equal sharing of goods? Tocqueville himself answered this question when he said, "I know of no country . . . where a profounder contempt is expressed for the theory of the permanent equality of property." [13]

At this point in the discussion of equality, someone, and very likely a businessman, is always likely to break in with the proposition that Americans believe in equality of opportunity—in giving everyone what is called an equal start, and in removing all handicaps such as illiteracy and all privileges such as monopoly or special priority, which will tend to give one person an advantage over another. But if a person gains the advantage without having society give it to him, by being more clever or more enterprising or even just by being stronger than someone else, he is entitled to enjoy the benefits that accrue from these qualities, particularly in terms of possessing more property or wealth than others.

Historically, equality of opportunity was a particularly apt form of equalitarianism for a new, undeveloped frontier country. In the early stages of American history, the developed resources of the country were so few that an equality in the division of these assets would only have meant an insufficiency for everyone. The best economic benefit which the government could give was to offer a person free access in developing undeveloped resources for his own profit, and this is what

13. Tocqueville, *Democracy in America*, I, 57–8.

America did offer. It was an ideal formula for everyone: for the individual it meant a very real chance to gain more wealth than he would have secured by receiving an equal share of the existing wealth. For the community, it meant that no one could prosper appreciably without activities which would develop undeveloped resources, at a time when society desperately needed rapid economic development. For these reasons, equality of opportunity did become the most highly sanctioned form of equalitarianism in the United States.

Because of this sanction, Americans have indeed been tolerant of great discrepancies in wealth. They have approved of wealth much more readily when they believed that it had been earned—as in the case, for instance, of Henry Ford— than when they thought it had been acquired by some special privilege or monopoly. In general, however, they have not merely condoned great wealth; they have admired it. But to say that the ideal of equality means only equality of opportunity is hardly to tell the whole story. The American faith has also held, with intense conviction, the belief that all men are equal in the sense that they share a common humanity— that all are alike in the eyes of God—and that every person has a certain dignity, no matter how low his circumstances, which no one else, no matter how high *his* circumstances, is entitled to disregard. When this concept of the nature of man was translated into a system of social arrangements, the crucial point on which it came to focus was the question of rank. For the concept of rank essentially denies that all men are equally worthy and argues that some are better than others—that some are born to serve and others born to command. The American creed not only denied this view, but even condemned it and placed a taboo upon it. Some people, according to the American creed, might be more fortunate than others, but they must never regard themselves as better than others. Pulling one's rank has therefore been the unforgivable sin against American democracy, and the American people have, accordingly, reserved their heartiest dislike for the officer class in the military, for people with upstage or condescending manners, and for anyone who tries to convert power or wealth (which are not resented) into overt rank or privilege (which are). Thus it is permissible for an American to have servants (which is a matter of function), but he must not put them in livery (which is a matter of rank); permissible to attend expensive schools, but not to speak with a cultivated accent; permissible to rise in the world, but never to repudiate the origins from which he rose. The most palpable and overt possible claim of rank is, of course, the effort of one individual to assert authority, in a personal sense, over others, and accordingly the rejection of authority is the most pronounced of all the concrete expressions of American beliefs in equality.

In almost any enterprise which involves numbers of people working in conjunction, it is necessary for some people to tell other people what to do. This function cannot be wholly abdicated without causing a breakdown, and in America it cannot be exercised overtly without violating the taboos against authority. The result is that the American people have developed an arrangement which skillfully combines truth and fiction, and maintains that the top man does not rule, but leads; and does not give orders, but calls signals; while the men in the lower echelons are not underlings, but members of the team. This view of the relationship is truthful in the sense that the man in charge does depend upon his capacity to elicit the voluntary or spontaneous co-operation of the members of his organization, and he regards the naked use of authority to secure compliance as an evidence of failure; also, in many organizations, the members lend their support willingly, and contribute much more on a voluntary basis than authority could ever exact from them. But the element of fiction sometimes enters, in terms of the fact that both sides understand that in many situations authority would have to be invoked if voluntary compliance were not forthcoming. This would be humiliating to all parties—to the top man because it would expose his failure as a leader and to the others because it would force them to recognize the carefully concealed fact that in an ultimate sense they are subject to coercion. To avoid this mutually undesirable exploration of the ultimate implications, both sides recognize that even when an order has to be given, it is better for it to be expressed in the form of a request or a proposal, and when compliance is mandatory, it should be rendered with an appearance of consent.

It is in this way that the anti-authoritarian aspect of the creed of equality leads to the extraordinarily strong emphasis upon permissiveness, either as a reality or as a mere convention in American life. So strong is the taboo against authority that the father, once a paternal authority, is now expected to be a pal to his children, and to persuade rather than to command. The husband, once a lord and master, to be obeyed under the vows of matrimony, is now a partner. And if, perchance, an adult male in command of the family income uses his control to bully his wife and children, he does not avow his desire to make them obey, but insists that he only wants them to be co-operative. The unlimited American faith in the efficacy of discussion as a means of finding solutions for controversies reflects less a faith in the powers of rational persuasion than a supreme reluctance to let anything reach a point where authority will have to be invoked. If hypocrisy is the tribute that vice pays to virtue, permissiveness is, to some extent, the tribute that authority pays to the principle of equality.

When one recognizes some of these varied strands in the fabric of equalitarianism it becomes easier to see how the concept has contributed to the making, both of the Jeffersonian American and the Tocquevillian American. For as one picks at the strands they ravel out in quite dissimilar directions. The strand of equality of opportunity, for instance, if followed out, leads to the theme of individualism. It challenged each individual to pit his skill and talents in a competition against the skill and talents of others and to earn the individual rewards which talent and effort might bring. Even more, the imperatives of the competitive race were so compelling that the belief grew up that everyone had a kind of obligation to enter his talents in this competition and to "succeed." It was but a step from the belief that ability and virtue would produce success to the belief that success was produced by—and was therefore an evidence of—ability and virtue. In short, money not only represented power, it also was a sign of the presence of admirable qualities in the man who attained it. Here, certainly, an equalitarian doctrine fostered materialism, and if aggressiveness and competitiveness are individualistic qualities, then it fostered individualism also.

Of course, neither American individualism nor American materialism can be explained entirely in these terms. Individualism must have derived great strength, for instance, from the reflection that if all men are equal, a man might as well form his own convictions as accept the convictions of someone else no better than himself. It must also have been reinforced by the frontier experience, which certainly compelled every man to rely upon himself. But this kind of individualism is not the quality of independent-mindedness, and it is not the quality which Tocqueville was denying when he said that Americans were conformists. A great deal of confusion has resulted, in the discussion of the American character, from the fact that the term individualism is sometimes used (as by Tocqueville) to mean willingness to think and act separately from the majority, and sometimes (as by Turner) to mean capacity to get along without help. It might be supposed that the two would converge, on the theory that a man who can get along by himself without help will soon recognize that he may as well also think for himself without help. But in actuality, this did not necessarily happen. Self-reliance on the frontier was more a matter of courage and of staying power than of intellectual resourcefulness, for the struggle with the wilderness challenged the body rather than the mind, and a man might be supremely effective in fending for himself, and at the same time supremely conventional in his ideas. In this sense, Turner's individualist is not really an antithesis of Tocqueville's conformist at all.

Still, it remains true that Jefferson's idealist and Tocqueville's conformist both require explanation, and that neither can be accounted for in the terms which make Jefferson's individualist and Tocqueville's materialist understandable. As an explanation of these facets of the American character, it would seem that the strand of equalitarianism which stresses the universal dignity of all men, and which hates rank as a violation of dignity, might be found quite pertinent. For it is the concept of the worth of every man which has stimulated a century and a half of reform, designed at every step to realize in practice the ideal that every human possesses potentialities which he should have a chance to fulfill. Whatever has impeded this fulfillment, whether it be lack of education, chattel slavery, the exploitation of the labor of unorganized workers, the hazards of unemployment, or the handicaps of age and infirmity, has been the object, at one time or another, of a major reforming crusade. The whole American commitment to progress would be impossible without a prior belief in the perfectibility of man and in the practicability of steps to bring perfection nearer. In this sense, the American character has been idealistic. And yet its idealism is not entirely irreconcilable with its materialism, for American idealism has often framed its most altruistic goals in materialistic terms—for instance, raising the standard of living as a means to a better life. Moreover, Americans are committed to the view that materialistic means are necessary to idealistic ends. Franklin defined what is necessary to a virtuous life by saying "an empty sack cannot stand upright," and Americans have believed that spiritual and humanitarian goals are best achieved by instrumentalities such as universities and hospitals which carry expensive price tags.

If the belief that all men are of equal worth has contributed to a feature of American life so much cherished as our tradition of humanitarian reform, how could it at the same time have contributed to a feature so much deplored as American conformity? Yet it has done both, for the same respect of the American for his fellow men, which has made many a reformer think that his fellow citizens are worth helping, has also made many another American think that he has no business to question the opinions that his neighbors have sanctioned. True, he says, if all men are equal, each ought to think for himself, but on the other hand, no man should consider himself better than his neighbors, and if the majority have adopted an opinion on a matter, how can one man question their opinion, without setting himself up as being better than they. Moreover, it is understood that the majority are pledged not to force him to adopt their opinion. But it is also understood that in return for this immunity he will voluntarily accept the will of the majority in most things. The absence of a formal compulsion to conform seemingly increases the obligation to conform voluntarily. Thus, the other-directed man is seen to be derived as much from the American tradition of equalitarianism as the rugged individualist, and the compulsive seeker of an unequally large share of wealth as much as the humanitarian reformer striving for the fulfillment of democratic ideals.

To say that they are all derived from the same tradition is by no means to say that they are, in some larger, mystic sense, all the same. They are not, even though the idealism of the reformer may seek materialistic goals, and though men who are individualists in their physical lives may be conformists in their ideas. But all of them, it may be argued, do reflect circumstances which are distinctively American, and all present manifestations of a character which is more convincingly American because of its diversity than any wholly uniform character could possibly be. If Americans have never reached the end of their quest for an image that would represent the American character, it may be not because they failed to find one image but because they failed to recognize the futility of attempting to settle upon one, and the necessity of accepting several.

12

AMERICAN INDIVIDUALISM
IN THE TWENTIETH CENTURY

Written a year or so after "The Quest for the National Character" and in some respects a sequel to it, this essay was prepared for a symposium held at the University of Texas in December 1962. It was published first in the Texas Quarterly, *summer 1963.*

AT THE BEGINNING of his essay, "Individualism Reconsidered," David Riesman remarks, "Such terms as 'society' and 'individual' tend to pose a false as well as a shifting dichotomy." [1] We might take Riesman's remark and extend it by observing that, in general, we tend to discuss questions too much in terms of antitheses, and frequently in terms of antitheses which are deceptive. Thus, we speak in polarities about liberty versus authority, dissent versus conformity, and, of course, individualism versus collectivism. But in fact we know all the while that no one intends to choose starkly between these alternatives. Liberty would be intolerable to the most independent-minded person without some measure of authority, or dissent without some conformity. In fact, human life presents us with a whole series of situations in which diverse and, to some extent, conflicting values must be kept in some kind of working relationship with one another. Two junior officers both bucking for promotion will presumably work together for the improvement of their unit while they work in rivalry with one another for advancement. Indeed, the principle of "antagonistic co-

1. David Riesman, *Individualism Reconsidered, and Other Essays* (Glencoe, Illinois: Free Press, 1954), p. 26.

operation" probably goes much deeper than this, for even nature seems to abound in situations where two elements are
linked in a relationship of tension and at the same time of interdependence. The basic case is the relationship of men and
women, eternally needing one another and eternally engaged
in a "battle of the sexes"; but there is also the case of youth
and age, with youth forever restive under its dependence upon
the elders, and the elders forever vexed by the brashness of a
youth which they have lost, and with each unwillingly drawing upon the other for qualities which it, itself, lacks. Along
with these classic dualisms, there is also the relationship between man alone, and man in society—man constantly strain-
ing against the compulsion imposed by the group, and man
continuously driven by need for identity with the group.
These conflicting needs must forever be mediated and accom-
modated, and the ultimate choice of either one to the complete
exclusion of the other would be equally unthinkable. In our
literature, any story of the complete isolation, either physical
or psychological, of a man from his fellow man, such as the
story of Robinson Crusoe before he found a human footprint
on the beach, is regarded as essentially a horror story. But the
tale of any man having his identity completely swallowed up
by total absorption into the group, as happened for the members of the Party in Oceania in George Orwell's *1984,* is also
regarded as a kind of nightmare.

    If this principle of balance or beneficent tension between
conflicting values has any validity in the cases which I have
mentioned, it might be argued that it has even more in the case
of individualism, especially in the United States. For is it not
notoriously true that historically American individualism has
always been sanctioned only within very sharply defined limits? The word "individualism," of course, has been included in
our litany of sacred terms, and in many respects, America has
placed an immense premium upon the individualistic values of
independence, self-reliance, and rejection of authority. But

American society has never, I believe, sanctioned the attempt
of a person to practice the kind of individualism which one
would find in a society with a recognized elite. An elite or
aristocratic individualist is likely to regard the principles of
individualism as conferring a franchise for self-indulgence as
well as for self-expression. This was the kind of individualism
which Lord Byron practiced—the kind which he defended in
his epic of Don Juan. It lends itself to the idea that the talented
man may become a superman and that he is quite justified in
sacrificing less talented men and in riding roughshod over
them. Nietzsche is unfavorably remembered for exalting this
superman version of individualism, and of course one finds the
ideal set forth also in Shaw's *Man and Superman*.

Individualism in this form seems profoundly alien to the
American tradition—so alien that we who are in the American
tradition do not usually even recognize it as a form of individualism. Yet occasionally we will find a traveler from overseas
who regards individualism as involving the right of the individualist to indulge his own impulses at the expense of others,
to attain self-expression regardless of its effect on other people.
Such a person is astonished that American individualism carries
no such franchise. The writings of Tocqueville abound in observations on the lack of real variety in American life, despite
all its claims to individualism. But the most vivid statement of
the point that I think I have ever seen was made by Tocqueville's compatriot, Michael de Chevalier, also in the 1830's:

> As for us [the French], who resemble each other in nothing
> except in differing from everybody else, for us, to whom
> variety is as necessary as the air, to whom a life of rules
> would be a subject of horror, the Yankee system would be
> torture. Their liberty is not the liberty to outrage all that is
> sacred on earth, to set religion at defiance, to laugh morals
> to scorn, to undermine the foundations of social order, to
> mock at all traditions and received opinions. It is neither the
> liberty of being a monarchist in a republican country, nor
> that of sacrificing the honor of the poor man's wife or

daughter to one's base passions; it is not even the liberty to
enjoy one's wealth by a public display, for public opinion
has its sumptuary laws, to which all must conform under pain
of moral outlawry; nor even that of living in private differently from the rest of the world.[2]

Just how serious Chevalier was in asserting the right to seduce a poor man's wife as one of the prerequisites of individualism in its Gallic form, I do not know. But his mere voicing
of this assertion gives us, I believe, a kind of benchmark which
may help to define the limits of individualism in its Yankee
form. This assertion of individualism would not do at all for
Americans; and why, we may ask, would it not? Why are
Chevalier's suggestions more or less offensive to us, and why,
particularly, does the suggestion about the poor man's wife
grate on us more than the proposal to "outrage all that is
sacred"? I would suggest that it is because Chevalier is implicitly denying the American proposition that men are intrinsically equal, even though their physical circumstances
may vary immensely. For a rich man to seduce the wife of
another rich man might be accepted in a spirit of joviality,
under the axiom that all is fair in love and war, but for him to
seduce the wife of a poor man is to treat a fellow man as less
than an equal simply because he is poor. In the American
creed this is, perhaps, the sin against the Holy Ghost.

It may seem that I am dwelling too much here upon what
may have been a random phrase in the writing of one French-
man now dead for more than a century, but I have lingered
over it because I believe it may illustrate, in a particularly
vivid way, the fact that American individualism has always
been limited and held in balance by other cherished principles
which were not entirely consistent with it. It could never be

2. John William Ward (ed.), *Society, Manners, and Politics in the United
States: Letters on North America by Michael Chevalier* (Garden City,
New York: Doubleday & Company, Inc. [Anchor Books], 1961), pp. 327–
328.

asserted in a way which would violate the principle of equality, and we will do well to look twice before we even assume that it placed the values of man in isolation ahead of the values of man in a group, or man in society.

At this point it may be necessary for me to pause and declare myself as to what I understand individualism to have meant in American life. If so, I must venture an assertion that American individualism in the nineteenth century and American individualism in the twentieth century have had two fundamentally different emphases, but that both of them have placed great weight upon the belief that individualism should serve as a means to group welfare rather than as a way of exalting man in isolation. This assertion may be difficult to prove, but let us examine it. To specify more fully, let me suggest that the individualism of the nineteenth century stressed the element of self-reliance while that of the twentieth century has stressed the element of nonconformity or dissent, but that in each case there was a strong emphasis upon the value of the quality in question for society as a whole and not simply for the individual apart from society.

Theoretically, perhaps, it might be supposed that these two emphases are not very different: that self-reliance and nonconformity would go together and would tend to converge. It is logical to argue that a man who does not depend on other people for his physical welfare will certainly not be very quick to borrow his ideas from them. If he has the habit of fending for himself, will he not also have the habit of thinking for himself? If he shows initiative in his endeavors to attain success, will he not also show initiative in forming his social ideas? If individualism equals independence and independence equals freedom and freedom equals dissent, then doesn't it follow that individualism equals dissent? Perhaps the plausibility of this kind of equation has led us to the fallacy of using one term, "individualism," to express the ideas of both self-reliance and nonconformity.

But history often mocks logic, and in our historical experience, the believers in self-reliance, in the sense of taking care of oneself, and the believers in nonconformity, in the sense of encouraging dissent, have often been far, far apart. In fact, these two types of individualists seem to be almost natural antagonists, for the "rugged individualist" of laissez-faire economics is likely to be what we call a conservative, as orthodox in his ideas of success as he is enterprising in his efforts to succeed, while the nonconforming individualist is likely to treasure unconventional forms of self-expression and to regard the orthodoxy of the laissez-faire individualist as a threat to such self-expression and to novel ideas in general.

As these two types of individualists feud with one another, it is ironical that the ultimate accusation which each makes is that the other is betraying the community. Thus, while each in his own way places the individual before the group, each at the same time pays inverted tribute to the importance of the group by making the betrayal of the group the basis of his rejection of the other. To the nonconforming individualist the sin of the laissez-faire individualist is that he sacrifices the weak to the strong and that he values the opportunity for private advantage more than he values the general welfare. To the self-reliant individualist, the sin of the nonconforming individualist is that he denies the community the means of protecting its values and the morale of its members against injury by hostile or irresponsible persons or groups. His concept of the right of dissent is so absolute that he extends it not only to responsible critics who want to improve the society, but also to enemies who want to destroy it and to exploiters who are alert to every chance for arousing and playing upon the anxieties, the lusts, and the sadistic impulses which society, from the beginning of time, has struggled to control.

But before looking further at the relationship of these two modes of individualism to one another, let us first look at the historical context of the two. The individualism of self-reliance was essentially the response or adaptation of a people who had an undeveloped continent in front of them and who lacked institutional or technological devices for conquering it. Society needed persons who were what we call self-starters, persons who would go ahead and tackle the wilderness without waiting for signals to be given or for arrangements that would make it easy. It needed qualities of initiative and of ruggedness. It needed the attitude of Stonewall Jackson when he said that he would care for his own wounded and bury his own dead. In the conditions of pioneer America, where the services of the police and the church and the school and the hospital and the specialized economic occupations were often not available, it needed a man who could tote his own gun, pray his own prayers, and learn to read, write, and cipher by the light of a pine-knot fire. Andrew Jackson's mother is said to have admonished him at the parental knee, "Andy, never sue nobody. Always settle them matters yourself."

America needed a breed of men who would swarm over a wilderness which was a continent wide, and it produced the adaptation that was needed—the frontier American, famous in song and story as well as in the classic formulations of Frederick Jackson Turner. He was, it appears, rugged; he was self-reliant; he seems to have been magnificently successful; and he did tame the continent in record time—with the important aid, it must be added, of a tremendously effective new technology of power and machines. But was his self-reliance individualism? And, insofar as it was individualism, what were the social costs of developing this kind of individualism to such a pronounced degree? These questions are somewhat harder to answer.

Turner himself suggested that the frontier experience stimulated innovation, which of course means a break with conformity, a break with the past. He offered the hypothesis, which research has failed to vindicate, that the frontiersmen showed great fertility in working out new and untraditional political devices for the governments of their new states. But in fact, the tendency to imitate and copy the older political models was high. Professor Walter P. Webb has made a considerably more tenable argument that the men of the Great Plains seized upon certain technological innovations: the six-shooter, barbed wire, and the windmill. But this seems more a matter of physical adaptation than of a capacity for independent or deviant thought. The status of the frontiersman as an independent thinker is questionable indeed. Perhaps, one might add, it is unfair even to expect of him that he should have been an independent thinker. The physical demands upon him were very rigid, and rigid demands necessarily require one specific response, thus limiting the range or spectrum or variety of response. Nonconformity and diversity in attitude will flourish where the demands of the physical environment are not so harshly rigorous, and where they leave more latitude for variation from man to man. Nonconformity implies the possibility of varied reactions to the same situation; but the frontier, with its rigorous conditions of life, was too exacting in its demands to allow much choice for the frontiersman in the mode of his reaction.

In the past generation we have come to see, with increasing clarity, that the individualism of the American frontier was an individualism of personal self-reliance and of hardihood and stamina rather than an individualism of intellectual independence and personal self-expression. Arthur Schlesinger, Jr., for instance, has argued, I think convincingly, that the frontier was slow to perceive the problems arising in connection with the application of democracy to an industrial society and slow to develop social ideas of reform, so that these ideas, in fact, developed predominantly in the cities. At the same time when we were recognizing this, we were also beginning to count the social costs of the individualism of self-reliance, so that there has grown up a tendency to doubt whether the frontier influence was altogether a beneficial one in American life. As far back as Alexis de Tocqueville, we were warned in the clearest possible terms that American equality, which is peculiarly identified with the frontier, was conducive to conformity rather than to freedom, since it places the stigma of arrogance upon any man who ventures to set his personal judgment against the judgment of a majority of his equals. Arthur K. Moore, in his study of the frontier mind as exemplified in the backwoodsmen of Kentucky, has shown how readily the practicality of the frontier took the form of a blighting anti-intellectualism.[3] Many writers have begun to say that the frontiersman was spiritually and culturally impoverished by his isolation and by his predilection for a society in which the ties of community life were so weakened that he ceased to be, in any adequate sense, a social being. One who has stated this most strikingly, and perhaps in the most controversial way, is Leslie Fiedler with his famous (or, as some citizens of Montana would say, infamous) comments on his earliest impressions of the people of that frontier state. Upon his arrival in Montana, says Fiedler:

> I was met unexpectedly by the Montana Face. What I had been expecting, I do not clearly know; zest, I suppose, naiveté, a ruddy and straightforward kind of vigor—perhaps even honest brutality. What I found seemed, at first glance, reticent, sullen, weary—full of self-sufficient stupidity; a little later it appeared simply inarticulate, with all the dumb pathos of what cannot declare itself; a face developed not for sociability or feeling, but for facing into the weather. It said friendly things to be sure, and meant them; but it had no adequate physical expressions even for friendliness, and the muscles around the mouth and eyes were obviously unprepared to cope with the demands of any more complicated emotion. I felt a kind of innocence behind it, but an innocence difficult to distinguish from simple ignorance. In a way there was something heartening in dealing with people who had never seen, for instance, a Negro or a Jew or a servant, and

3. Arthur K. Moore, *The Frontier Mind* (Lexington: University of Kentucky Press, 1957).

were immune to all their bitter meanings; but the same people, I knew, had never seen an art museum or a ballet or even
a movie in any language but their own, and the poverty of
experience had left the possibilities of the human face in
them completely unrealized.[4]

Here, in effect, is the assertion that society had to pay too
high a price for frontier individualism—that men as a group
were penalized for the freedom of men as separate beings, and,
in short, that individualism is not justified if it serves only individuals. It must serve society. Our conviction that it must is
why we have never had any elite individualism that amounted
to anything, and is also a striking commentary upon the paradoxical elements in the fact that we are committed to individualism at all.

Along with frontier individualism, the nineteenth century
also subscribed to the economic individualism of *laissez-faire*.
The two had a great deal in common. Both exalted strength
and stamina and scorned weakness or lack of practicality. Both
enjoined the individual to fight for his own aspirations first
and to subordinate consideration for the group to consideration for the enterpriser acting alone. Both made a virtue of independence, but their independence meant a self-propelled
drive toward the goals which society had prescribed rather
than any real independence of mind in setting the goals for
which to strive. Both were individualistic in a sense—certainly
in the sense of "rugged individualism"—but it was an individualism that was more conservative than liberal, more hostile to
dissent than favorable toward it.

It is a notable fact about *laissez-faire* individualism, however, that while it exalted the virtues of unregimented, uncon-
trolled, independent action by man acting alone, it never for a
moment contended that the success of the unusual individual
was more important than the welfare of the community. In-

4. Leslie A. Fiedler, *An End of Innocence* (Boston: The Beacon Press,
1955), pp. 134–135. Courtesy also of the *Kenyon Review*.

stead, it constantly stressed the idea that the bold enterpriser served the community by daring to undertake projects which the community needed but which the rank and file were too unimaginative to initiate. The argument was much like that of the modern nonconforming individualist who defends dissenters not on the ground that the dissenter matters and that the conventional thinkers from whom he dissents do not, but that the community needs ideas which the conventional or orthodox thinkers cannot supply.

There is no need for me to recite here the elaborate arguments which Adam Smith stated so ingeniously, and which nineteenth-century publicists so dearly loved to repeat, that a providentially designed economic system (the unseen hand of God at work) took the selfish impulses and selfish actions of individuals and translated them into results which served the welfare of the community. This concept that the antagonistic rivalries of selfish and competing producers would create an optimum relationship between the social need for goods and the economic supply of goods is not only a subtle but by no means a preposterous economic theory. It is also a renewed testimony that even the ardent individualists of the nineteenth century were not willing to base their faith in individualism upon any concept of the primacy of the interests of the individual over the interests of the group. Instead they made the interests of the group—that is, the society—the ground for their insistence that society must not be deprived of the contribution which the independent-minded individual can make.

During the Great Depression, a great many Americans grew to doubt that laissez-faire individualism really did serve the interests of the whole society. Our government under the New Deal abandoned it, and though we have had a span of a quarter of a century since that time, with two Republican administrations in the interim, there is no indication that we will return to the old faith in self-reliance and private action. Richard Hofstadter has subtitled his essay on Herbert Hoover

"The Last Stand of Rugged Individualism," and there are probably not many, even among the conservatives, who would quarrel very much with this verdict.

In saying that the individualism of self-reliance has passed its high tide, I don't mean to suggest by any means that it has disappeared, or even that it does not remain, in some forms, a very dominant American attitude. Anyone who thinks that it is becoming extinct might well ponder over an analysis which Martha Wolfenstein and Nathan Leites made only a few years ago of the plots of a year's crop of American motion pictures of the A grade.

> The major plot configuration in American films [they wrote] contrasts with both the British and the French. Winning is terrifically important and always possible though it may be a tough fight. The conflict is not an internal one [as in Hamlet]; it is not our own impulses which endanger us nor our own scruples that stand in our way. The hazards are all external, but they are not rooted in the nature of life itself. They are the hazards of a particular situation with which we find ourselves confronted. The hero is typically in a strange town where there are apt to be dangerous men and women of ambiguous character and where the forces of law and order are not to be relied on. If he sizes up the situation correctly, if he does not go off half-cocked but is still able to beat the other fellow to the punch once he is sure who the enemy is, if he relies on no one but himself, if he demands sufficient evidence of virtue from the girl, he will emerge triumphant. He will defeat the dangerous men, get the right girl, and show the authorities what's what.[5]

We all know that American boys, from the early years of childhood, are taught to stand up and fight back. Margaret Mead, incidentally, has commented cogently on this point.[6] So

5. Martha Wolfenstein and Nathan Leites, *Movies: A Psychological Study* (Glencoe, Illinois: Free Press, 1950), p. 298.
6. Margaret Mead, *And Keep Your Powder Dry: An Anthropologist Looks at America* (New York: William Morrow & Company, Inc., 1942), p. 141.

long as this is true, and so long as the self-reliant protagonist in the movie gets the desirable girl, it would be premature indeed to suggest that all the bark has been rubbed off the tradition of individualism in its rugged form. But certainly the tradition has come under attack and certainly it is, as we might say, selling at a discount.

Now what is the basis of our discontent with the tradition of self-reliance? This is certainly a complex and difficult question, to which it may be brash to venture a simple answer, but in many respects it appears that the point of the criticism is that stress on self-reliance was carried to a point where it emphasized private goals and private values too much at the cost of community goals and community values. The coherence of the community was impaired, the vitality of the community was lowered. Leslie Fiedler's men with the Montana face are essentially men who have been starved of the psychological nourishment which community life could offer.

This criticism can be detected, I think, in quite a number of different forms. For instance, Stanley Elkins, in his comparison of slavery in North America and in South America, comments on the fact that in South America certain community institutions such as the church and the government were strong enough to assert a concern for the slave, and to stand, as it were, in certain respects, between the slave and his master.[7] But in North America, the naked authority of the master was tempered in hardly any way by the institutional force of the community. This amounts to saying that private values had eclipsed public values in the United States. Many other writers have expressed concern about the lack of corporate *esprit* among Americans, and some of the concern about the lack of reciprocal support for one another among American prisoners of war in Korea, as contrasted, for instance, with that among Turkish prisoners of war, was also addressed to the fear that

7. Stanley M. Elkins, *Slavery: A Problem in American Institutional and Intellectual Life* (Chicago: University of Chicago Press, 1959), pp. 27–80.

we have emphasized private values, or what may be called privatism, too much and community values not enough. The old Yankee prayer:

> God save me and my wife,
> My son John and his wife,
> Us four and no more

may have expressed an attitude that was rooted too deep for comfort.

Many of the comments that we have had on privatism as an unfortunate dimension of American individualism have been expressed in strong and somewhat controversial terms, but Gabriel Almond, in his *The American People and Foreign Policy*, gave us what might be regarded as a sober and measured statement of this point.

> The American, [said Almond] is primarily concerned with "private values," as distinguished from social-group, political, or religious-moral values. His concern with private, worldly success is his most absorbing aim. In this regard it may be suggested by way of hypothesis that in other cultures there is a greater stress on corporate loyalties and values and a greater personal involvement with political issues or with other-worldly religious values.[8]

With the twentieth century, as I have already tried to suggest, American individualism took on a new emphasis. The frontier was disappearing, and *laissez-faire* was having its wings clipped. According to a well-known phrase which is perhaps a trifle too pat, human rights were replacing property rights. The new expounders of the American tradition re-examined the sacred documents and concluded that the priceless feature of our heritage was the principle of nonconformity, or dissent. Of course, they had perfectly sound historical grounds for tracing the principle of dissent far back in Amer-

8. Gabriel A. Almond, *The American People and Foreign Policy* (New York: Harcourt, Brace and Company, Inc., 1950), p. 48.

ican history. Puritanism itself was a fairly radical form of dissent, as well as a harsh system for enforcing conformity. Ralph W. Emerson, that great apostle of individualism, had not only exalted self-reliance; he had exalted dissent also. "Whoso would be a man," Emerson said, "must be a non-conformist." In our own day, the sanction which we give to dissent is suggested quite clearly in the antithesis which we constantly set up of liberty versus authority and of self-expression versus conformity.

The exponents of this new kind of individualism went forward rejoicing, for quite some time, that individualism was now purged of the taints of privatism and of conformity. For the spokesmen of the individualism of nonconformity were very often men who could in no sense be accused of indifference to the interests of the group, of society. Most of them are what we call liberals—using the term with a fairly clear understanding of what kind of people we mean, even if we cannot quite define their exact quality—and the liberals were so concerned with the welfare of the group that they often gave it a priority over the rights of the individual. Their opponents offered an implicit recognition of this fact by angrily denouncing them as "collectivists." How could a man whose fault, if he has one, is that he is too collectivist—too group-minded—legitimately be accused of privatism? How could a man who supports the American Civil Liberties Union and consistently disparages the bourgeoisie be suspected of conformity? The new individualism, then, was an emancipated individualism, cleansed of its old, middle-class sins of privatism and of conformity.

Yet before we accept the conclusion that the nineteenth-century doctrine of progress has been vindicated again, and that individualism has reached a new and perfected condition, it may be worthwhile to apply one of the weapons of dissent, the weapon of skepticism, and to ask in a truly searching way whether conformity and privatism are really dead, whether true self-expression has come into its own at last, or whether, to some extent, conformity and privatism have merely found new modes of expression.

To pursue this question, as it relates to conformity, one would have to ask whether we have ceased to follow the crowd, or whether we have to some extent merely changed the crowd which we follow? Have we ceased to be cultists, or have we primarily changed our cults? Does the liberal who makes a fetish of his nonconformity actually show much more readiness to get out of step with his fellow liberals than does the avowedly conformist conservative with his fellow conservatives?

Stated a little differently and a little more abstractly, conformity is the faithful, unquestioning compliance with the standards imposed by a group. But to say this is to say that whether you call a man a conformist or a dissenter is very often not a question of his intrinsic independence, but a question of what group you measure him by. A Communist, for instance, measured by the reference group of the American public, is a dissenter and a nonconformist, but measured by the reference group of his own adoption, the Communist group, he is the supreme conformist—more so than a Baptist or a Rotarian, for he has completely abdicated his capacity to judge questions on their own merits and has embraced, *verbatim et literatim*, a whole body of doctrine which, like medieval theology, has answered all questions before they arise.

David Riesman has dealt with this point with sharp perception in his essay "The Saving Remnant," where he says, "The Bohemians and rebels are not usually autonomous; on the contrary, they are zealously tuned in to the signals of a defiant group that finds the meaning of life in a compulsive nonconformity to the majority group." [9] In an extraordinarily acute article called "The Bored and the Violent," Arthur Miller has

9. Riesman, *Individualism Reconsidered*, p. 117.

discussed this point in connection with extreme manifestations of sadistic violence among juvenile delinquents. Miller makes the striking point that, among these youths, who are responding to society by defiance in its most extreme form, the real pattern is not one of deviation but of conformity—a blind, abject conformity to the expectations of their peers. As Miller says, "The delinquent, far from being the rebel, is the conformist par excellence. He is actually incapable of doing anything alone." [10] His reliance upon his gang is, of course, the measure of this lack of capability. Here, one is reminded of a cartoon in the *New Yorker* some time ago showing a young woman, attractive and appearing very much an average American girl, speaking somewhat crossly to her husband, who was dressed in the prescribed uniform of a beatnik. Her question to him was, "Why do you have to be a nonconformist like everyone else?"

If there is any group in our society which makes a truly earnest effort to cultivate real intellectual freedom and fearless inquiry, it is no doubt the academic and intellectual community. Yet even here, do we not have a certain incidence of what might be called academic conformity? Would not an academic who in 1960 spoke out loud and clear for Richard Nixon have shocked the sense of propriety of a gathering of academics as much as an overt glorification of the New Frontier would shock a group of investment bankers? Do not even the academics have their orthodoxies and their conventions? Do not these conventions require that in the case of a novelist, for example, he make a conforming obeisance to nonconformity by following the practice of employing as frequently as possible the monosyllabic words for the functions of sex and bodily elimination which have now become almost trite but which still have a gratifying capacity to startle a good many readers and to attract a good many buyers who hope to be

10. Arthur Miller, "The Bored and the Violent," *Harper's Magazine* (November, 1962), pp. 51–52.

startled? And do not the conventions also require that the book reviewer also conform and prove that he too is an emancipated spirit by dutifully praising the fearless realism of the author without reference to whether his work has merit?

One more illustration may be in order here—the case of an academic of irreproachable standing. When Hannah Arendt published an article questioning whether the integration of public schools ought to be attempted by the exercise of public authority, the result was not, as one might have hoped, a rough-and-tumble scrimmage between her and persons who disagreed with her. It was rather a shocked silence, a polite looking in the other direction as if no one had noticed. It was, indeed, the same reaction as if she had belched in church. Miss Arendt had questioned a point on which liberals have established a dogma to which they require conformity, and they were shocked in a prudish way to hear this dogma questioned.

If there is some question about the completeness of the triumph of nonconformity, there is perhaps also a question concerning the finality of the victory over privatism. Surely the old nineteenth-century brand of rugged individualism is gone for good, and we will no longer sacrifice the interests of society to the individualism of *laissez-faire*. But can any generation, even our own, completely reconcile the social needs of the group with other personal needs of the individual? And must we not expect that even the new style of defense of individual right will sometimes be conducted at the expense of what might best serve society as a whole? The new individualism firmly repudiates all the nineteenth-century freebooters who used to exploit the public economically, but it still thinks, and perhaps ought to think, in terms of man as separate rather than of man in the group. Thus, when it is confronted with what we call crime—the large-scale incidence of violence in our society—it seems more concerned with the rehabilitation of the deviant individual who has committed the violence than with safeguarding those anonymous persons upon whom the violence is committed. When confronted with the sale in every drugstore of magazines which exploit sex, it does not really ask whether it would be better for society if the drugstores did not purvey this material. It does not ask whether the publisher who makes a fast buck by this shoddy commercial enterprise is different from a patent-medicine manufacturer who also makes a fast buck by selling nostrums but is regulated, hopefully, by the Pure Food and Drug Act. It asks instead who will dare to violate freedom of the press in maintaining an informed public opinion.

Perhaps this is the right question to ask. I would hesitate to say that it is clearly wrong. But what I do venture to suggest is that the freedom of the individual, in relation to his society, cannot be absolute, basically because the individual and the society are not really separate. The individual acquires his full identity only as a member of society, and society itself is, in the last analysis, a multiplicity of individuals. The American tradition, which rejected elite individualism from the beginning, has always shown enough concern for the social values to seek to justify its individualism—whether self-reliant or nonconformist—in social terms. Thus the competitive system in economics was defended not on the ground of the great profits which it would bring to some individuals, but with the claim that it would assure economic vigor for the society. Similarly, the sanctions which have surrounded dissent were based less upon approval of the dissenter than upon the need of society for an unrestricted "free trade in ideas." Moreover, each school of individualism cared enough for social values to attack the other for betraying them. Thus the dissentients accused the self-reliants of sacrificing the weak to the strong and the community to its predatory members, while the self-reliants accused the dissentients of sacrificing the strong to the weak and the community to its aberrant members. Perhaps both accusations have been justified, for both groups have remained primarily committed to a strong individualistic emphasis, and in the long struggle between two schools of individualism, the values of the community have often lacked effective defenders on either side. Neither form of individualism has had enough genuine concern for real group values, shared community values, to hold a proper balance between the centrifugal and the centripetal forces.

Neither one has been willing to recognize that the tension between the individual and the group can never be treated as a simple antithesis, involving a simple choice. For each, in its logically pure form, contains implications which are unacceptable to most of us. The emphasis on the individual essentially implies a component of privatism which would sacrifice the interests of the group to the interests of a limited number of its members, and this implication is not acceptable in the long run to a democratic society; the emphasis on the group implies the subordination of the qualities of the mind and spirit of man, standing by himself, to the pressures of men in a herd, and this implication, too, is unacceptable to a people who believe that society exists for man and not man for society. Therefore, we can never make a clearcut, exclusive choice in favor of either individualism, as it is called, or collectivism, as it is called. While philosophers are engaged in pursuing one or the other of these two to their logical extremes and even their logical absurdities, people in everyday life will go on, trying in the future, as they have tried in the past, to accommodate these two and imperfectly to reconcile the indispensable values which are inherent in them both. As Riesman stated it, "Such terms as 'society' and 'individual' tend to pose a false, as well as a shifting dichotomy."

13

AMERICAN WOMEN AND
THE AMERICAN CHARACTER

*Have generalizations about the "American character" been
drawn more or less exclusively from observation of American
males? Beginning with this question, David Potter proceeded
to a wide-ranging examination of the changing role of women
in American society, producing a seminal essay now recognized as a miniature classic in the field. First presented as
a lecture at Stetson University in 1959, it was published in
the University's* Bulletin *of January 1962.*

THERE IS AN OLD RIDDLE which children used to ask one another concerning two Indians. One was a big Indian, the other was a little Indian, and they were sitting on a fence. The little Indian, the riddle tells us, was the big Indian's son, but the big Indian, was not the little Indian's father. How, asks the riddle, can this be?

Boys and girls for a long time have found that this riddle succeeds very well in mystifying many people. And the fact that it does presents another puzzle as to why the riddle is hard to answer. If we were to state the question in more general terms: there are two human beings, one adult and one child; the child is the son of the adult, but the adult is not the father of the child, probably no one would have much difficulty in recognizing that the adult is the mother. Why then do the Indians on a fence perplex us? If we examine the structure of the riddle, I think we will find that it contains two devices which inhibit our recognition that the big Indian is a female. First, the two Indians are described as being in a very specific situation —they are sitting on a fence. But women, at least in our culture, do not usually sit on fences; if the two Indians had been roasting some ears of corn, or mending their teepee, how

much easier the riddle would have been. Second, we are perhaps especially prone to think of Indians as masculine. If the
riddle had said two South Sea Islanders, or perhaps, two Cir-
cassians, the possibility of their being female might occur to
us much more easily.

But most of all, the riddle owes its baffling effect to the fact
that our social generalization is mostly in masculine terms. If
we said that the little Indian is the big Indian's daughter, but
that the big Indian is not the little Indian's mother, the possibility that the big Indian is the father would come to mind
readily enough. For in our culture, men are still in a general
category, while women are in a special category. When we
speak of mankind, we mean men and women collectively, but
when we speak of womenkind, we mean the ladies, God bless
them. The word humanity is itself derived from *homo*, that is
man, and the species is *Homo sapiens*. Neuter nouns or general
nouns which are ambiguous as to sex—nouns like infant,
baby, child, sibling, adolescent, adult, spouse, parent, citizen,
person, individual, etc.—all take masculine pronouns. In our
culture, a woman, at marriage takes her husband's name.
Though born a Cabot, if she marries Joe Doaks, Mrs. Joe
Doaks she becomes and Mrs. Doaks she remains, usually for
the rest of her life.

This masculine orientation is to be expected, of course, in a
society which is traditionally and culturally male-dominated
—in what we call a patriarchal rather than a matriarchal society. Even women themselves have connived at maintaining
the notion of masculine ascendancy, and in the rather numerous concrete situations in which they actually dominate
their men, they often dissimulate their control by pretending
to be weak, dependent, or "flighty." In such a situation one
must expect that men will be regarded as the normative figures
in the society, and that, in popular thought at least, the qualities of the masculine component in the society will pass for
the qualities of the society as a whole.

If this habit were confined to popular thought, it would hardly be worth examining. But it also sometimes creeps into academic and scholarly thought, which ought to have more rigor, and when it does so, it can sometimes distort our picture of society. Thus a writer may sometimes make observations on the traits or values of American men, and then may generalize these as the traits or values of the American people. If he did this deliberately, on the theory that since male values dominate the society, they must therefore be American values, we would have to concede that he is aware of what he is doing, even though we might question his results. But when he does so unconsciously, his method may easily lead him to assume first that since American men are dominant, the characteristics of American men are the characteristics of the American people, and that since women are people, the characteristics of the American people are the characteristics of American women, or in short, that the characteristics of American men are the characteristics of American women.

To avoid this trap, when one meets with a social generalization it is frequently worthwhile to ask concretely: Does it apply to women, or only to the masculine component in the population? Does the statement that Prussians are domineering mean that Prussian women are domineering, or only Prussian men? Does the statement that Americans are individualistic mean American women as well as American men? The question seems worth asking, for it appears more than possible that many of our social generalizations which are stated sweepingly to cover the entire society are in fact based on the masculine population, and that if we took the feminine population into account, the generalization might have to be qualified, or might even run in an entirely different direction.

A notable example of this can perhaps be found in Frederick Jackson Turner's famous frontier hypothesis, stated so brilliantly at Chicago almost seventy years ago. The gist of Turner's argument was, of course, that the frontier had been a basic influence in shaping the character of the American people. Primarily, as he saw it, the frontier provided economic opportunity in the form of free land. When this free land was suddenly conferred upon a people who had previously been held in dependence by the land monopolies of the Old World, it made the American economically independent and this independence made him more individualistic and more egalitarian in his attitudes. Also, the necessity for subduing the wilderness by his own personal exertions, in a situation where he could not call upon doctors, dentists, policemen, lawyers, contractors, well-drillers, repairmen, soil analysts, and other specialists to aid him, made him more self-reliant.

Not even Turner's harshest critics deny that there was much truth in his observations, but many of them have pointed to his lack of precision, and it is fair to question to what extent Turner's generalizations applied to all frontier people, or to what extent they applied restrictively to frontier men. Sometimes it becomes clear that the life-process which he identifies with the frontier was primarily though not wholly an experience shared by men rather than by women. There is one famous passage, for instance, which begins, "The wilderness masters the colonist." Now *colonist* is a neuter noun, and could apply to a female colonist. But the passage continues to say that the wilderness, finding the colonist "European in dress, industry, modes of travel, and thought, . . . takes him from the railroad car and puts him in a birch canoe [This sounds progressively less as if it could be a woman.]. It strips off the garments of civilization and arrays him in the hunting shirt and the moccasin." Soon, this colonist hears the call of the wild almost as clearly as Jack London's dog, and when he does, "he shouts the war cry and takes the scalp in orthodox Indian fashion." [1] Here, at least, the pioneer in question is hardly a woman.

1. Frederick Jackson Turner, *The Frontier in American History* (New York: Henry Holt and Co., 1920), p. 4.

Certainly it is true that the frontier offered economic opportunity, and certainly, also, frontier women shared in some of the social consequences which flowed from the fact that this opportunity was available to their men. But is it not true, in cold fact, that the opportunities offered by the West were opportunities for men and not, in any direct sense, opportunities for women? The free acres of the West were valuable to those who could clear, and break, and plow and harvest them. But clearing and breaking, plowing and harvesting were men's work, in which women rarely participated. The nuggets of gold in the streambeds of California in 1849 represented opportunity to those who could prospect for them. But the life of the prospector and the sourdough was not a woman's life, and the opportunities were not women's opportunities. Similarly, the grass-covered plateau of the Great Plains represented economic opportunity for those who could use it as an open range for the holding and grazing of Longhorn cattle. But the individuals who could do this were men; the Cattle Kingdom was a man's world. Thus, when Turner says that "so long as free land exists, the opportunity for a competency exists," he means, in effect, an opportunity for males.

Again, it may bear repeating, there is no question here that the frontier influenced women as well as men. It had its Molly Pitcher and its Jemima Boone, as well as its Davy Crockett, and its Kit Carson. It left its stamp upon the pioneer women as well as the pioneer men. But when Turner states that it furnished "a new field of opportunity, a gate of escape from the bondage of the past," one must ask, exactly what was the nature of women's participation in this opportunity? Before this question can be analyzed, it is perhaps necessary to recognize that women's place in our society is invariably complicated by the fact that they have, as men do not, a dual status. Almost every woman shares the status of the men in her family—her father or her husband—and if this is a privileged position, she is a recipient of some of the privilege. This is an affiliated status, but if her men gain, she gains with them. Thus, if her family became landowners on the frontier, she participated in their advancement, and no one can deny that free land was, in this indirect sense, opportunity for her also. But woman also has a personal status, which is a sex status, as a female. As a female, on the frontier, women were especially dependent upon having a man in the family, for there was no division of labor there, as there was in settled communities, and most of the tasks of the frontier—the hunting, the wood-chopping, the plowing—could hardly be performed by women, though many of them, of course, rose to these tasks in time of emergency. In fact, the frontier was brutally harsh for females, and it furnished its own verdict on its differential impact upon the sexes. "This country," said the frontier aphorism, "is all right for men and dogs, but it's hell on women and horses."

If we accept Turner's own assumption that economic opportunity is what matters, and that the frontier was significant as the context within which economic opportunity occurred, then we must observe that for American women, as individuals, opportunity began pretty much where the frontier left off. For opportunity lay in access to independent employment, and the employments of the frontier were not primarily accessible to women. But in the growing cities, opportunities for female employment began to proliferate. Where the work of the frontier called for the strong back and the powerful muscles of a primeval man, the work of the city—clerical work, secretarial work, the tending of machines—has called for the supple fingers and the ready adaptability of a young woman, and it was in this environment, for the first time in America, that women found on any scale worth mentioning, access to independent earning power. Once a woman possessed access to such earning power, whether she used it or not, the historic basis for her traditional subordination had been swept away. The male monopoly upon jobs was broken, and the breaking of this monopoly was no less significant for American women than the breaking of the landlord's monopoly upon fertile soil had been for American pioneer men. As a symbol, the typewriter evokes fewer emotions than the plow, but like the plow, it played a vital part in the fulfillment of the American promise of opportunity and independence. The wilderness may have been the frontier for American men, and the cabin in the clearing the symbol of their independence, but the city was the frontier for American women and the business office was what gave them economic independence and the opportunity to follow a course of their own.

Another social generalization which is often stated as if it applied to all Americans, men and women alike, is that our society has experienced a vast transformation in the occupational activities of its people, and that we have passed from the independent, self-directed work, of the kind done by a landowning farmer, to the regimented, externally-directed activity of the employee who labors for pay. In 1850, 63% of the gainfully employed workers in the United States were engaged in agriculture, and a high proportion of these were landowning farmers—perhaps as nearly independent as people can be. In the past the farmer, more than most of his fellows, was in position to plan, decide, and act for himself— to maintain his own values without regard for the approval or disapproval of his fellow man, to work at his own pace, to set his own routine. But today, as the census figures show, the American who labors is no longer self-employed. In 1958, it was estimated that 50,000,000 people gainfully employed in the United States received salaries or wages, while only 8,000,-000 were self-employed, which means that in general the American worker does not work for himself. He works under direction in an office or a factory. He does not decide what to do, when to do it, or for what purpose, but he waits for instructions which come to him through channels. Even the junior executive, despite his prestige, is no more a self-employed man than the factory worker, and if we may believe *The Organization Man* he is in fact considerably less independent after hours. With these ideas in mind, we speak in broad terms about the disappearance of the old forms of autonomous, self-directed activity.

Yet none of this applies in any sense to women, except for women who are employees, and although female employment has increased steadily to a point where nearly one-third of all women are employed it is still true that two out of three American women are not employees, but find their occupation chiefly in the maintaining of homes and the rearing of children. Millions of housewives continue to exercise personal choice and decision not only in arranging their own time-table and routine but also in deciding what food the family shall have and how it shall be prepared, what articles of purchase shall have the highest priority on the family budget, and, in short, how the home shall be operated. Despite strong tendencies toward conformity in American life, it is clear that American women exercise a very wide latitude of decision in these matters, and everyone knows that there are great variations between the regimes in various American homes. Indeed it seems fairly evident that the housewife of today, with the wide range of consumer goods available for her purchase and the wide variety of mechanical devices to free her from drudgery, has a far broader set of alternatives for her household procedure than the farm wife of two or three generations ago.[2] Moreover there are now great numbers of women working independently in their own homes, who a generation ago would have been working very much under direction as do-

2. Robert Lynd, "The People as Consumers," writes that there is "probably today a greater variation from house to house in the actual inventory list of family possessions . . . than at any previous era in man's history." *Recent Social Trends in the United States* (New York: McGraw-Hill, 1933), pp. 857-911.

mestic servants in the homes of other women. If we based our social generalizations upon the experience of women rather than that of men, we might drop the familiar observation about the decreasing independence of Americans in their occupational pursuits. Instead we might emphasize that in the largest single occupational group in the country—the group which cooks and keeps house and rears children—there is a far greater measure of independent and self-directed work than there was in the past.

Closely connected to this question of the disappearance of the independent worker is another commonplace generalization, namely that the American people have become the victims of extreme specialization. Everyone is familiar with the burden of this lament: American industry has forced the craftsman to abandon his craft, and with it the satisfaction of creative labor, and has reduced him to operating a machine or to performing a single operation on the assembly-line as if he were a machine himself. Further, the complaint continues, modern conditions provide fewer and fewer opportunities for a worker to be an all-round person of varied skills and resources, as the American farmer used to be, and instead conditions make of him a diminished person, a narrow specialist hardly fit for anything save his narrow specialty.

Despite the exaggerated and somewhat hackneyed character of this outcry, it contains an important element of truth as regards the work of American male workers. But this generalization, too, is in fact applicable largely to the male component in the population rather than to the American people as a whole. For the American housewife is not a specialist, and in fact her modern role requires that she be far more versatile than her grandmother was, despite the greater skill of the grandmother in cooking, sewing, and other household crafts. A good housewife today must not only serve food to please the family palate, but must also know about calories, vitamins, and the principles of a balanced diet. She must also be an economist, both in her knowledge of the quality of the products offered to her and in her ability to do the impossible with a budget. She must not only maintain a comfortable home, but must also possess enough skill in interior decoration to assure that her own menage will not seem dowdy or unappealing by comparison with the latest interiors shown in Hollywood films. She must not only rear children, but must also have mastered enough child psychology to be able to spare the rod and still not spoil the child. She must not only get the children ready for school, but must also, in many cases, act as a kind of transportation manager, participating in an elaborate car pool to convey them to and fro. In addition to all this, society now enjoins her not to rely upon the marriage vows to hold her husband, but to keep her personality and her appearance so attractive that he will have no incentive to stray. Whatever else she may be, she is certainly not a specialist, and even if she fails to meet all these varied demands upon her, her mere effort to do so would remove her from the category of specialists. If we based our social generalizations upon women rather than upon men, we might quite justifiably affirm that the modern age is an age of diversified activity rather than an age of specialization.

The profound differences between the patterns of men's work and women's work are seldom understood by most men, and perhaps even by most women. In terms of the time-tables of life, however, the contrasts are almost startling. For instance, man usually begins work in the early twenties, labors at precisely timed intervals for eight hours a day and five days a week, until he is sixty-five, when his life as a worker may be cut off with brutal abruptness and he is left idle. Woman, also usually begins work in the early twenties, perhaps in an office on the same time-table as a man, but after a very few years she becomes a wife, whose work is keeping house, and a mother whose work is rearing children. As such she labors often for from fifty-one to fifty-six hours a week, and she does not have the alternation of work and leisure which helps to lend variety and pace to the life of her husband. Her work-load will continue to be heavier than her husband's until the children are older, after which it will gradually diminish, and she may ultimately re-enter employment. But most women do not; they continue to keep house.[3] And as long as a woman does keep house, either as a wife or as a widow, she never experiences the traumatic, sudden transition from daily work as the focus of life to enforced idleness—the transition which we call retirement.

Another far-reaching consequence of the difference between man's work and woman's work is forcibly expressed in a public interest advertisement in *Harper's Magazine* by Frank R. Neu, entitled "We May Be Sitting Ourselves to Death." Neu presents some very impressive data about the poor physical fitness of a large percentage of American men, and about the deleterious effects of the sedentary life of Mr. Joe Citizen as an office worker whose principal exercise is to go around a golf course on an electric cart on the week-end. Then Mr. Neu says, "Let's consider Jill, Joe's wife, for a moment. Chances are, on the basis of current statistics, Jill will outlive Joe by anywhere from five to 25 years. Medical science is not sure yet whether this is because Jill has different hormones from Joe or whether it is a result of the different roles which Joe and Jill fulfill in our society.

"The average suburban Jill is likely to be a homemaker responsible for rearing two or more children. It is safe to assume that any woman with this responsibility is going to get a lot of daily exercise no matter how many gadgets she has to help

---

3. In 1957, of the 21,000,000 women in the work force, 11,000,000 were wives. Female employment was highest (45%) in the age brackets 20 to 24, declined to 39% in bracket 25 to 44, rose to 40% in the bracket 45 to 64, and declined to 10% in the bracket 65 and over.

her do the housework. A homemaker does a lot of walking each day merely to push the buttons and start the machines that wash the clothes, cook the meals, and remove the dust. And she also does a good deal of bending each day to pick up after Joe and the junior members of the family. All in all, Jill is likely to get much more exercise than Joe. This may have a significant relationship to Jill's outliving Joe, who no longer hikes the dusty trail to bring home the buffalo meat and hides to feed and clothe his family." [4]

In the light of differences so great that they may radically alter the duration of life, it is again evident that a serious fallacy results when generalizations derived from the experience of American men are applied indiscriminately to the American people in such a way as to exclude the experience of American women.

As a further illustration of the readiness with which one can fall into a fallacy in this way, let me suggest one more generalization about Americans which has been widely popular in recent years. This is the proposition, formulated by David Riesman in *The Lonely Crowd*, that the American has been transformed, in the past century, from an inner-directed individual to an other-directed individual. A century or so ago, the argument runs, the American learned certain values from his elders, in his youth. He internalized these values, as matters of principle, so that, in Riesman's phrase, they served as a kind of gyroscope to hold him on his course, and he stood by them throughout his life whether they were popular or unpopular. When these values were involved, he did not hesitate to go against the crowd. Thus he was inner-directed. But today, says Riesman, in a universe of rapidly changing circumstances, where the good will of our associates is more important to our

4. *Harper's Magazine*, Vol. 223 (Nov., 1961), p. 23.

success than it ever was to the nineteenth-century farmer, the American no longer internalizes his values in the old way. Instead, he responds very perceptively, very sensitively, to the values of others, and adjusts his course to meet their expectations. Indeed their expectations are a kind of radar-screen for his guidance. Thus he is other-directed, or to use an older and less precise term, he is much more a conformist.

Riesman does not discuss whether his thesis about "the changing American character" is applicable to American women, as well as to American men.[5] But we are entitled to ask, does he really believe that American women were so inner-directed as his analysis would suggest? Perhaps yes, if you believe that women have been more steadfast than men in defending the values on which the security of the home is based. But on the other hand, woman, historically, was a dependent person, and as a dependent person, she developed a most perceptive sensitivity to the expectations of others and a responsiveness in adapting herself to the moods and interests of others. She has always had a radar screen. If women are quicker to conform to the expectations of a group of other women than men are to a group of other men, and if we should say that this has been true in the past, what it would mean is that women have been other-directed all along, and that when Riesman says Americans are becoming other-directed, what he means is that American men are becoming other-directed. As women gain more economic and social independence, it might be supposed in terms of Riesman's own analysis, that more than half of the American people are becoming less other-directed rather than more so. With

5. David Riesman, "*The Lonely Crowd:* A Reconsideration in 1960" in Seymour Martin Lipset and Leo Lowenthal, eds., *Culture and Social Character: The Work of David Riesman Reviewed* (Glencoe, Ill.; The Free Press, 1961), p. 428, discusses an investigation by Michael S. Olmsted which showed that Smith College girls regarded themselves as more other-directed than men and regarded other girls as more other-directed than their group, but Riesman does not state what his own belief is in this matter.

the gradual disappearance of the so-called "clinging vine" type, who dared not call her soul her own, this is, in fact, apparently just what is happening.

If many of the generalizations which apply to American men, and which purport to apply to Americans generally, do not actually apply to American women, anyone who attempts to study the American character is forced to ask: to what extent has the impact of American historical experience been the same for both sexes, and to what extent has it been dissimilar? Viewed in these terms, the answer would probably have to be a balanced one. Certainly the main values that have prevailed in American society—the belief in individualism, the belief in equality, the belief in progress, have shaped the thought of American women as well as of American men, and American women are no doubt more committed to individualism, and to equality, and to progress, than women in many other societies. But on the other hand, some of the major forces that have been at work in American history have impinged upon men and upon women in differential ways. For instance, as I have already suggested, the frontier placed a premium upon qualities of brute strength and of habituation to physical danger which women did not possess in the same degree as men, either for biological or for cultural reasons. The result has been a differential historical experience for American men and American women which must be analyzed if there is any basis to be found for asserting that there are differences in the character types of the two sexes.

What then, we might ask, have been the principal transformations that history has brought in the lives of American women? Surprisingly enough, this is largely an unexplored field, but there are certain answers which appear more or less self-evident.

One of these is that our society has, during the last century and a half, found ways to do most of its heavy work without the use of human brawn and muscle. Water power, steam power, electric power, jet power, and the power of internal combustion have largely eliminated the need for brute strength and great physical stamina in most forms of work. This transformation has emancipated men in a revolutionary degree, but it has even more strikingly emancipated women, for women are physiologically smaller than men, and they lack the muscular strength and physical endurance of men. As the factor of hard labor in human work is reduced and the factor of skill is enhanced, therefore, women have found that inequality in ability to meet the requirements of work is greatly diminished. This basic fact, by itself, has probably done more than anything else to promote the equality of women.

But if this is the most fundamental effect of the mechanization of work, mechanization has also had a number of other sweeping consequences. One of these is that it has destroyed the subsistence farm as a unit of American life, and the disappearance of the subsistence farm, in turn, has had the most far-reaching implications.

To appreciate this, we must remember what life was like on the subsistence farm. The only division of labor that existed in this unit was the primitive division between men and women. The men constructed the dwelling, planted and cultivated the crops, raised the cattle and hogs and poultry, sheared the sheep, and chopped wood for the stoves and the fireplaces. In short the man was the producer—the producer of food, of fuel, of the raw materials for clothing. The farm wife, in turn, not only cooked, kept house, and cared for the children, as modern wives still do, but she also performed certain other tasks. She used ashes to make her own soap, she put up vast quantities of preserved food, she spun fibers into cloth, and made cloth into clothing. In economic terms, she and her daughters were processors. Together, they worked in a small, close-knit community, in which all lived very much together.

It hardly needs saying what happened to this typical unit of life in an earlier America. The use of machinery, the increased specialization of labor, and the development of an economy of exchange superseded it, and rendered it almost obsolete. Today a limited number of farmers with machines raise enough food for the entire population. Men go out to work instead of working on their own place, with their own sons, and their reward is not a harvest but a weekly wage or a monthly salary. Instead of "making a living" they make an income. All this is obvious, and oft-repeated. But what are the implications for the American woman?

Some embittered critics have retorted that modern woman, no longer a processor of goods, has lost her economic function, and that she retains only a biological function as mate and mother and a social function in the family. This loss of function, they would say, accounts for the frustration and sense of futility which seems to plague modern woman even more than it does modern man. But if we take a hard look at this argument, clearly it will not stand up. What has happened is that women have acquired a new role, in a new division of labor. With her husband away from the home, held by the compulsions of the clock, it falls to her, first of all, to use the family's income to take care of the family's needs. In short, while her husband has changed from a producer to an earner, she has changed from a processor to a consumer in a society where consumption is an increasingly important economic function.

The responsibilities of the consumer are no mean task. To handle them successfully, a person must be something of a dietitian, a judge of the quality of many goods, a successful planner, a skillful decorator, and a budget manager. The business of converting a monthly sum of money into a physical basis for a pleasant life involves a real art, and it might be counted as a major activity even if there were not children to rear and meals to prepare. But the increased specialization of the work

of men at offices and factories away—frequently far away—
from the home has also shifted certain cultural duties and certain community tasks in ever-greater measure to women.

In the Old World, upper-class men, claiming leisure as the
principal advantage of their status, have made themselves the
custodians of culture and the leaders in the cultural life of their
communities. In America, upper-class men, primarily businessmen, working more compulsively and for longer hours than
any other class, have resigned their cultural responsibilities to
women and then have gone on to disparage literature and the
arts because these pursuits, in the hands of females, began to
seem feminine. Women have shouldered the responsibility,
have borne the condescension with which their cultural activities were often treated, have provided the entire teaching
force for the elementary schools, and most of the force for the
secondary schools, and have done far more than their share to
keep community life alive. This is another of the results, im-
pinging in a differential way upon women, of the great social
transformation of the last two centuries.

So far as we have examined them, all of these changes would
seem to operate somewhat to the advantage of women, to have
an emancipating effect, and to diminish her traditional subordination. No longer handicapped by a labor system in which
biceps are at a premium, she has moved into the realms of employment, and has even preempted the typewriter and the
teacher's desk as her own. If she has exercised a choice, which
she never had before, and has decided to remain in her home,
she has encountered a new economic role as a consumer rather
than as a processor, with a broad range of activities, and with
a new social role in keeping up the vigor of the community activities. In either case, the orbit of her activities is far wider
than what used to be regarded as women's sphere, and it has
been wide enough in fact to lead some optimistic observers to
speak of the equality of women as if it were something which
had reached some kind of absolute fulfillment and complete-

ness about the time of the ratification of the woman's suffrage amendment in 1920.

Yet before we conclude our story with the ending that they all lived happily ever after, it is necessary to face up to the fact that women have not found all these changes quite as emancipating as they were expected to be. Indeed, much of the serious literature about American women is pessimistic in tone, and makes the dissatisfactions and the sexual frustration of modern American women its principal theme. Great stress is laid upon the fundamental dilemma that sexual fulfillment seems to depend upon one set of psychological attitudes—attitudes of submissiveness and passivity—while the fulfillment of equality seems to depend upon an opposite set—attitudes of competitiveness and self-assertion. At its grimmest level, this literature stresses the contention of Sigmund Freud that women instinctively envy the maleness of a man and reject their own sex. There is no doubt that these psychoanalytic views are important and that attention to questions of the sex life of an individual is basic, but a very respectable argument can be and has been made that what women envy about men is not their maleness in purely sexual terms but their dominance in the society and their immunity from the dilemmas which the needs of sexual and biological fulfillment on one hand and of personal fulfillment on the other pose for women.[6]

6. Probably the best of the literature which emphasizes the sex frustration of the modern American woman is found in professional publications in the fields of psychology and psychoanalysis which do not reach a popular audience. In the literature for the layman, probably the best presentation of this point of view is Simone de Beauvoir's excellent *The Second Sex* (New York: A. A. Knopf, 1953), but other items have enjoyed a circulation which they hardly deserve. Two cases in point are Ferdinand Lundberg and Marynia F. Farnham, *Modern Woman: The Lost Sex* (New York: Harper, 1947) and Eric John Dingwall, *The American Woman: an Historical Study* (New York: Rinehart and Co., 1958). Denis W. Brogan's judicious and yet precise evaluation that Dingwall's book is "strictly for the birds" would be equally applicable to Lundberg. For an able argument

The inescapable fact that males can have offspring without either bearing them or rearing them means that the values of family life and of personal achievement can be complementary for men, where they are conflicting values for women.

This one immutable and timeless fact, more than anything else, seems to stand forever in the way of the complete and absolute equality of men and women. Political and legal emancipation and even the complete equality of women in social relations and in occupational opportunities could not remove this handicap. So long as it remains, therefore, no one who finds a measure of inequality still remaining will have to look for an explanation in social terms. But it is legitimate to ask whether this is the only remaining barrier to emancipation, or whether other factors also serve to maintain adverse differentials against woman, even in modern America, where she seems to be more nearly equal than she has been in any other time or place, except perhaps in certain matriarchal tribes.

There are, perhaps, two aspects of woman's role as housekeeper and as consumer which also contribute, in a new way historically, to work against the prevailing tendencies toward a fuller equality. These aspects have, in a subtle way, caused society to devalue the modern activities of women as compared with those of men, and thus may even have contributed to bring about a new sort of subordination.

One of these is the advent of the money economy, in which income is the index of achievement, and the housewife is the only worker who does not get paid. On the farm home, in the days of the subsistence economy, neither she nor her husband got paid, at least not very much, and they were economic partners in the enterprise of making a living. But today, the lowliest and most trivial job which pays a wage counts as employ-

---

that the condition of modern woman must be understood partly in social terms, and that the concept of "genital trauma" has been overdone, see Mirra Komarovsky, *Women in the Modern World: their Education and their Dilemmas* (Boston: Little, Brown and Company, 1953), pp. 31–52.

ment, while the most demanding and vital tasks which lack the sanction of pecuniary remuneration do not so count. A recent, and in fact very able book entitled *Women Who Work* deals, just as you would expect, not with women who work, but with women who get paid for their work. Sociologists regard it as an axiom that the amount of income is as important as any other criterion in measuring social status today, and in one sense, a woman's status may reflect the income of her husband, but in another sense it should be a corollary of the axiom that if income is esteemed, lack of income is followed by lack of esteem, and even by lack of self-esteem. If it needed proving, Komarovsky has shown that the American housewife tends to disparage herself as well as her work, as both being unworthy because they do not receive recognition in terms of cash income.[7]

If woman does not command respect as an earner, she is also likely to incur a certain subtle lack of respect for herself in her role as a consumer. For there is a strong tendency in some phases of American advertising to regard the consumer as someone who may be flattered or may be bullied, but who need not be treated as a mature person. Insofar as the consumer is an object of condescension, someone to be managed rather than someone to be consulted, someone on whom the will of the advertiser is to be imposed by psychological manipulation, and insofar as consumers are primarily women, it means that women become the objects of more than their share of the low esteem in which the consumer is held, and more than their share of the stultifying efforts to play upon human yearnings for prestige and popularity or upon human psychological insecurities. Anyone who recalls the recent publications about the rate at which the blinking of women's eyes increases when they view the display of goods in a supermarket, and the extent to which this display causes them to spend im-

7. Komarovsky, *Women in the Modern World*, pp. 127–153.

pulsively, rather than according to need, will recognize that the role of the consumer has not enhanced the dignity of women.[8] This aspect was very clearly and wittily recognized by Sylvia Wright in an article in *Harper's* in 1955, in which she dealt ironically with the assertion which we sometimes hear, that America has become a woman's world.

"Whatever it is," she wrote, "I'll thank you to stop saying it's mine. If it were a woman's world, people wouldn't yammer at me so much. They're always telling me to do, be, or make something. . . .

"The one thing they don't want me to be is me. 'A few drops of Abano Bath Oil' they say, 'and you're not you . . . you're Somebody New lolling in perfumed luxury.' But I'm not allowed to loll long. The next minute I have to spring out in order to be Fire and Ice, swathed in satin, not a thing to do but look stark, and wait for a man to pounce. Turn the page, I've got to make sure it's Johnson's cotton buds with which I swab the baby. A few pages later, the baby gets into the act yelling for fullweight diapers. . . .

"I'm supposed to use a lot of make-up to keep my husband's love, but I must avoid make-up clog. I'm supposed to be gay, spontaneous and outgoing, but I mustn't get 'expression lines' [Expression lines are to wrinkles as morticians are to undertakers.] . . .

"In the old days, I only had to have a natural aptitude for cooking, cleaning, bringing up children, entertaining, teaching Sunday School and tatting . . .

"Now I also have to reconstitute knocked-down furniture and build on porches."[9]

If woman's status is somewhat confused today, therefore, it

8. Experiments on the rate of eye-blink, as conducted by James M. Vicary, a leading exponent of motivation research, were reported in Vance Packard, *The Hidden Persuaders* (New York: David McKay Co., 1957), pp. 106–108.

9. Sylvia Wright, "Whose World? and Welcome to It," in *Harper's Magazine*, vol. 210 (May, 1955), pp. 35–38.

is partly because, at the very time when efforts to exploit her as a female began to abate, the efforts to exploit her as a consumer began to increase. And at the time when the intrinsic value of her work was gaining in dignity as compared with that of the male, the superficial value as measured in terms of money income was diminishing. The essential strength of her position has increased, but the combined effect of the manipulation by the media and the emphasis upon monetary earning as a standard for the valuation of work has threatened her with a new kind of subordination, imposed by the system of values which she herself accepts, rather than by masculine values imposed upon her against her will.

If a woman as a consumer in a world of producers and as an unpaid worker in a world of salaried employees has lost some of the ground she had gained by emancipation as a female in a world of males, even the emancipation itself has created some new problems for her. For instance, it has confronted her with a dilemma she never faced in the days when she was confined to her own feminine sphere. This is the dilemma that she is now expected to attain a competence in the realm of men's affairs but that she must never succeed in this realm too much. It is well for her to be intelligent, but not intelligent enough to make a young man feel inferior; well for her to find employment and enjoy it, but not enjoy it enough to be unwilling to give it up for the cradle and the sink; well for her to be able to look after herself but never to be so visibly able that it will inhibit the impulse of the right man to want to look after her; well for her to be ambitious, but never ambitious enough actually to put her personal objectives first. When a man marries, no one expects him to cease being a commuter and to become a farmer because it would be good for the children—though in fact it might. But when a woman marries, her occupation becomes an auxiliary activity.

Here we come back to the presence of a fundamental dualism which has made the so-called "emancipation" of women different from the emancipation of any other group in society. Other emancipated groups have sought to substitute a new condition in place of an old one and to obliterate the old, but except for a few of the most militant women in a generation of crusading suffragettes, now almost extinct, women have never renounced the roles of wife and mother. The result has been that their objective was to reconcile a new condition with an old one, to hold in balance the principle of equality, which denies a difference, and the practice of wifehood and motherhood which recognizes a difference in the roles of men and women. The eternal presence of this dualism has not only caused a distressing amount of confusion and tension among women themselves; it has also caused confusion among their many volunteer critics. The result is that we encounter more wildly inconsistent generalizations about modern American women than about almost any other subject.

For example, modern woman, we are told, is gloriously free from the inferiority of the past, but she is miserable and insecure in her new freedom. She holds the purse strings of the nation and has become dominant over a world of increasingly less-masculine men who no longer trust themselves to buy a suit of clothes without their wife's approval. But also she does the routine work at typewriter and sink while the men still run the universe. Similarly, we are assured that the modern woman is an idle, parasitic, bridge-playing victim of technological unemployment in her own mechanized home, and also that she is the busy manager of a family and household and budget whose demands make the domestic chores of the past look easy by comparison. She escapes from reality into the wretched, petty little world of soap opera and neighborhood gossip, but she excels in her knowledge of public affairs and she became an effective guardian of literary and artistic values when her money-grubbing husband defaulted on this responsibility. She is rearing the best crop of children ever produced on this planet, by the most improved methods ever devised, while her over-protectiveness has bred "momism" and her unwillingness to stay at home has bred delinquency.

Clearly, we are still a long way from having arrived at any monotonous unanimity of opinion about the character of American women. Yet if we will focus carefully upon what we really know with some degree of assurance, we can perhaps begin the process of striking a balance. We certainly know, for instance, that many of the trends of American history have been operative for both men and women in somewhat the same way. The emphasis upon the right of the individual has operated to remove legal disabilities upon women, to open many avenues to gainful employment, to confer the suffrage, and so on. Even our divorce rate is an ironic tribute to the fact that the interests of the individual, and perhaps in a majority of cases the individual woman, are placed ahead of the protection of a social institution—namely the family. The rejection of authority in American life, which has made our child-rearing permissive and has weakened the quality of leadership in our politics, has also meant that the relation of husband and wife is more of a partnership and less of an autocracy in this age and in this country than at any other time or place in Western civilization. The competitive strain in American life has impelled American women as well as American men to strive hard for their goals, and to assert themselves in the strife—indeed European critics complain that they assert themselves far more strenuously than European women and entirely too much for the tranquility of society.

On the other hand, we also know that the experience of women remains in many ways a distinctive experience. Biologically, there are still the age-old facts that women are not as big as men and not as strong; that the sex act involves consequences for them which it does not involve for the male; that the awareness of these consequences conditions the psychological attitudes of women very deeply; and that motherhood is a biological function while fatherhood is, in a sense, a cultural phenomenon. Historically, there is the formidable truth that the transformations of modern life have impinged upon men and women in different ways. The avenues of employment opened to men are not the same as the avenues of employment opened to women. The revolution in our economy has deepened the division between work in the home and work outside the home by according the sanction of monetary reward to the one and denying it to the other—thus devaluing in a new way work which is distinctively woman's. The economic revolution, while converting most men from producers to earners, has converted most women from processors to consumers, and the exploitation of the consumer has, again, added a new devaluation to women's role. Society has given her the opportunity to fulfill her personal ambitions through the same career activities as a man, but it cannot make her career aspirations and her family aspirations fit together as they do for a man. The result of all this is a certain tension between her old role and her new one. More of an individualist than women in traditional societies, she is by no means as whole-heartedly individualistic as the American male, and as a study at Berkeley recently showed, she still hesitates to claim individualism as a quality of her own.[10] If she enters the competitive race, she does so with an awareness that the top posts are still pretty much the monopoly of men, and with a certain limitation upon her competitive commitment. In short, she is constantly holding in balance her general opportunities as a person and her distinctive needs as a woman, and when we consider how badly these two go together in principle can we not say that she is maintaining the operative equilibrium between them with a remarkable degree of skill and of success?

The answer to my childish riddle was that the big Indian is

10. John P. McKee and A. C. Sheriffs, "Men's and Women's Beliefs, Ideals, and Self-Concepts," *American Journal of Sociology*, LXIV (1959), 356–363.

the little Indian's mother. To say that she is a squaw is not to deny that she is an Indian—but it is to say that she is an Indian for whom the expectations of the masculine world of Indians, or of Americans, do not apply. It is to say that her qualities and traits, whether she is an Indian, or an American, will reflect the influence of the same sweeping forces which influence the world of men, but that it will reflect them with a difference. In this sense, what we say about the character of the American people should be said not in terms of half of the American population—even if it is the male half—but in terms of the character of the totality of the people. In this sense, also, attention to the historic character of American women is important not only as a specialty for female scholars or for men who happen to take an interest in feminism, but as a coordinate major part of the overall, comprehensive study of the American character as a whole. For the character of any nation is the composite of the character of its men and of its women and though these may be deeply similar in many ways, they are almost never entirely the same.

14

THE ROOTS OF AMERICAN ALIENATION

*From the consideration of individualism it was not, in the
later twentieth century, a long step to the consideration of
alienation. The word "alienation" was already coming into
its present vogue when David Potter wrote this essay in 1963,
but outside the disciplines of sociology and psychology his
major themes were probably much less familiar then than
they are today. Although "alienation" has recently acquired
a bewildering cluster of denotative and connotative meanings,
Potter uses it here in a fairly strict sense—that is, the psychological condition, together with the social factors presumably
producing that condition, in which an individual cannot form
effective personal relationships with the people around him.
Potter does not, except occasionally by implication, expand
the word to include associative concepts like normlessness, or
associative phenomena like social disaffection. The condition
to be explained is the private one of "isolation and loneliness,"
and the principal explanations are found in the social changes
wrought historically by industrialization and urbanization.
Yet Potter also expresses uncertainty as to whether alienation
is primarily "the historical condition of modern man" or
"the human condition of universal man." And in his closing*

*paragraphs he returns to the theme of individualism, specu-
lating about its possible contribution, as one of America's
supreme traditional values, to modern alienation. First presented as two lectures at Emory University in April 1963,
the essay, after some revision, was published in the University's* Quarterly *for winter 1963.*

MAN IS NOTORIOUSLY A SOCIAL ANIMAL, and man's accomplishments have been achieved through human society. To say this is to say that man's effectiveness has depended upon his capacity for forming adequate relationships with his fellow men, and that his society's effectiveness depends upon its capacity to provide groupings, contexts, or institutions within which such relationships can be nourished. Traditionally, our society maintained this capacity so effectively that it was almost taken for granted, but from the profound social changes of the past century or more, one of the many problems that have emerged is the impairment of many of the social contexts within which human relationships were nurtured, and the resulting psychological isolation, or alienation, as it is called, of those who can no longer form adequate relationships. This problem has an historical aspect, of course, and this essay is concerned with the historical side of the problem of alienation in modern society, and especially in American society.

The conspicuous feature of alienation is that it imposes isolation and loneliness upon those who cannot form effective psychological ties with those with whom they come in contact. But there is more to alienation than this: most of us, if not all of us, fulfill ourselves and realize our own identities as persons through our relations with others; we are, in a sense, what our community, or as some sociologists would say, more precisely, what our reference group, recognizes us as being. If it does not recognize us, or if we do not feel that it does, or if we are confused as to what the recognition is, then we become not only lonely, but even lost, and profoundly unsure of our identity. We are driven by this uncertainty into a somewhat obsessive effort to discover our identity and to make certain of it. If this quest proves too long or too difficult, the need for identity becomes psychically very burdensome, and the individual may be driven to escape this need by renouncing his own identity and surrendering himself to some seemingly greater cause outside himself.

If, through giving himself to this external cause, he is then able to find himself, like St. Paul after his experience on the road to Damascus, the surrender is psychologically rewarding, and proves ultimately not to have been a surrender at all. But if the external cause impels him to renounce his individual personality, to sacrifice his own identity to the movement, as for instance, Naziism, or Soviet Communism, or as some fanatical forms of religion have required, then his alienation is merely confirmed, institutionalized as it were, and he has accepted a substitute for personal identity. It is our awareness of this substitution which imparts the quality of horror to such a society as we see pictured in Orwell's *1984*: no one in the society of Oceania has fulfilled the potentialities of his own personality; the members of that society are not even permitted to conceive that they have personalities which might be enriched by fulfillment.

This isolation, sense of loss of identity, and questing for either real identity or a substitute, is what is meant by alienation. Anyone who understands it in this way will recognize at once that alienation cannot possibly be a wholly new phenomenon. The human quest for self-discovery is as old as history, and there have always been a certain number of failures in this hazardous quest. The crisis of adolescence, which we commonly view as a crisis of sex, is in fact a crisis of identity and probably not a crisis of sex at all, for there are many societies in which puberty produces no crisis and the adolescent exhibits few strains. But in our society, adolescence is the point at which the child can no longer look to his mother and his father to tell him who he is, but is challenged to find out for himself. This challenge is a very traditional one in Western society, and wherever it has prevailed, alienation was the indicated penalty for failure to meet the challenge. That is why it seems to me important to emphasize that alienation is not and could not possibly be an entirely new phenomenon.

Yet social thinkers today show a concern with the problem of alienation which indicates conclusively either that it has become a far more urgent and central problem than in the past, or else that our understanding of the human condition has made us far more aware of it. Perhaps both of these contingencies apply. Certainly there is no doubt that alienation has fixed the anxious attention of a very large proportion of our most thoughtful minds, in a wide variety of fields. Most of the giants of creative literature—men like Thomas Mann, James Joyce, T. S. Eliot, Franz Kafka, perhaps William Faulkner, have been deeply preoccupied with the isolation of modern man from his fellow men. One could easily prove the point without turning to those special groups—the Existentialists and the Beatniks—who evince this preoccupation in its most acute form. In theology, the rediscovery of Soren Kierkegaard and the influence of Paul Tillich both result partly from the fact that these two thinkers have tried to grapple with the problem of alienation in religious terms. In the social sciences, Emile Durkheim attained eminence partly because he recognized and stated so clearly how an emphasis upon individualism tended logically to isolate human beings from one another. Similarly, Elton Mayo has stood in the top rank of students of industrial relations because of his investigations of the importance of a sense of group identity among workers as an incentive to productivity and as a bulwark of morale. In psychology, Sigmund Freud pioneered in emphasizing the fact that civilization carried with it significant sources of discontent, but it has remained for the post-Freudians, Karen Horney, Harry Stack Sullivan, and Erich Fromm, to argue with great effectiveness that the psychological problems of modern man arise less from the conflict, which Freud emphasized, between biological impulses and social inhibitions, than from the relationships and lack of relationships between human beings in a culture that is sometimes very impersonal. Professor Robert A. Nisbet, of the University of California at Riverside, has written an important study, *Community and Power* (originally entitled *The Quest for Community*), concerning some of the social consequences of alienation, and one of his conclusions is that: "A concern with cultural disorganization underlies almost every philosophy of history in our time." Meanwhile, Eric and Mary Josephson, in a book entitled *Man Alone*, have summarized the same point by saying: "This theme of the alienation of modern man runs through the literature and drama of two continents; it can be traced in the content as well as the form of modern art; it preoccupies theologians and philosophers, and to many psychologists and sociologists it is the central problem of our time."

The Josephsons, it may be worth noticing, do not say that historians have given their attention to the problem of alienation. The omission is significant, and well-justified, for in fact, historians have been slow to come to grips with this problem. When they have dealt with alienation at all, it has usually been indirectly, as, for instance, when intellectual historians have given attention to major thinkers who were concerned with alienation, or when social historians have investigated problems of social disorganization which seemingly arise because of the widespread incidence of alienation. This does not mean that many writers, both historical and otherwise, have not offered what may be described as spot explanations of various kinds which would contribute to the understanding of alienation. But such explanations, instead of attempting a comprehensive view of the overall phenomenon, have usually hit upon and emphasized some one isolated factor which may pertain to it. Thus, as one sociologist remarks, modern alienation has been explained by various writers in terms of machinery, art, language, original sin, the decline of religion, and even sociology. He could also have added the abandonment of breast feeding for infants, the decline of the small town, the impact of radio and television, and the degree to which people move about from one job to another or from one place to another in modern society.

All of these points may constitute raw materials out of which to formulate an explanation. But they need putting together in a coherent pattern, and while it would be much too ambitious to attempt a full explanation of the complex forces which have shaped this phenomenon, it is perhaps not too much to attempt to put the existing fragments of explanatory discussion together in a coherent pattern. That is what I shall attempt to do in the remainder of this analysis.

Perhaps the most obvious factor in the development of alienation, and one of the most important, is the transformation, in modern times, in the pattern of social organization, and the displacement of the smaller, more permanent, more integral, and more intimate units of organization, such as the family, the neighborhood, or the church community (the primary groups, as the sociologist calls them), by larger, more transitory, less coherent, and more impersonal agglomerations such as the population of a city, the body of employees in a large factory, or the members of some voluntary association such as a recreation club, a fraternal order, or the like.

The elements which made the primary groups so strong in the relatively recent past, and the new forces which nevertheless undermined them are, in general terms, fairly well understood, and can be suggested briefly. The neighborhood, whether in town or country, owed its strong cohesion to the solid reality that the radius of mobility for most people was the distance which they could conveniently walk. Men walked to work; women walked to market; children walked to school; when a boy and girl became romantically attached to one another, they were sometimes said to be "walking out together." Consequently, in any population, focal centers developed within a space such that people could walk to them, such as a neighborhood school, a neighborhood store, a neighborhood church. Such units were necessarily small and served a rather limited number of people—so limited that personal acquaintance amongst them all was easy, and face-to-face association was general. But all this was predicated upon a limited range of mobility, and when modern technology began to extend this range, first with such relatively inflexible devices as the street car, and later with a completely flexible one, the automobile, the neighborhood as a controlling unit received a fatal blow: the consolidated school and the supermarket replaced the little red schoolhouse and the corner grocery; the necessity of living close to one's work or the desirability of living near one's friends went by the board; and we began to build the bedroom suburbs which house men and women who spend most of their active lives far away from the dwellings where they are said to live.

Probably the erosion of the neighborhood contributed substantially to weaken the structure of the church community, for the church had always been a social focus for the small community, and a context for the relationship of the community's members. Many people lived within this context all their lives, meeting life's crises in one another's presence. Here people were baptized, married, and ultimately buried; and, in the interim, encouraged, reproved, sustained, and kept under surveillance by one another. For many of its members, the church's social features—its ladies' missionary society, its young people's associations, its chicken suppers, its Sunday school picnic at the appropriate season, and its rousing hymns, in which the members sang along with one another rather than with a television screen, probably counted for more than its ecclesiastical features—its tedious sermons or its formal creed. The church served one function, which almost no institution now serves, of bringing old people and young people together, and preventing the social segregation of age groups. It strengthened the cohesiveness of a neighborhood community, but also it reflected and depended upon the cohesiveness of such a community, and it usually held in somewhat reluctant thralldom, a certain number of secular spirits who consciously or unconsciously resented its supervision of their lives and morals. When the neighborhood started to disintegrate, and when secular forces in the world grew in influence, the church community began to lose its character as a primary group. To say this is, of course, partly to beg the question, for it leaves in abeyance the whole vast problem of what the secularizing forces were and where they came from. But waiving that problem for purposes of this inquiry, it is certainly valid to observe that as the small community waned, the church community began to change, and no matter how much vitality the church may or may not now have as a result of today's so-called "religious revival," it certainly no longer occupies the place which it once had as a primary group.

Most important of all the primary groups, by far, of course, was the family. The family, historically, was not the family of today—the pitiable little aggregate of father, mother, and offspring, who are scattered for most of the day between office, school, and home, and are finally gathered at the rump end of the day in the communion of the television set. It was something far different. First of all, the family ramified out into a confusing network of grandparents, uncles, aunts, and cousins and all of their kin by consanguinity or by affinity, as the genealogists say. This extended family, as it is called, formed a small community in itself. It was a mediatory link between a child and his society. Within its limits, the child first found his identity as a member of the group. His family might be harsh and hateful or kindly and understanding, but even a harsh and demanding family could do a great deal to make a child very certain of who he was. Further, if the family was a farm family, economic life and family life were not separated. Father worked on the place, and the boys worked with him, learning how to be farmers themselves later on. Here there was none of the spurious intimacy and forced camaraderie of father-and-son-get-togethers. Instead of planning to get together, they planned what work had to be done, and when the work was finished, it frequently turned out that they had gotten together more than they could ever have done on a contrived basis. The same thing, I think, is true for mothers and daughters, for if the men were the producers in this little economic unit, cultivating the crops, raising the cattle, chopping the wood for fuel, women were the processors, putting up the preserves, making the clothes, and even spinning the thread and weaving the cloth. A family had many reasons to exist, aside from fulfilling the emotional needs of its members for "togetherness," and as Robert Nisbet has observed, this broad functional basis of family life made the need for emotional congeniality seem less an object of frantic, obsessive, psychological demand, since this need was not, as it seems to be today, the only real basis of family stability.

To some writers, who believe thoroughly in a maximum of individualism, this change in the nature of the family does not necessarily seem a change for the worse. They would argue that people are best related by purely voluntary ties rather than by institutional bonds which may be involuntary. Their view is well expressed in the title of a recent sociology textbook, *The Family, from Institution to Companionship.* Up to a point, of course, their position is hard to contest. It is certainly a good thing, for instance, that modern women, by gaining earning power, have escaped their former total dependence upon men. But the emotions, by themselves, lack structural rigidity, and it is unfortunate for men and women and their offspring, who need the supportive relationship of the family, when all the stresses upon the family structure have to be sustained by the emotions, without any institutional buttresses worthy of the name. This, however, is a digression. The point, so far as alienation is concerned, is that, as a primary group, the family has been both attenuated and weakened by the loss of its economic function. It survives to meet the needs of society for a system of rearing the young, and the needs of individuals for companionship and the sharing of life. But it survives in a much diminished form. Today, many children do not know their cousins and have no idea of clan. Also, many of them not only do not share in the work of their parents, but they have only the vaguest notion of what their father does to gain the family income. To many old world families, who handed on an occupation from father to son, generation after generation, today's social unit, in which the offspring will go their own separate ways soon after puberty, would hardly seem a family at all.

Nothing is more commonplace than the recognition that these traditional primary groups have been very much weakened within the past century, or even half-century, and the observation, by itself, would hardly be worth making. But the process that has weakened them and has loosened the bonds of human association is probably less well understood. Indeed the problem is often discussed as if it were purely a

moral question: why do *we* countenance divorce, sexual lax-
ity, lack of discipline in the young? Why do *we* not uphold
the standards which our fathers upheld? In certain personal
contexts these may be legitimate questions, but historically
considered, every institution owes its strength to its functional usefulness and owes its decline to the social changes
which impair this usefulness. A father and son who go on
separate paths cannot be related in the same way as a father
and son who work together, regardless of their moral attitudes
toward their relationship. A husband and wife whose home
is not an economic unit cannot have the same kind of home
which they would have if it were an economic unit, regardless of their moral attitude toward their home. Historically, if
we are to explain the withering of the primary groups and
the resulting alienation or estrangement for the human beings
who found their significant relationships to their fellow man
within these groups, we must look to the changes in the way
in which man goes about accomplishing his objectives—doing
his work—and to the ways in which these changes have
forced him to modify the structure of his society.

If we go at the problem in this fashion, the first, and most
obvious, and certainly most basic change that we are bound
to notice is that, in innumerable ways, we have moved from
a system in which individuals could operate separately or in
very small groups to one which requires that the activities of
large numbers of people should be synchronized and their
efforts concentrated. In such an economy of subsistence farming as prevailed in Thomas Jefferson's day, most men would
say they "made a living," and that was exactly what they
meant. By their own muscle, and the muscle of a work animal, they produced the food and the necessities which kept
them and their families alive. The idea of an income, in the
sense in which the Internal Revenue Service understands it,
would have been very foreign to them.

So long as this state of affairs prevailed, of course, the individual could operate without very much accommodation or adjustment to other individuals outside his immediate community. As far as economic necessity permitted, he could follow his own bent. His life brought him into relationship with only a limited number of other people, but the context of the relationship was a highly personal one, which encouraged him to recognize and even to savor the human qualities —the personal identity—of those whom he encountered, while they, in turn, looked for and recognized the human qualities in him. Thus, the workings of society were conducive to a very limited range of human relationships but to a high degree of self-expression and of recognition of personal factors within these relationships.

But then the great transformations of modern technology set in. As they did so, they left on the farm only a fraction of those who had been farmers. Machinery and power and science made it possible for one cultivator of the soil to feed a score of families instead of feeding only his own, and it released the other nineteen to do other things. It also provided other things for them to do. They could work in factories, which made the countless new products which the people in an increasingly affluent society wanted to buy. Or they could work in the ever-more-important business of moving all these products from the places where they were made to the places where they were used. Or again, they could join the ranks of the army of middlemen, brokers, wholesalers, retailers, and other intermediaries whose services were increasingly vital when no one consumed the products of his own work and everyone consumed the products of someone else's work, and nothing could realize its usefulness until it had been exchanged. Before long, as the process of specialization developed apace, there was room for another army of persons who performed all kinds of services for people who could not perform these services for themselves, either because the people had become too specialized or the services had become too complex and technical in their nature.

What has this to do with alienation? It bears upon alienation because it organized people in a new and profoundly different pattern of relationships. One aspect of this pattern was the concentration of people in large numbers. Concentration resulted partly from the new sources of power—steam, electricity, the internal combustion engine. Before such power became available, men did much of their work, such as spinning or weaving, wherever they happened to live, scattered over the countryside. But when the behemoths of power machinery came in, men went to work where the machinery was housed. This meant that they moved in from their scattered abodes and clustered near the factory. The new power was apparently the first cause of concentration, but concentration also resulted from a new specialization and a new interdependence, as mankind shifted from an atomized economy consisting of millions of more or less independent units to one in which the various parts and functions were involved with and contingent upon one another. This interdependence, however, meant that the various elements must be coördinated with one another, and must interact readily, without too much inconvenience or friction. Hence came further concentration, since centralization of control is conducive to coördination, and bringing together many economic facilities in one place makes their interaction easier.

The accumulation of people in the new centers of concentration—the centers of production and exchange, the big cities—was spectacular, and, in part, its effect upon the individual was obvious. Uprooted and overwhelmed by the numbers of his fellows surrounding him whom he could no longer know personally, he was likely to have a sense of anonymity, and of being all the more alone because he was in a crowd. This loneliness was poignant, and it has attracted much attention from observers of society. Clearly it contributed in an important way to the process of alienation. But the mere concentration of people by itself, need not profoundly alter the nature of personal relationships between people. It did not do so in the medieval cities like London and Paris and Bologna, and if a change in density of population were the only problem, one might suppose that men and women would have adjusted to it without any fundamental alteration in the nature of human relationships.

But along with the concentration of people in cities there went another change, less visible and less dramatic, but perhaps in the long run far more significant. This was the change by which indirect and fragmented relationships were substituted for direct and integral relationships, and the projection of personality into these relationships was inhibited, rather than encouraged.

In a situation involving only a handful of people, and a simple relationship, the group can readily adjust and adapt itself to the personal quirks and peculiarities of an individual member, and it will do so. But in a highly complex situation involving thousands of people, it becomes intolerable to take into account the personalities of each one of thousands of participants, especially when these participants are constantly being replaced by new participants. Therefore, a large organization (an army is the classic example) tends to treat its personnel—note that it calls them personnel, rather than members—as so many indistinguishable units, rather than as so many unique personalities. This in turn makes it necessary that the men and women involved should conduct themselves, for many purposes, as if they were indistinguishable units and not human personalities. This is what is sometimes called the rationalization—which means the depersonalization—of the relationships in an institutional structure. In a system of interchangeable parts, man himself became an interchangeable part. This meant that for man, as for the other parts, the rough edges must be smoothed off, the adjustment with other parts must be made easy, involving a minimum of friction, and the range of situations into which the individual unit would fit must be a broad one. Thus, a premium would come to be placed upon men who work best as interchangeable parts in the mechanism of a rationalized society. This is very nearly what we mean when we praise a man for being quickly adaptable, for being a good team member, for making a good first impression, for being well-adjusted—he is a good interchangeable part.

We have recognized for a long time now, that these new concentrations were at odds with the traditional structures of association—that under the impact of these new forces, the old structures, the stable and ordered community of neighborhood, or village, or church congregation, or extended family must give way. But what we have not fully recognized, I believe, is that this transformation altered the entire pattern of human relationships. Now it brought the individual into direct or indirect relationship with an almost infinite number of other people, but often without any personal contact at all, and where there was contact, it was frequently of such an attenuated and fractionalized and impersonal nature that the recognition by the parties involved, of one another's personalities was inhibited. Thus, while the range of human relationship was vastly expanded, the degree of personal identification and self-expression within the range of relationships was immeasurably reduced, and the relationship which had once involved a personal nexus ceased even to be relationships, except in a theoretical sense. Thus, there were still producers and consumers, as of old, but the labor of production was so highly subdivided that the worker could hardly visualize the relation of his labor to the product, and of course he had no contact with the consumer at all. Karl Marx recognized this fact, and argued that since the work was a projection of the worker's personality, this severance of the work from the worker would deprive him of part of his personality, and thus "alienate" him. In fact, Marx, borrowing from a metaphysical concept of Hegel's, and setting forth his adaptation of this idea in 1844 in his *Economic and Philosophical Manuscripts* (which have been recently translated), was apparently the first person to conceive of alienation as we understand it today. In his thinking, it was related, as was almost everything else, to the economic exploitation of the worker. This emphasis was so strong that occasionally one still encounters, among the more orthodox adherents to Marxism, the view that alienation is an occupational malady of the proletariat. But it is evident that this is far too narrow a view. Alienation has impinged just as heavily, if not more heavily, among those who never turned a lathe and never punched a time clock, as it has among the workers of the world.

The process which Marx noted as afflicting the worker did, of course, afflict the worker, and Marx's analysis may well have been correct so far as it went. But this same process impinged upon people at every level of economic activity, and not solely upon the workers. If producer and consumer no longer know one another, neither do shipper and carrier, sender and receiver, extractor and processor, buyer and seller. Elaborate distributional mechanisms instead of market days, electronic communications instead of face-to-face dealings, and most of all, impersonal money exchange instead of direct negotiation between the man who can provide a commodity and the man who needs it, have all contributed to minimize the individual personality as a factor in the economic process, and even to make it something of an impediment. Money itself is completely impersonal, and where goods are exchanged for money, or money for goods, it is more efficient not to recognize those who engage in the transaction as human individuals, but to regard them merely as the party of the first part and the party of the second part. But this is equivalent to saying that where a man is a buyer or seller, his personality

is irrelevant—his membership in the community is irrelevant
—even his status has no meaning. In proportion as the importance of buying and selling increases, then, the importance
of individual identity, of personality, of membership, will
diminish. To depersonalize relationships is to alienate the individuals who engage in the relationships, and this must mean
that the great modern system of money exchange has contributed much to accentuate the problem of alienation in
modern society.

A number of the important social thinkers of our times
have recognized this factor. Georg Simmel, for instance, had
much to say about the depersonalizing impact of the money
system upon traditional moral and social relationships. Max
Weber worked out with care the process by which all bureaucratic structures seek to rationalize their arrangements and
to eliminate the human equation as far as possible, so that in
effect, men are reduced to interchangeable units in a bureauc-
racy just as machine-produced pistons are reduced to interchangeable parts in a machine shop.

Some writers on alienation have used this factor of the
economy of money exchange as a basis for blaming capitalism
for alienation. This line of argument is basically rather similar
to Marx's argument about the alienation of the worker, except that it regards all buyers and sellers, and not merely all
workers, as being the targets of a force that works toward
alienation. It is not strange that opponents of capitalism should
use this argument, when money exchange is such an important feature in capitalism. Nor is it strange that some
writers should treat the exchange economy and the capitalist
economy as if they were the same. An example appears in a
discussion of the depersonalizing effects of the exchange economy which Erich Fromm published in 1955 in *The Sane
Society*, and which has recently been reprinted under the
title "Alienation under Capitalism." Yet, in this discussion
Fromm writes less about the effects of private property and

the competitive system than he does about a system of impersonal exchange, repetitive work, and bureaucratization—all of which are prominent features of socialist or communist economies, quite as much as, if not more than, of capitalist ones.

This does not mean that either the conditions of factory labor in particular, or of modern capitalism in general, are unrelated to alienation. Probably, both are related to it in a very real and significant way, and it is part of the social price we pay for the high productivity of our economic system. But there is nothing diagnostic about the role of capitalism. What is diagnostic to the problem of alienation is the system of mechanized production or mass production. This does not mean, of course, that the conditions of modern capitalism are unrelated to alienation. The profit system and the competitive system, which are distinctive to capitalism, may accentuate alienation by creating a sense of rivalry or adverse relationship between individuals. But the economic features which are usually stressed by writers on alienation, such as factory labor, mechanized production, mass production, and the division and rationalization of labor, are, if anything, more prevalent in collectivist economies than free enterprise economies, and are in no sense distinctive to capitalism. The evidence indicates, moreover, that the psychological problems of alienation may be just as acute in the workers' paradises as they are under our own regime.

To say that the machine economy of modern times has weakened and impaired the primary associations in which Western man found his most meaningful relationships, and that it has substituted a system of depersonalized activities and "contacts" or "interactions," might seem a sufficiently sweeping indictment in the search for the causes of alienation, but no analysis could be complete without reference to some additional features.

One of these is the way in which modern specialization of function and elaboration of skills which require intensive training have steadily reduced the body of common lore and shared culture which gave to people a common ground on which to communicate, and a common field of reference for the interpretation and understanding of their own lives. As an illustration of this, consider for instance, the place which the King James version of the Bible once held in our culture —entirely without reference to religion as such. The Bible furnished a vast storehouse of human situations which were analogous to almost any situation that might arise in the experience of an individual. It provided an eloquent, deeply evocative, and spiritually supportive commentary on almost all of the tribulations and the problems of life. Men shared a familiarity with this book; they quoted it to one another on the stump and at the bar as well as from the pulpit, and it must have aided their psychological as well as their merely linguistic communication with one another. Similarly with many other things. Two generations ago students in a given class at a given college would all take the same course at the same time under the same professor. Compared with the richness of the curriculum today, it was a narrow education, a very limited one, and it would not for a moment enable us to meet today's demands for varied skills and expertise, in what we correctly recognize as a complex and pluralistic society. No one would propose to go back to it. But the classmates who shared a common curriculum for four years, again, possessed an inestimable basis for a closer relatedness to one another. This kind of shared lore and common field of reference is much diminished in our lives today. Indeed, it is so diminished that C. P. Snow has asserted that we confront a kind of cultural schizophrenia in which our scientific culture and our humanistic culture can no longer communicate with one another. Perhaps the loss of a common culture is not quite so complete as Snow suggests, but certainly a significant loss has occurred. Carl Bridenbaugh, in his address as President of the American Historical Association in 1962, offered some striking evidence in support of his assertion that we have been losing what he called "the priceless asset of a shared culture."

Almost all discussion of alienation is focused upon the nature of human relationships, for it is assumed that the individual finds his identity in his relations with others. As a major premise, this assumption is no doubt correct, but the communion of man with man is perhaps not the only communion. Certainly a strong case can be made that many people have found their identity in a communion with God. In the realm of spiritual aspects, there is also communion with nature, and even a kind of communion with the past. The role of religion in this connection is a major subject in itself, but again, beyond the scope of this essay, and I will not attempt to discuss it further than to note that at the same time when modern forces were making effective relationship between man and man more difficult, they were also, through the secularization of life making the immediacy of God seem somewhat less real to most people, and thus making self-discovery through religion somewhat more difficult.

As to the role of nature, it is notable that there have been times in the past when many observers believed that man did relate to nature, and could discover himself through the relationship. At the hands of a romanticist like J. Fenimore Cooper, one suspects that this potentiality was somewhat exaggerated, and that the noble savages—whether Indians or frontiersmen—found less psychological fulfillment in nature than the litterateurs supposed. But mankind's oldest ties are the ties with nature, and until a relatively recent moment in history, it is worth recalling, the human creature was a natural man. His work was timed to the rhythm of nature —to the rising and the setting of the sun, to the sequence of the seasons, to the heat and the cold, the long days and the short days, the times of bounty and the times of scarcity. Man felt himself part of the order of nature, planting according to the seasons, fishing according to the tides, hunting according to the cycles of the wild creatures. But the new technology put the clock in place of sunrise and sunset; it put the furnace and later the air-conditioning unit in place of the seasons; it put electric lights in place of the short days; and it erected a vast secondary environment of pavements, masonry, steel construction, plumbing, artificial illumination, mechanical substitutes for horses and oxen, so that the old adjustments to nature withered and atrophied.

In some ways, communion with the past was akin to communion with nature, for the past, like nature, was at one time almost part of the environment. The elders had learned how to adjust to the problems and the vicissitudes of life, had incorporated this learning in their lore, and had handed it down through the children to the children's children. In this pattern, human existence was an affair where the individual held a kind of tenancy on life, between his parents and his offspring. For many a man, his own identity merged imperceptibly on one side into the identity of his forebears and on the other into that of his posterity. This is what C. Vann Woodward has meant when he finds a special distinctiveness in the identity of the Southerner, as treated by the Southern novelists: they conceive of man, "not as an individual alone with his conscience or his God, as the New Englanders were inclined to do, or alone at sea with a whale or a marlin, or alone in a ring with a bull, but as an inextricable part of a living history and community, attached and determined in a thousand ways by other wills and destinies of people he has only heard about."

In a society where the ties of personal relationship were strong, and the pace of change was slow, such a fusion of past and present could almost occur, and instead of the sense of personal identity being sharply and anxiously focused upon the ego, it could almost be diffused to extend beyond one's personality as an individual. But when social change is very rapid, it necessarily destroys this psychic continuity. What one generation has learned about meeting the problems of life is often not really relevant for the next generation. When this condition arises, it breaks the links between the young folk and the old folk, and forces people to look to the technicians and the experts. But a person cannot identify himself with his physician (not even with his psychiatrist) or with his marriage manual, as he could with his father, or with his God, and to this extent again, the roads which lead to self-discovery through relationship are blocked—not only the main highways of relationship between persons, but even the alternatives of relationship with God, with nature, and with the past.

In preceding sections I have tried to trace some of the factors in modern society which have made alienation seem a serious problem, even for our problem-ridden age—a problem acute enough to lead responsible thinkers to call it "the central problem of our time." I myself would not want to exaggerate its seriousness, though I believe it to be major, and I believe that alienation may have long-range effects which will not overtake society in the first generation after the primary groups begin to crumble or the relation with nature begins to falter. But a number of points arise which might to some degree qualify the pessimism with which we view this problem, and might help us to view it, as an overall problem, in perspective.

First of these points is that while we lack precise information about the incidence of alienation in the present, we are very ignorant as to its incidence in the past. In fact, it is hard to be sure at what stage of his historical development the human creature began to have a sharply-focused awareness of his distinctive identity as a separate individual with a personality of his own. Historians like Jacob Burckhardt have suggested that this awareness was not evident in ancient and medieval times, and that it is only as recently as the Renaissance that man's self-discovery of himself as an individual begins. Yet it seems questionable whether modern psychology would accept the view that the nature of the psyche in Western man experienced a basic transformation between the fourteenth and the sixteenth centuries. Until we understand more about this, we can have no idea how much alienation may have existed among slave populations in the past, or even among people who found themselves unable to adjust to the requirements of their societies—requirements far more rigid and prescriptive, if far less difficult and confusing, than the voluntaristic and alternative-ridden requirements of ours.

A further point is that if alienation is part of the historical condition of modern man, it is perhaps also part of the human condition of universal man. Universal man has always faced one unwelcome and inescapable reality—the reality of death—which gave a certain urgency to his quest for identity and warned him of his inevitable defeat, at least on earth, in that quest.

Still another point which may be worth watching is that alienation is a preoccupation of the intellectuals, and they are notoriously a disaffected class, prone to project their disaffection upon society as a whole. The rank and file of people may not be so cankered by alienation as the intellectuals suppose them to be.

Still further, alienation may be set down in part as a price we have paid, not entirely unknowingly, for certain gains by which we set great store, such as an economy with a high rate of production, a society which allows the utmost mobility for its members, and even a society which maximizes freedom. Indeed, some of freedom's ideological champions tend to regard all the outcry about alienation as a cryptic, indirect way of pleading for such reactionary objectives as a class society, an authoritarian state, and a traditionalist system of values.

All these considerations have a certain weight, and all may enter into the formation of a balanced judgment about the problem of alienation. But allowing for all of them, it still remains a demonstrable fact that within the past two centuries we have profoundly altered the nature of the groups within which human beings established their relationships to one another. In place of the old primary groups, involuntary and few in number, we have now placed a far greater range of loose, transitory, and wholly voluntary groups, giving the individual greater freedom, but also depriving him of relationships of the depth, intensity, and continuity which the old groups offered. It is also a demonstrable fact that a large number of the contacts and activities of life are now conducted on a depersonalized basis, so that functions which once brought personal relationship into play are now conducted in such a depersonalized way that they involve no relationship whatever.

Thus, by any calculation, the problem of alienation remains. It remains as a feature of modern society in a mechanized world. But it is also believed by many critics to show itself in an especially acute form in American society. The distinctive impact of this problem in American life cannot be explained in the broad and general terms of an Industrial Revolution which has swept over the entire Western world, and therefore, if we are to understand the peculiar intensity of alienation as a problem of our own country, it may be necessary to consider how American conditions and American values have distinctively contributed to the problem.

In tracing the connection between American values and alienation, we do not have the relatively easy recourse of blaming a force like mechanization, which no one likes and everyone regards as inevitable. Instead we have to assess the responsibility of values which we have traditionally cherished and have regarded as sources of unqualified strength in our society. If we make such an assessment, we will have to scrutinize closely the role, in this connection, of two of the sacred concepts of the American system—American equalitarianism and American individualism. A full scrutiny of these pervasive themes would fill a book, and only the directions which it might take can be suggested here.

But without exhausting the subject, it is easy to see that equalitarianism has had an operative role in this connection. At the same time when the principle of equality assured the American that he was inferior to no one, and must be himself, it also warned him that he was superior to no one, and therefore must not presume to be really different from his fellows. Ever since Tocqueville, thoughtful students of American society have known that conformity has been the price that we pay for equality, and conformity, of course, inhibits the individual in the effort to express his own fullest potentialities and discover his own fullest identity. Moreover, equality has denied the validity of clearly defined groups or classes within the society. Ethnic groups, occupational groups, class groups, even regional groups, are not necessarily equal, and are therefore bad. Consequently, the individual must not identify himself too strongly with them. In fact he must not even identify himself with his family strongly enough to interfere with the demonstration of his own equality through success and upward mobility. But if he is only permitted to identify with a homogenized population of nearly two hundred million Americans, all reduced by equality to their lowest common denominators, the possibility of his achieving a strong self-realization through close identification with a tangible, sharply-defined group is greatly diminished.

If equalitarianism is almost sacrosanct in the American canon, the one other quality which is enshrined with the same degree of veneration is individualism. The two are held as

twin values, and Americans have piously averted their gaze
from the fact that they sometimes conflict with one another.
Individualism, then, has been almost a fetish in our society—
one of the few fetishes venerated by so-called conservatives
and so-called liberals alike. Of course, the two parties have
not meant the same thing when they spoke of individualism,
for to the conservative it has traditionally meant that everyone has an obligation to seek success and that no one must be
restrained from getting ahead of other people, nor deprived
of the advantages of getting ahead of them; to the liberal, on
the other hand, it has meant that the individual must be protected against society in his rights—his rights as the member
of a minority, as a non-conformist, as a dissenter; above all,
whatever is done with reference to him must always be done
solely on the basis of his own merits as a separate person, and
never on the basis of his being put into a category or of his
membership in a group. To deal with a person on the basis
that that person is a female, or a Negro, or an atheist, or a
property-owner, is, in the eyes of the liberal, wrong. In one
sense, the liberal and the conservative have little sympathy
for one another. The liberal suspects the conservative of a
willingness to sacrifice the freedom of the community to the
interests of its most selfish and hard-fisted members; the conservative suspects the liberal of a willingness to sacrifice the
interests of the community to the freedom of its most irresponsible and disloyal members. But both, it should be noted,
agree in giving a priority to the rights of the singular person,
apart from the group.

Thus, all parties have joined in celebrating the individual,
whether as go-getting exponent of the free enterprise economy or as dissenting exponent of minority rights. And accordingly, all have distrusted the group. The liberal, in the
tradition of Rousseau, regarded society as a source of corruption, while man apart from society was innocent. The conservative regarded any heavy emphasis upon the welfare of

the group as "socialism" or "collectivism." Thus both arrived, from opposite directions, at a common distrust of society. As they did so, they developed a sweeping indictment of the trammels which the group may impose upon the individual. Society, it was said, inhibited the full development of man; it repressed him, limited him, stultified him, and sometimes smothered him. It fettered him by the irrelevant bonds of status and social class. By classifying him as the member of a clan or a family connection, it refused to recognize him on the personal terms of his own merits. Hence, anything that recognized men in groups rather than men as solitary persons fell under suspicion.

With many factors combining to devalue the group and to exalt the individual apart from the group, America embraced a cult of the individual, in an extreme form. A symbol of this cult was that American folk-hero, the frontiersman, who illustrated, in a dramatic form, the principle of man alone against the universe. From the time of Daniel Boone and of Fenimore Cooper, we have idealized the frontiersman, creating two fictions about him: one, that he was anti-social and wanted to live where he could not hear his neighbors' dogs bark; two, that his free life gave to him a fuller and richer personality than could be attained by those who were bound by the fetters of society. But in fact, the frontiersmen aspired to nothing so much as to be social builders, and in fact, instead of being enriched in personality by his isolation, the frontiersman was impoverished.

During the present century, we have grown to exalt individualism much less than in the past. When, in 1933, the individualism of *laissez-faire* seemed to be working injury upon a large part of our population, we put severe restraints upon it, and have kept them there ever since. When, in times of national crisis, the individualism of dissent or non-conformity has taken a form which seemed to the majority to endanger the community, restraints have been put upon freedom, and probably would be again, in comparable circumstances, despite the protests of liberal exponents of individualism. Pragmatically, we always refused to follow our theories very far if it meant sacrificing the values of men in groups to the values of men in isolation. But though, in action, we have never followed logic to all its conclusions, our thinking is to some extent warped by the very word, individualism. Starting with the premise that we will prize most highly that which will enhance the worth of man, we have added the assumption that isolation somehow gives value to the human person and that association with "the herd" somehow devalues him. If we could recognize that man may be enhanced as much by membership as by isolation, by association as by separation, we would see at once that there is sometimes (though not always) a false antithesis in such dualisms as freedom versus conformity, or individualism versus collectivism, and that the result is to condemn the group value by definition, rather than on its merits. If, instead of speaking of individualism versus whatever it may be, we should speak of separatism versus memberism, we would then recognize at once that the human being has a stake in both: he must be separate in some things, and must be capable of standing alone, but he must also be part of a group in some things, so that his need for relatedness will not be denied; for it will not help him even as an individual to deny it.

Our historic distrust of groups, our attribution of corruption to society and of innocence to man alone has run through our national thought like a scarlet thread through a cloth. We find it in a thousand forms—Huck Finn on the Mississippi, Abraham Lincoln walking at midnight—a man alone—and all the folklore of man on his own against the universe. These attitudes are not without their value, and one part of our tradition, the part which sees the fulfillment of man through freedom is buttressed by them. But they should not be held in so literal or exaggerated a form as to impair another part of our tradition—the fulfillment of man through his participation with his fellow men. That they have been held in such a form has, I believe, contributed somewhat to make the problem of alienation not only a human problem, which it is because of the nature of man, or a modern problem, which it is because of the vast forces of industrial society, but also, and not altogether inevitably, an American problem as well.

15

REJECTION OF THE
PREVAILING AMERICAN SOCIETY

In 1964–65, with a grant from the Carnegie Corporation, David Potter set to work at a major historical study of alienation in American culture. Other writing commitments and a term as department chairman impeded his progress, but he returned to the project in 1968–69, when he held fellowships from the National Endowment for the Humanities and at the Center for Advanced Study in the Behavioral Sciences. During the latter part of that year, he put some of his thoughts into a manuscript of sixty-four typewritten pages, now published for the first time. Intended primarily for his own future reference, it was not the beginning of a draft of the final study. Indeed, Potter himself started out calling the piece an "outline," but it proved to be both something more and something less—in certain respects, perhaps, a fragment of the finished work he had in mind. Of course the campus revolution and other historical developments of the late 1960's added new meanings to the word "alienation" and greatly affected Potter's conception of his project. The principal object of his attention here is no longer the more or less passive psychological victim upon whom isolation and loneliness are "imposed" by historical forces; it is rather the person who has by deliberate choice placed himself in opposition to the existing social order and the values underlying it. Potter's full title for this fragment was: "Historical Aspects of the Rejection of or Disaffiliation from the Prevailing American Society."

THE POINT of departure of this study is an assumption, the validity of which I will seek to test and demonstrate, though not exhaustively. The assumption is that a significant proportion of people in American society, especially young people, do not accept the society as it is; and further that the proportion who reject it overtly is higher than in the past.

In connection with this assumption, it will be important to examine whether the rejection of the prevailing norms is distinctively and restrictively related to American society, or whether it is universally present in the modern world, or whether America seems to manifest earlier and more conspicuously, a phenomenon which is appearing in less pronounced form in other parts of the world.

It will also be important to inquire to what extent the phenomenon of rejection of society is new, and to what extent such rejection was widespread in the past but took forms quite different from the highly visible forms of protest and demonstration which it takes today. For instance, membership in the monastic orders represented a kind of rejection of society, but one which is difficult to equate with the modes of rejection which we find today.

Finally, it will be necessary to analyze the question of what constitutes "rejection" of society, and to arrive at a kind of definition. In dealing with the groups who are dissatisfied with society, some writers tend to distinguish between the "alienated," who are often somewhat apathetic toward society, tending to withdraw from social involvement, and the "committed," who are activistic, highly politicized, highly involved. This distinction may be valid, but it must be recognized, I believe, that no categorical distinctions are possible between those who want to alter the society drastically and those who want to destroy it. One man's alteration is another's destruction. Sometimes the distinction between the two is as tenuous as the wavering line between optimistic hope that recognized evils can be corrected by the society itself and pessimistic despair of correcting them. ("Do I really want," asks James Baldwin, "to be integrated into a burning house?" The question whether it is really burning influences his acceptance or rejection of the house.) But while recognizing the very real difference between angry protest against the evils of a society which the protestor feels to be his own, and total rejection of the society by a person who disaffiliates—even without anger —we should also recognize that there is a very real difference between a "committed" person who accepts the society as it is and a "committed" person who would accept it if it were fundamentally different. Almost anyone would accept a society built according to his specifications, and it means little to say that this is all that protestors want, and therefore that they are not really alienated. A sense of membership in a group, it would seem, conditions the mode of opposition to the other members, and the mode of opposition may be the best key, in terms of overt action, to the difference between the discontented and disaffiliated.

In this connection it may be worth observing that the degree of radicalism of a given protestor may be a less reliable index of the extent of his alienation than the question whether he rejects the life style of a society. The rejection of a life style is usually expressed symbolically rather than substantively—for instance, by rejecting the standard manner of dress of a society (e.g., by wearing beads, long hair, beards, sandals, et cetera), or by the calculated and sometimes ostentatious violation of the society's taboos (e.g., by the use of obscene or scatological words). It is, of course, unfortunate that conventional folk become excited at a certain amount of long hair or hippie dress, but it is by no means unrealistic for them to sense that these items may be a challenge to their values, quite as much as if the values were challenged in philosophical discourse.

There is, however, a difficulty in construing the meaning of the rejection of a society's life style. This difficulty lies in the fact that once real disaffiliates have adopted dress, speech, and music which presents a clear alternative to the modes of the prevailing style, such features will be taken up by many other people merely because they are stylish, and not to express a rejection of the society. Similarly, once taboos are violated, the violations will be taken up, for instance by publishers of pornography, not because they reject the society, but because they will sell out anything, including the values of their society, for a price.

It is an unfortunate fact that explanations of dissent in terms of overt circumstances and rational thought tend to justify the dissent (e.g., "young people reject the 'system' because they regard the Vietnam War as evil" or "because they regard racism as evil"), while explanations in terms of psychological circumstances or sub-rational responses tend to discredit the dissent (e.g., "young people reject society because of an impaired capacity for relatedness with other people" or "because they have not achieved satisfactory development of the ego and cannot face adulthood"). One explanation is in terms of rational and perhaps also moral ideas, the other in terms of personality difficulties. Further, the two are so disparate that writers who explain attitudes in terms of social ideas seldom even recognize the existence of psychological factors and vice versa. In the present study I have no magic formula for relating rational factors to irrational ones, but at a pragmatic level, it seems clear that American society has a number of important unsolved problems and unsatisfactory conditions, and these problems and conditions must contribute significantly in some fashion to rational dissatisfaction with the society. Since I shall later discuss the significance of irrational factors at some length, I think I ought here to say something further about the real urgency of rational reasons for fundamental dissatisfaction with the society.

I do not, of course, plan to treat any of these problems in detail, but I expect to indicate briefly something about the following features of American society, and why they are conducive to social estrangement.

1. The society has dealt in a discriminatory way with various minorities, including the blacks especially. Such discrimination, amounting almost to denial of membership in society, has naturally weakened the capacity of those discriminated against to identify with the society psychologically as their own. A less severe form of discrimination against immigrants, especially against Jews—most acute perhaps around the beginning of the century—has also left its heritage. A great many Americans tend to reject the society because the society rejects them, or did reject them, or the group with which they are identified, in the fairly recent past.

2. The society is a "technological" and scientific society in the sense of being very highly industrialized, mechanized, and bureaucratized, to the end that it has achieved the highest levels of physical production and control of the environment ever attained by man. This high productivity brought a material standard of living which, at one time, appeared to validate the society completely. But it is now evident that all the

gains were at a high price not yet paid, and that they created problems not yet solved. The boon of control over the death rate has brought acute overpopulation. The capacity to convert "resources" into "products" has brought with it devastation and pollution of the environment. The dynamic of a technological society has made rigorous psychological demands upon human beings, that they be achievement-oriented and consumption-minded, that they adapt themselves to bureaucratization, that they be ready to live where employment requires them to live, that they work readily in close and demanding coordination with others, that they be constantly responsive to competitive situations in their social lives as well as their employment, in childhood as well as in adulthood. These demands are, in many cases, inconsistent with the psychological and physiological predispositions of the human creature, and, in short, many human values have been sacrificed to technological values. This sacrifice has evoked articulate criticism from a few, and inarticulate frustration, resistance, and negativism from a great many others.

3. When mankind developed a technology that could control the environment before developing a social organization that could control the technology, a very dangerous situation was created. With the development of atomic energy, and also of instruments of chemical and biological warfare, the human race achieved a triumphant potentiality for its own extinction. The contingency of potential destruction has unquestionably influenced social thought today: the possibilities not only of hydrogen bomb warfare, but of poisoning the human race with pesticides, of warming up the planet until we melt the polar ice cap, of riding overpopulation to its sequel of mass starvation, or of bringing on destruction by the unperceived side effects of some other phenomenon of our technology— all these things lend an apocalyptic tone to any speculations about the future. They perhaps generate, and certainly support the kind of anxieties which might motivate a person to

reject the society. Just how pervasive the sense of the uncertainty of life may be, no one can say, but one recent writer has argued that the diagnostic feature of the "generation gap" is the fact that people "who had passed puberty at the time of the bomb . . . were incapable of conceiving of life *without* a future, [while those] . . . who had not yet reached puberty at the time of the bomb were incapable of conceiving of life *with* a future."

It is, I believe, important to be very cautious in tossing about generalizations about the sense of security which people felt in the past and the sense of insecurity which they feel today. It seems quite possible that psychological anxiety has little correlation to actual physical danger, and that one of the devices which enable us to survive in a life certain to terminate in death, is a psychological capacity for disregarding hazards when they are not immediately and visibly at hand. Thus, paradoxically, the Bomb may have served more as a receiver or focus for floating anxieties than as a generator of anxieties based on realistic dangers. Also, people in previous generations faced unheralded death far more constantly than we do, and many of them believed very emotionally in a Second Coming which would end the world as they knew it. But in any case, no one is likely to argue that the potentiality of the Bomb has left either the world or social thought unchanged; no one is likely to doubt that a "system" which may use the Bomb forfeits some of the psychological support which people within the system might otherwise have given it.

It is not intended here to give detailed treatment to the injustices of the prevailing society, to the discontent which a coercive technology may evoke, or to the effects of insecurity about the future upon social estrangement. But I do want to make explicit the fact that a reasoned view of our society presents the most urgent grounds for dissatisfaction with many of the society's features, and a person might reject the society for purely rational reasons. But the fact that such reasons exist by no means demonstrates that they are the primary causes which prevent many people from identifying with the society. The fact that given reasons would be valid reasons does not mean that they are the operative reasons. Indeed, the indications are that identification with a society is a sub-rational process, which would not be much influenced directly by a rational contemplation of the Bomb, though it might be influenced by social changes which the existence of the Bomb could bring about.

Writers who discuss the "breakdown of community," the "disintegration of the family," and the "loss of identity," in the modern world, frequently seem to assume that there was a golden age in "the world we have lost." In that age, everyone was sustained by his status or membership in his community, received psychological support from a glorious "extended family," had a deep awareness of his existence as a link in "the great chain of being," and lived and died with dignity, even though he was humble and obscure.

The indications are that this idealization is false for a vast proportion of those who lived in previous centuries. Not only were exploitation and deprivation chronic (these conditions are not necessarily inconsistent with the belief in the psychological supports offered by a status society), but warfare, private violence, sadistic cruelty, prejudice, treachery, and deception cursed almost every community. There was realism in Burns's lament over "man's inhumanity to man" and in Hobbes's characterization of life as "short, brutish, and nasty."

It seems unrealistic to suppose that in such a society everyone felt a sense of membership, fellowship with his neighbors, and commitment to the system. The appalling and very widespread persecution of "witches," which barely touched American history for a moment at Salem, is a case in point. In view of conditions such as these, it would be very unsafe to suppose that the proportion of people who psychologically reject their society today is any greater than the proportion who rejected it in, say, the fifteenth, sixteenth, seventeenth, or eighteenth century—though I am assuming that Americans now reject it in greater proportion than they did in the nineteenth century. But, while the degree of rejection may differ, what differs spectacularly, I believe, is the mode of rejection.

Essentially, the people of previous centuries were repressed people—more directly and overtly repressed probably than people today, for today's repressions, though perhaps not less, are more subtle and diffuse. But although repressed, people in the past abstained from acts of public defiance of the "system," either because of a conscious awareness that such acts would bring swift and harsh punishment, or, more likely, because they had internalized their own repression through inhibitions. They were like human beings of other times and places in the sense that they were subjected to frustrations, and that they responded with impulses toward aggressions, but instead of projecting these aggressive impulses, in "activist" fashion, against institutionalized authority, they re-directed the impulses, and turned them against parties who could not retaliate —against scapegoats, such as Jews or "witches"; against women; against members of their own family, even, with feelings of guilt for their own aggression, against themselves, with the conviction of sin.

Not only did they find substitute objects of aggression, but they also found substitute modes. Women, who were denied almost all opportunity to fight or to express direct hostility, might express it indirectly in whispered gossip. Pious folk might express it, religiously, in a hatred of "sin," which often included hatred of any pleasures that had been denied to them, and in fantasies of the eternal torment of "sinners" (those who had enjoyed such pleasures) in a hell to come. This concept of indirect venting of aggression is well known in Freudian psychology under the term "displacement" and is as familiar as the figure of the bullied clerk, who, after submitting meekly to a tongue lashing from his boss comes home to yell at his wife and kick the cat. But it has perhaps not been recognized that a major quantitative change in the modes of direct expression or displacement of aggression might be one of the most significant alterations, historically, in the functioning of a society.

When we examine, therefore, the phenomenon of rejection of the society, it will be important to recognize that what appears to be a new degree of aggressiveness against the "system" may, in fact, be, in significant part, a new way of expressing an attitude that is not so new. I believe, tentatively, that the increase or decrease of what may be called the total social quantum of discontent is only one factor in the increase of expressions of hostility toward the established order, and that a no less important factor is the revolutionary change that has occurred in the sanctioned forms of aggression. If this is true, the inquiry must turn to an examination of the historic changes which have led to a situation where almost any kind of discontent is permitted to take a public form, or, as the phrase goes, to be politicized.

In a broad sense, what happened in the last two centuries, I believe, is that American society has had two kinds of authority in historical sequence, both of which possessed means of inhibiting or displacing direct expressions of rejection or of aggression toward the society. First, it had the hierarchical authority of a system which possessed direct coercive power to compel social compliance with the dominant values. Later, it had what may be called consensual authority which possessed only very limited coercive powers, but which invoked the social pressure of the majority in the society to induce people to *conform* to the dominant values. Thus, conformity replaced coercion as the sanction by which authority sustained itself. But now, both coercion and conformity have lost their potency, and authority no longer possesses any real sanction.

Examining these two forms of authority in more detail, one might observe that in Western Europe before the industrial age, land was the principal form of wealth, and the ruling classes based their domination upon the effective control of land, which they held in a kind of monopoly and which provided the basis of their ascendancy. But in America, land was too abundant to be monopolized, and the whole system of privilege and hierarchical authority began to lose its force in colonial America, primarily because land was almost free. Land-owning farmers could not be held in subordination. As economic authority weakened, political authority weakened also. The War of Independence was the act by which the Americans repudiated monarchical authority, and, along with it, all special privilege and special rank. They did not repudiate the rights of property ownership, however, nor could they eradicate the deeply instilled deference with which many Americans still regarded men of wealth and social influence. The society, therefore, did not cease to be a deferential society, but it did cease, essentially, to be a coercive one. In a hierarchical society, it was always in order for the gentle folk to impose their will forcibly on the common folk, but once formalized social rank had been abolished, overt coercion was no longer really acceptable. Once government became a democratic affair, with the conduct of public affairs vested in citizens who were elected by their fellow citizens, the officials of government no longer had any real stomach for applying coercive controls. The United States became notoriously a country that dealt leniently with violators of the law. In fact, coercive institutional controls have not been a major instrument for the enforcement of American norms for more than a century and a half.

One might suppose that the decline of coercive power meant the deterioration of social control, and led directly to what is now commonly described as a permissive society. But, in fact, this is not true. Hierarchical control in America declined gradually, because hierarchy was supported by a considerable measure of influence on the part of the wealthy and of deference on the part of ordinary folk, even after it ceased to be supported by coercive power. As it declined, it was replaced, as has been stated above, by consensual authority. Consensual authority should not be confused either with pure majoritarian rule or with permissiveness, for on the one hand, it required the majority to heed the wishes of any substantial minority *of the recognized members of the society* and to make concessions to them, but, on the other hand, it also required the minority to acquiesce in the settled values of the majority and to show their acquiescence by conformity. The functional pressures toward conformity were strong, for, as Alexis de Tocqueville observed, the principle of equality in America decreed that each man was no better than any one of his fellows, and therefore not as good as a number of them combined. In a society of equals, every man must be extremely sensitive to what the majority of his equals expect of him. With the old, hierarchical status system swept away, the only status which any person could attain was that which his fellows would accord to him. Hence, "free" men who scorned official authority, nevertheless submitted eagerly to the social authority of the prevailing mores, and Americans became conspicuous for a compulsive conformity by which they made themselves more obedient and tractable than any official coercion could possibly have made them. The values, practices, habits, and prejudices of the majority came to have an overwhelming power over the individual in matters both fundamental and trivial.

For more than a century in America, the authority of compulsive conformity continued to prevail. During this time, public order was well maintained, and the society showed no evidence that it lacked any truly effective means, other than social pressure, for enforcing its values. But in fact, no other means existed; social compliance was essentially voluntary; and the society flourished with less of a direct coercive power, perhaps than any society in history.[1] Political disputes were settled by an elaborate system of compromise, and political leadership was a form of brokerage. The American Civil War formed the one major exception to this rule, but even then, Union victory was followed by an agreement by which the South accepted the principle of union (which it had never really opposed), while the North accepted the principle of subordination of the blacks (which it had never really opposed either). Once again, government was, in the fullest sense, government by consent of the recognized members of society. Labor disputes were settled by negotiation between employers and workers, in which, for a long interval, workers were much the weaker party, sometimes tempted to violence to compensate for their weakness, but for the last three and a half decades, labor and management have been able to solve their disputes voluntarily, by arrangements made at the expense of the consumer rather than of one another. In the most pervasive sense, the American system was a voluntaristic one. Some components which were excluded from full participation in the society did not disturb the arrangements made by those who did participate, because they hoped to gain participation fairly soon (as in the case of the immigrants) or because they lacked the means for expressing a collective voice, and were apathetic (as in the case of the blacks). While it lasted, this state of affairs, despite its sordid aspects, provided a wonderfully attractive spectacle of freedom from antagonism and friction, as well as from coercion, but it meant that the body politic

1. This statement is a controversial generalization, and some critics will certainly argue that the ruling elements used coercion freely and violently. They will cite the frequency of occurrences of vigilantism, lynching, and Ku Kluxism, and the use of militia against strikes and radical demonstrations. Recognizing that such actions certainly qualify the generalization, I nevertheless believe that, on balance, American society has, historically, resorted to a minimum of coercion, and especially of institutionalized coercion.

existed without any antibodies against the kind of fundamental resistance which would reject both consensus and conformity. If the society ever encountered opposition from groups which would not bargain, which scorned the prevailing values, which made demands that were, in fact, non-negotiable, it would be without means of defending itself against such opposition.

The vulnerability of an institution is never discovered until it is attacked, and the vulnerability of American society was not revealed for a century and a half after the consensual control replaced the hierarchical one. But at last a revolution occurred. It was a peaceful-appearing transformation, unlike the dramatic and bloody overturns which are so readily recognized as revolutions. But it resembled other revolutions in the basic reality that it occurred when the distribution of social control ceased to correspond to the distribution of actual power in American society.

Power had been very broadly diffused and, as I have indicated, had been rendered instrumentally quite weak in traditional American society, because of democratic distrust of concentration of power as a device of hierarchical authority. But power did exist, nevertheless. Socially, in the nineteenth century, power resided in the traditional "old stock" (i.e., Anglo-Saxon Americans whose religion was Protestant, with strong Puritan overtones, and whose values were the abstemious, achievement-oriented, pleasure-condemning values of the Protestant Ethic). Their style was rural; their strongholds were on the farms and in the small towns; and they distrusted the city as a sink of iniquity. Economically, in the nineteenth century, power resided in a class of entrepreneurs, or as they were called, businessmen. This class was immensely important in the rapid opening up and exploitation of a new country which was experiencing two prolonged booms simultaneously —the boom of "developing" a rich, virgin continent, and the boom of converting an agricultural society into an industrial one. The businessmen came almost wholly from the Protestant, Anglo-Saxon stock, and they held firmly to the Protestant Ethic, partly because it was their heritage and probably even more because its values of enterprise, of initiative, of industriousness, of conformity, and of the repression of impulsive pleasures, were admirably adapted to the kind of demanding, self-denying, reward-deferring economic program which they were conducting.

As the United States came into the twentieth century then, the social power of white, Anglo-Saxon, Protestant, rural society, had combined with the economic power of a "business civilization," as it was called, to give overwhelming moral ascendancy to the Protestant Ethic with its system of values. The people of America acquiesced almost totally in this system of power, and their submission was expressed through the pervasive system of conformity which was such a conspicuous feature of American life. This was consensual authority at its zenith.

But during the first third of the twentieth century, both the social power and the economic power of what now appears as the Old Order began to deteriorate. First of all, the cities continued to grow, and after a while it became evident that they were no longer mere aggregations of country folk come to town. Urban America challenged the ascendancy of rural America; secularism challenged orthodox Protestantism; and the allurements of sophisticated pleasure challenged Puritan condemnation of pleasure as sin. At the same time, the cities swelled with a population of immigrants and children of immigrants who grew to constitute a majority of the total population in a state like New York. These immigrant-stock Americans were not culturally compatible with the system of WASPish values, but, with a dominating wish to become and be accepted as Americans, they practiced an almost compulsive conformity. There was no rebellion in them, but as they discovered that they still were constantly reminded in both great and small ways that they remained outsiders, no matter how zealous their conformity or how successful their adaptation, they began to react against the society which, at least partially, still rejected them.

By the 1920's, the tension between old-stock Americans and immigrant-stock Americans began to take a highly palpable form. The old-stock component, alarmed by the prospect that it might lose its ascendancy, reversed the traditional immigration policy, and in 1921 and 1924 secured legislation which greatly curtailed the flow of immigration and also frankly discriminated in favor of immigrants from Britain and Western Europe who were most compatible with the old stock. This discrimination continued in force until 1960. At the same time, the old-stock Americans also sought to constitutionalize their moral ascendancy by amending the Constitution to prohibit wine, beer, and spirituous liquors. Prohibition remained on the books for fourteen years, and incidentally it destroyed the saloon, which had been an important social institution for immigrant-stock Americans. But the cities never accepted Prohibition; it was more widely and openly flouted than any other law in American history; and in 1933 it was repealed. The ultimate failure of Prohibition today receives minor attention in the text books, but it marked the beginning of the end of the old-stock ascendancy. Perhaps the strongest remaining sanction for that ascendancy was no longer in the power of rural and small-town elements, but in the unquestioned leadership of the "captains of industry," the WASPish businessmen who presided over the capitalistic system of production, with its magic capacity constantly to raise the American "standard of living." American business, by this time, provided a stronger bulwark for the Protestant Ethic than American Protestantism was able to provide.

But in 1929, the Old Order sustained another crippling blow as the Great Depression set in. American businessmen had always practiced a kind of brinkmanship in maintaining prosperity in a business cycle of boom and bust, which is inherent in a pure capitalistic economy and which they could not really control. But in 1929, the phenomenon of bust exceeded all past disasters, and businessmen were badly discredited by the futility of the incantations with which they sought to exorcise a demon that they did not understand. Before the Depression had been dispelled, as it finally was ten years later by the economic stimulus of the Second World War, a regulated economy had begun visibly to displace the free market economy. Regulation, as such, was not unwelcome to businessmen, who, through trade associations, had imposed limited controls of their own for several decades, but they objected strenuously to sharing the regulatory function with a new class of bureaucrats in Washington.

After the Second World War, the revolution was complete. The control of the institutions—governmental, business, educational—was still, socially, in the hands of the old-stock Americans, and, economically, in the hands of the businessmen, but both had lost the potency which had previously enabled them to set up their values as the unquestioned standards of conformity. There was no longer a regnant majority capable of applying monolithic social pressure to elicit conformity to a set of accepted values. Consensual authority, like hierarchical authority, had lost its sanctional force. American society was left with a variety of competing values, each of which commanded the moral support of a part of the population, and, of course the traditional values continued to receive the allegiance of vast numbers of people, including many who were neither WASPs nor businessmen. But none of these values was vested with any prescriptive authority. Thus, more than a century and a half after the leaders of the War of Independence effectively neutralized the power of coercion as a sanction of public authority, American society at last came to the jarring reality of a situation where, though there was official jurisdiction, there was no real authority which anyone was bound to respect. Consensual authority had apparently followed hierarchical authority into the dustbin of history. This was the unseen revolution of the 1920's and 1930's.

The Old Order might have survived the failure of Prohibition, the social trauma of the Great Depression, and the swing toward a regulated economy, if the Anglo-Saxon leadership and the leadership of businessmen had retained its remarkable vigor. But, in fact, the greatest vigor now seemed to reside elsewhere. In business, a new managerial class, who did not own the enterprises which they conducted, and who therefore lacked a proprietary sense of both power and (sometimes) responsibility, replaced the old entrepreneurs. In the increasingly complex technological system, a new class of engineers, technicians, personnel managers, social scientists, and other assorted "experts" acquired a more and more dominant voice in the conduct of affairs. Research and Development became the key to industrial growth, and scientifically trained research men, from no one knew which side of the railroad tracks, called the tune. These men were university-trained, and suddenly the traditional, beloved, sleepy, futile "colleges" of nineteenth-century America became dynamic and indispensable suppliers of research personnel and social expertise. College faculties—as impotent a class as had ever been accorded a status of gentility—suddenly began to feel the stirring of virile power. What happened, in short, is that the pedagogues became intellectuals—the first sizable cadre of intellectuals that America had ever known. As intellectuals have a way of doing, they soon began to throw their weight around.

These new intellectuals, like the immigrant stock—and a disproportionate number in fact were of immigrant stock—stood in opposition to the existing order, and not without reason. If the immigrants had been simply excluded from the mainstream of society, the academics had traditionally been underpaid, condescended to, and ignored. But now academia suddenly received an opportunity to render its verdict on the system, and indeed to inculcate this verdict in the sons of the entrepreneurs. Perhaps most intellectuals are, by nature, skeptics and idol-smashers, and perhaps all successful societies build up elaborate folklores about their own virtue and superior merit. Whether this is true or not, the American society had certainly done so, and American academics began zeroing in to do a demolition job on the folklore, without, perhaps, considering exactly why they were doing it, or indeed what it was that they were doing.

Justifiably aware of the evils of primitive, unregulated capitalism, academia assailed the venerated captains of industry as "robber barons" and spoilers who had gotten rich by using other people's money, without risking their own. Outraged by the genteel exclusiveness and the covert but pervasive discrimination of the WASPish establishment, intellectuals launched an assault on every aspect of race distinction, from the immigration quotas, through "select clienteles," to the concept of genetically inherited differentials in human potential. By nature hostile to "Philistinism," the intellectuals, who were antagonized by the repressive Puritan strain in the Protestant Ethic, flourished the works of Sigmund Freud and went far beyond Freud himself, to denounce all forms of repression. The bourgeois values of middle-class business America and the evangelical values of rural Protestant Americans were castigated with a scorn which reflected a new sense of power on the part of the scornful. All the old figures were turned upside down: pillars of society became stuffed shirts; munitions manufacturers became merchants of death; young men who went willingly to war became not heroes, but suckers; the legendary frontiersman ceased to be a "pioneer," and became an exploiter and a looter of the environment.

The significance of all this is not merely that we had a wave of what was called "debunking," but much more. Every society has a myth of its own identity, full of objectively unrealistic beliefs which serve a realistic social or psychological function. The myth is to the society almost what a sense of personal identity is to the individual. The fictions and unrealities of the myth are as needful to the society as certain fantasy notions of the self may be to the personal identity. The indiscriminate destruction of myth, therefore, may cause a serious deterioration in the society. But oblivious to such possible impairment, American intellectuals, during the 1920's and later, set busily about laying their axes to the mythic underpinnings of the American identity.

The myth-destroyers hardly intended to pull the props from under their society, and if it had been a coercive or regimented society, their activities might not have had such a destructive effect. Or, if the spokesmen of the majority had been prepared to fight back, and to seek more realistic or more rational grounds for defending the prevailing values, as the mythic grounds were swept away, the society might have been shored up quite effectively. But the custodians of power lacked conviction. They lacked it fundamentally because they believed in philosophical principles which were inconsistent with many of the realities of American life, and therefore they could not mount a whole-hearted defense. They believed in equality, and they could not reconcile this with racial discrimination; they believed in the perfectibility of man, and they could not reconcile this with the existence of war and preparations for war, or with the poverty and exploitation which still existed in American society. Because of these contradictions, most of the leadership, consisting, at least in political, academic, and ecclesiastical circles, of what we call liberals, exhibited acute guilt feelings. This guilt, arising from their justified unwillingness to excuse the shortcomings of the society, reduced many of them to a state of mind where they could not defend even the society itself.

If the defenders of the society were disarmed by their conviction of its failure to fulfill its own ideals, they were disarmed also by their broad, absolutist, and somewhat indiscriminate ideas of the right of dissent. The concept that freedom of speech, freedom of the press, and freedom of assembly are unlimited rights had taken shape in an earlier time, when controversy had operated within the framework of a broad agreement upon the basic goals of society. Public dispute had related to means rather than to ends. It had operated subject to the consensual pressures which inhibited dissenters from pushing their dissent to an extreme. The centrifugal effects of controversy had been held within the offsetting centripetal orbit, as it were, of consensus. In operative terms, freedom to dissent had meant a franchise to enter into rational argument about the best means of attaining agreed-on social goals. As such, it had been accepted as an unmitigated benefit to society ("the free market in ideas") and as an inviolate right of the individual. Because of these qualifying circumstances, the full social effects of a system of unlimited dissent had never been demonstrated.

But by the 1960's, consensual common denominators had to a great extent been broken down, and freedom of dissent began to be invoked by groups or individuals who were committed to a total rejection of the society. In this new situation, freedom of dissent was put to the purpose not merely of correcting evils in the society but of assailing the society as such; not merely of argumentation to persuade adversaries, but of abuse and vilification to destroy their claims to legitimacy. The implications of dissent, never before closely examined, were now fully exemplified: the right of dissent, construed as broadly as the judiciary construed it, meant, of course, the right to protest; the right to protest meant the right to concentrate aggressive crowds and the right of vitriolic denunciation—in short, the right to demonstrate, given any real latitude proved, in effect, to amount to a right to intimidate and a right to disrupt. The power to disrupt is, in a very direct sense, a power to discredit the institutions and the officials of the society. This point may not appear obvious, but one of the

attributes of high status in any society is that the person holding it shall not be subjected to public insult, infamy, or hu-
miliation, and that he shall be heard in a way that enables him
to speak effectively, without the feeling of being hunted
which verbal insult and abuse produce and are intended to
produce. Open and deliberate expressions of contempt have a
psychological effect of demonstrating the power of those who
express it and the weakness of those toward whom it is expressed. On this score, it may suffice to note that after about
1966, two Presidents, Mr. Johnson and Mr. Nixon, found it
inadvisable to appear in public, or even to attend church,
except under the most carefully controlled conditions. This
had not happened before in the United States. But though
they had reason to dread appearances in the country of which
both were Chief of State, they could present themselves in
public, with much less cause for apprehension, in Mexico and
in Romania. The power to disrupt is the power to discredit.
And in public affairs, the power to discredit is the power to
destroy.

For purposes of this discussion, the point is not just that
rejection of the society was being expressed very widely, publicly, and aggressively, but that the society had reached a point
where it accorded a kind of sanction to such expressions. This
sanction was seldom specific, but it was rather like the sanction which Victorian society used to give to sex escapades by
young boys. The escapades were, of course, "wrong" and had
to be "disapproved" of, but it was good for boys to be high-
spirited, boisterous, and a little bit wild. They needed, after all,
to "sow their wild oats" before they settled down. In short,
the specific act could not be certified as proper, but the general attitude which gave rise to it could be condoned. Similarly, today, liberal spokesmen in education, the church, the
mass media, and politics express disapproval of disruptive activities of militants on the Left, but they do not view these

with any of the real distaste and revulsion with which they view violence from the Right. They do not deny the angry assertions that the society is "sick" nor the angry implications as to whose fault the sickness is. They view without real repugnance the cult which glorifies Ché Guevara and Eldridge Cleaver. They prefer the social ferment which disrupts prestigious universities to the social orthodoxy which gives peace to blander and less eminent institutions. In the light of all that is badly wrong in society, perhaps they are correct in believing that strong medicine is needed. This discussion is not intended to deny that it is. But it might be observed that they have cherished two very simple fallacies: first, the clock stopped for a good many of them a third of a century ago, during the New Deal, and they cannot conceive that society might have any real enemies anywhere except on the Right; second, they also cannot conceive that people with ideals are capable of doing just as much damage, if the ideals are misplaced, as people with evil natures and malevolent designs.

But again, for purposes of this discussion, the point is not to discuss whether liberals do a disservice to society by giving a franchise to the radicals. They are certainly correct in believing that freedom is meaningless unless it is extended to the spokesmen of unpopular causes. The point, rather, is that the institutions of the society seem actually to place a kind of premium upon militant rejection of the society, and this premium will have a profound effect upon the channels into which all forms of social discontent are directed. An example of the premium placed upon militant rejection is found in the news media which, after all, control what shall receive the attention of the American public. But though they control in a sense, the media are supported by advertising and therefore live under a necessity to hold the attention of a mass audience, which is the life blood of advertising. They have long since learned that reasonable ideas and reasonable people are often unexciting and will disperse a mass audience in droves. But bizarre, outrageous, or sensational ideas or people engage the fascinated though perhaps shocked attention of vast numbers of citizens. Hence television gives to the bizarre, sensational, or outrageous a national platform which it would never provide to the moderate, the reasonable, and the realistic. This has been well stated in *New York Magazine*: "Television had made an enormous impact . . . and because of the nature of that medium—its preference for the politics of the theatre, its seeming inability ever to explain what is happening behind the photographed image—much of their [the working-class whites'] understanding of what happens is superficial. Most of them have only a passing acquaintance with blacks and very few have any black friends. So they see blacks in terms of militants with Afros and shades, or crushed people on welfare. Television never bothers reporting about the black man who gets up in the morning, eats a fast breakfast, says goodbye to his wife and children, and rushes out to work. That is not news. So the people who live in working class white ghettoes seldom meet blacks who are not threatening to burn down America, or asking for help, or receiving welfare, or committing crime."

When major institutions such as the communications media offer the intoxicating prize of national celebrity (even if this celebrity is, in a subtle way, notoriety) to militants, the net effect is to give a sanction to the expression of discontent in the form of overt rejection of the society. Psychologists are, of course, perfectly familiar with the concept that there is a paradoxical relationship between the sources and the objects of discontent. Discontent has many sources. One of these is social injustice, which might be called a public source of discontent. But there are many others, some of which may be called private: an individual may be discontented because of emotional friction with members of his family, because he has not attained some desired goal, because his mother weaned him too soon, because she did not wean him soon enough, because of an awareness of some personal inadequacy or defect, or because of random disasters that may have befallen him. To say that he is discontented is to say that he is frustrated, and he must express this frustration by some form of aggression. He may become a tyrannical father, a religious fanatic, a road-hog with his automobile, a sexual sadist, or perhaps simply an alcoholic who has turned his aggression against himself. All that one can be reasonably sure of is that he is not likely to express his aggression in any way which society interdicts, either by severe overt punishment or by psychological inhibition. If he were, for instance, of the older generation of ancestor-worshipping Chinese, he would not express aggression by acts designed to humiliate his parents. If he were a citizen of a highly militaristic totalitarian state, he would not express it by public denunciation of the army. On the contrary, impulses of aggression have customarily been directed against objects which can be attacked with physical and psychological impunity—objects which are weak or which lack protective sanctions, such as scapegoats, witches, strangers, or, historically, Catholics in Protestant countries, Protestants in Catholic countries, or citizens of a country with which the aggressive person's country is at war.

All these various examples of the sources of aggression and the objects of aggression are mentioned for the purpose of emphasizing the curious hiatus between sources which cause discontent and objects which become the outlets for discharging the aggression which is generated by discontent. As has already been suggested, attention to this hiatus is not lacking in psychology, where the concept of displacement is well known. But psychology has tended to examine such phenomena primarily in terms of the implications for the individual personality, and not in terms of social implications. For purposes of this discussion, it is the neglected social and historical implications which matter, and the social implications may be stated as follows.

First, all societies have a certain quantum of discontent

among their members. The amount of discontent will vary according to the differential between what the members of the society believe that they are entitled to experience and what they believe that they actually experience. When fulfillment falls short of expectation they will blame something, or someone, perhaps including themselves, and the quantum of discontent will increase or decrease as this differential increases or decreases in the society. But there will always be a certain quantum.

Second, in any society, a certain portion of the discontent will be rationally derived from dissatisfaction with conditions which are wrong in the sense that they cause human wretchedness and suffering which is not necessary in terms of the capacities of the society. This kind of discontent is ideologically inspired. It can be discharged only against the condition which aroused it; and it is public in its nature. Because it is rational and because it has an intellectual content which is what it purports to be, historians, who enjoy exercise with intellectual concepts, and who still harbor eighteenth-century ideas about the rationality of man, frequently treat all discontent as being of this kind, which lends itself to explanation purely in rational-intellectual terms. But in any society, another portion of the discontent will arise from problems of a personal, less public nature: family tensions, the failure of the individual in some deeply committed effort, the strains of competition, personal inadequacies, or the stress resulting when the individual finds that two of his values or his goals cannot be reconciled with one another. This kind of discontent is emotionally generated; it does not recognize its own source and therefore is not specifically directed toward that source but is a free-floating discontent, ready to be discharged as aggression against any object which is not protected by superior strength or by inviolable psychological sanctions. Historians have usually ignored this kind of discontent, partly because they despised it for its lack of intrinsic intellectual content, and partly because they failed to perceive that, though it may originate in the private or personal sphere (which history seldom reaches), it often finds the channels for its discharge in the public sphere where it may affect the course of history. But although the latter kind of discontent has been largely overlooked by historians, the fact is that both kinds of discontent exist in every society, in varying proportions from one society to another, and with strong indications that the latter kind may be quantitatively more significant in many situations than the former.

Third, it follows from the above that the degree of discontent in any society is not necessarily correlated to the degree of injustice or evil in the institutions of the society. This means that historical explanation which explains social discontent wholly in terms of the rational recognition of substantive evils is fallacious. In short, the degree to which men reject society does not necessarily depend upon the degree to which something is wrong with the society.

Fourth, it also follows from the above that the degree of social protest in any society is not necessarily correlated with the degree of discontent in the society, for a society with less discontent may have it all channeled into social protest, and a society with more discontent may discharge almost all of it into channels other than social protest. This means that historical explanation which treats an increase in the volume of social protest as an indication of rising discontent may be fallacious, for in fact an increase of protest may indicate only that a greater proportion of the existing discontent is going into protest and a lesser proportion is going into other channels through which aggression is discharged. This point has more than a theoretical aspect, for it is clear that the sanctions which gave the American society immunity from attack have diminished and the acceptability of the act of rejecting the society has increased. As this happened, of course, the proportion of discontent finding expression in attacks upon social institutions has increased, while the proportion finding other expressions has diminished. To take a historical example, in the nineteenth century, a great deal of the aggression which had been generated by frustration led to guilt feelings on the part of those who repressed their aggressions, and these guilt feelings were often discharged at the revival meetings of the evangelical churches. In short, revivals may have been a major device by which society handled the impulses of discontent. But this device became almost negligible in the latter half of the twentieth century. In view of all the sources of discontent and all the channels for discharging it, it would be a plausible hypothesis to suppose that in the past, when expressions of hostility to society were strongly tabooed, much of the discontent which had its source in the injustice of public institutions (e.g., slavery or segregation) found its expression in private forms of aggression (e.g., violence practiced by blacks upon one another), but that by now the tables are turned and that much of the discontent which arises from private or personal circumstances finds its expression in quasi-sanctioned attacks upon public institutions. Where at one time discontent was, on balance, deflected from the public sphere into the private, it now spills over from the private sphere into the public. This concentration of diverse forms of frustration and discontent upon public issues is pretty much what we mean by the politicization of American life.

Fifth and finally, historians have tacitly assumed that the kind of discontent which arises from public sources and which has an ideological content will also influence public events, and is therefore historically important; while the kind of discontent which arises from private sources and which lacks ideological content will play itself out in the private sphere, and therefore is of no real interest to historians. But this assumption is fallacious, not only because discontent which is generated in the private sphere may be discharged in the public one, but also, most emphatically, because historic changes may alter private circumstances, and may indeed alter large numbers of sets of private circumstances in the same direction. The collective result of a sufficient number of such cases, though private in their separate occurrence, will be public in their cumulative impact, and will produce historic change. For instance, social change may pose conflicts between old and new values in a society; when it does so, it will, as Karen Horney pointed out, increase the degree of neuroticism in the society. Social change may intensify the competitive demands in a society; this, in turn, may lead to a greater total measure of insecurity in the society. Social change may alter the patterns of interpersonal relationship in a society—by, for instance, transferring economic functions from the family to other institutions, and thus diminishing the economic supports of family cohesion. Or it may do this by a bureaucratization of social and economic organizations, which will deal with individuals indiscriminately as so many units which are to be treated impersonally and which are expected to respond in an impersonal way. Again, it may convert a society from a system in which family life is integrated with occupational life to one in which several roles—the family role, the business role, and others—become isolated from one another, so that life is fractionized instead of being integrated. Any such changes can have profound social impact and historical importance, even though the change occurs, privately, to a great multiplicity of individuals, and not publicly to the society as a whole. But perhaps one of the most subtle and important ways in which social change can impinge upon a whole population with transforming results is by altering the processes through which individuals develop their identities as persons and at the same time as members of society. This matter of the process of identity formation is closely related to the problem of the rejection of society; for it appears that traditional processes of developing social identity have tended to produce a high proportion of men and women who attained their identity by adopting, quite readily, the roles which the society expected of them. The adoption of such roles was, itself, a way of accepting the society, and the act of adoption tended to strengthen ties with members of the society. There is considerable evidence that many people today do not, for whatever reason, adopt expected roles and that they react negatively even to behaving as the role which they have adopted requires them to behave. If the nature of interpersonal relationships has changed in a way that would somehow impair the capacity of human beings to find and form identities compatible with the society in which they are to live, it would be one of the most crucial factors in explaining the number of people in America who reject the prevailing society. It would also be, historically, a social change of unparalleled importance.

One of the difficult problems of intellectual history is to understand why, in the case of a given movement such as the antislavery crusade, one individual will support the reform, while another individual, exposed to the same intellectual appeals, and comparable to the first in his education and social and economic status, will oppose the reform. The difficulty is increased by the fact that many historians still cling to the unstated assumption that human motivation is controlled by rational thought, and that men's positions on public questions are determined either by the altruistic rationality of ideals or by the selfish rationality of cold calculation. In application, however, neither of these formulae of rationality is sufficient by itself. History abounds in instances where men made sacrifices for a cause and did things which ran counter to their economic self-interest. And it is not really tenable to suppose that all antislavery men were responsive to ideals while all proslavery men were unresponsive. A simple assumption that antislavery attracted the virtuous, while opposition to antislavery attracted the evil, may satisfy ideologues posing as historians, but it is not borne out by a close scrutiny of the personal qualities of the individuals who composed the two camps.

One step toward solution of the problem would be for historians to recognize that response to public issues is the product of both the general ideas (probably rational ideas) which are directed at a man *and* of the nature of the psychic apparatus (probably non-rational in some respects) of him who receives the ideas and reacts to them. The ideas, stated in terms of commonly shared values, will have a fairly uniform appeal to all to whom they are directed; but the diverse psychic apparatuses which receive them will reflect a wide spectrum of personality differences in different individuals, and therefore will respond in different, even in opposite ways. For instance, an argument that John Brown was striving for human freedom, and therefore that his attempt to organize a slave revolt was laudable, might appeal uniformly by its invocation of the ideologically accepted idea of freedom; but it would nevertheless have a very different impact, on the one hand, upon individuals whose personality structures predisposed them to crave security and to identify psychologically with authority figures, and, on the other hand, upon individuals who had internalized in their personalities attitudes of resentment toward authority and of identification with under-dogs, outsiders, and oppressed persons who shared an adverse relationship to authority.

To say that the historian should examine not only the ideas to which people respond, but also the kinds of personalities which are responding—not only the nature of the force which causes a reaction but also the nature of the mechanism which does the reacting—may sound quite plausible. But it presents great difficulties to the historian. For the ideas to which people react are rational, and the analysis of ideas can be conducted in the rationalistic terms which historians have conventionally used. But the nature of people's reactions is psychological, which is equivalent to saying that they are, to a great degree, non-rational, and therefore not susceptible to historical analysis with the kinds of criteria customarily applied by historians. Further, even if historians should learn to handle the historical record left by non-rational phenomena, they would still face an immense problem in finding a way to relate the rational aspects of human experience and behavior to the non-rational aspects.

The problem of finding some equation for this relationship brings us back to the main theme of these pages—the rejection of society by a significant and increasing proportion of the people who compose it. Earlier, I indicated briefly, but very distinctly, that there are certainly a number of things vitally wrong with the society and that awareness of these things must generate a certain amount of rational and well-justified dissatisfaction with the society. Then I attempted to show that the nature of authority has altered in a way which permits personal discontent to be expressed in the form of rejection of the society's dominant modes, rather than in alternative forms for the expression of frustration-aggression. But to say that there are objective conditions which might rationally be conducive to acute social unrest does not quite mean that any social unrest which may happen to exist is therefore the result of these objective conditions. It may be the result of non-rational factors, and here the problem of the relationship between rational and non-rational (psychological factors) becomes critical.

To state the same point in a different way, what historians are concerned with, in a broad sense, is social change over time. The kinds of changes which they have conventionally handled best are changes in institutions, changes in overt modes of human conduct, changes in technology and in the adaptation of economic and social practice to technological change, changes in the formal structure of society, and changes in rational thought. Each of these themes is immense, and historians would have much more than they could manage if they confined themselves just to them. Operating primarily with rational concepts and with the data of overt action, they have seldom attempted to deal with changes—perhaps non-rationally induced changes—in the patterns of human relationship. By "patterns of human relationship," I mean the web of interpersonal affiliations which distinguishes a society from a mob or a herd, and gives it its distinctive texture or structure. An understanding of the web of affiliations must derive from an understanding of the way in which individuals form relationships with other individuals, the social contexts which are necessary to these formations, and the processes of identification and bonding which operate within the personality and also contribute vitally to its further development.

Psychology is, in most respects, especially equipped to deal with the patterns of relationship, and historians have no doubt been well advised to leave the analysis of these patterns to the psychologists. But at the same time, alterations in such patterns must be explained partially by the processes of historical change. Further, some kinds of historical change cannot be explained without a recognition of the consequences of the alteration of the patterns. For instance, the diminution of the role of the family has been caused, to a great extent, by the historic shift from an agrarian society, in which the family was a functional economic unit, to an industrial society in which the family's function is much less evident. Psychologists, talking about what has happened to the family are likely to oversimplify and to make naïve assumptions about historic changes in the social context, just as historians, talking about what has happened to the family, are likely to be naïve about the psychological consequences of changes in the social fabric. But no matter what the division of labor may be, there have been historic changes in the patterns of relationships, and a recognition of these changes may well be vital, in turn, to an understanding of historic changes in conditions which are determined in part by the pattern of relationships. Specifically, such recognition may be vital to an understanding of changes in the cohesion of a society or in the degree of estrangement which will develop within a society.

Through the long history of man, the human species has exhibited an incredible diversity of attributes and characteristics in different human cultures. Few features have been constant in all human societies. But among these few, three are prominent. First, man is less guided by instinct than any animal, and whatever he knows about how to stay alive in the world has to be learned—learned primarily from other human beings. Second, the young of the human species has a longer period of immaturity and dependency, in proportion to his total life span, than the young of any other animal. Third, man is a simian, and as a simian (unlike, for instance, the felines), he has a strong propensity for associating in groups larger than the little nucleus of the mating pair and their young.

These three features have constantly shaped the conditions, practices, and structures of human organizations. The lack of any innate capacity of young humans to take care of themselves, and the long duration of immaturity led to a very special relation between the adults and the young (almost invariably the parents and the offspring), in which the adults provided nurture and also rearing or training which would enable the young to attain the kind of skills and capacities necessary to them if they were to lead self-sufficient lives. In this process, the mother usually provided nurture for the young during their infancy, while they were being fed at her breast. But at the later stages of rearing, the mother cared for the young females and the father took an increasing responsibility for the rearing of the young males. During this stage of development, the young showed a notable capacity to learn by imitation what they did not know by instinct. The process of learning by imitation was greatly facilitated by a psychological reaction which caused the male and female children to want to be like the adults of the same sex. The attachment of the boy to the father and the girl to the mother was explained by Freud with a theory of active infant sexuality, manifesting itself in two phases. First the infant would desire to possess sexually the parent of the opposite sex (the Oedipus complex in males, the Electra complex in females) but later the male child, feeling guilty for his impulse to violate a taboo against an illicit relation, and feeling fear of punishment (castration) by his powerful rival, the father, would cease his primary attachment to the mother (i.e., the complex would be *resolved*) and then he would later *identify* with the father. The identification might reflect fear of the father's authority or envy of the father's strength quite as much as love for the father; but in any case it would make the child *want to be like* the father. This would clear the path for imitative learning, and would also mean that the child had experienced the important developmental step of forming a strong and significant relationship with another person.

One might suppose that identification with the father could be explained more directly and easily, without becoming involved with questions of infant sexuality and the Oedipus complex, simply by supposing that the male child perceives in the male adult a model of what he must attempt to be—a model enviable in strength and competence—and that he identifies with his model. But the concept of the Oedipus complex adds some necessary dimensions that will become significant later in this discussion. It suggests that there is an ambivalence in the young child between attachment to the mother and attachment to the father, and if the ambivalence is not resolved, the primary identification with the mother may persist, with some resultant confusion in sex role for the child. It suggests, too, that the identification with the father is not only an important interpersonal relationship but also an identification

with the male principle and an identification with authority—
for there is much awe of the father's strength in this identification.

The identification with the father, however, is not the only
important interpersonal relationship formed by the male child,
for as has been observed above, the human animal has a propensity for group association. But the gregariousness of the
male child in the period of sex latency which precedes puberty
is not a random sociability which indiscriminately embraces all
other humans of every age and sex. It is a sociability of pre-
pubescent males. Maleness is the criterion of membership, and
since none of the membership is mature enough to be confident of virility or to express it sexually, the group has traditionally demanded that the abilities which it associates with
maleness—readiness to incur danger, capacity to bear pain,
willingness to take the lead, physical prowess—should be
clearly evident, even in an exaggerated form. If these qualities are not evident, membership in the group may be denied.
This means that, although we speak of interpersonal relations,
these young males do not relate in a general way as persons.
They relate in a specific way, as males, or they do not relate
at all.

After puberty, the conspicuous exclusion of females breaks
down. Those wedding bells ultimately break up that old gang.
But for the rest of their lives, at social gatherings, the men
gravitate to one side of the room and the women to the other,
just enough to make one wonder whether there is one group
or two, and whether a person can attain membership through
affiliation with the group as a whole, or only through affiliation with one of the two entities which meet together so often
but never show any sign of merging.

Throughout all of the prehistory of man and all but the last
century and a half of his history, males have dominated most
human societies. Psychologically, they have buttressed the system of male domination by their identification with the prin-

ciple of authority as symbolized by the father, and by their identification with the principle of virile masculinity as symbolized by the male group. These facts have been recognized, more or less. But what has seldom been recognized is that interpersonal relations were mediated through groups which were so self-consciously male that if a person of male gender did not present enough masculine credentials to satisfy such a group, he was excluded from the only existing access to interpersonal relations of a social nature. A human male might be gregarious simply as a human, but he could fulfill his gregariousness and identify with other humans only as a male.[2]

Yet the exclusiveness of this situation was not as restrictive as might appear, for most boys understood clearly what role was expected of them, and were so eager to fulfill the role that, given allowance that boyish tests of masculine prowess were not nearly so demanding as the boys pretended, most boys could meet the tests. In fact what was demanded was not so much the physical demonstration of manliness as the psychological acceptance of the male role. Their acceptance by their peers made young males members of the brotherhood, safe from estrangement and sufficiently aware of the value of their membership to be on guard against forfeiting it by any neglect of their expected roles.[3]

From prehistoric times until early in the nineteenth century, the conditions of life for man, or at least for Western man, were such that these arrangements sketched above were realistic and worked very well socially. Human existence was geared to a pastoral-agricultural economy, with some hunting and fishing at one end and some craft work with wood, leather, and metals at the other. In this world, so very recent and so

---

2. The alternative to establishing interpersonal relations through the medium of the male group was social estrangement.

3. A man might, of course, relate to a woman in a deep and meaningful way, but this is not the same as to say that he could find his own identity in such a relationship.

incredibly remote, real physical strength was needed for many of the tasks—breaking a horse or a mule to harness, plowing a field, lifting a weight, toting a bale—and adult males took a dominant position because they had physiques which fitted them for these tasks better than the women (in women's physiques the capacity for bearing and nursing babies took a priority over the capacity for feats of strength). Not only were adult males dominant, but also they showed their strength in situations on the farm or in the field, where the boys would observe, understand, and admire. Naturally, most of the adult males became real authority figures for their off-spring, and identification with the father came naturally. (Again, this need not mean affection for the father at all, but rather a desire to be like him, and an acceptance of him as a model to be copied.) As experienced workers in an economy whose operations were relatively simple, fathers knew most of the things which boys, who were destined to be the same kind of workers in the same kind of economy, needed to learn. Further, as the system operated, the son usually followed the occupation of the father, which meant that if the father possessed specialized knowledge or skill—if, for instance, he made shoes for his living—what he knew would still be what his son needed to learn. Thus the authority figure also became a mentor who, more by example than by precept, taught his male offspring a great many things both general and particular —how to plow a straight furrow, how to slaughter a hog, how to behave at weddings and at funerals, how to handle responsibility, how to act in a crisis, how to treat women. Father was not a trained pedagogue and he may have lacked skills as an instructor, but fortunately, the imitative talent of the boys, which they had developed to compensate for their lack of instinct, made it easy for them to learn. Their dependence upon the father for training and guidance reinforced their acceptance of him as an authority figure and their identification with him.

If the relation with the father was functional, the social orientation of the pre-pubescent boy to a group of other boys was functional also, for it completed his indoctrination in the roles which he was expected to assume, and it gave him the kind of affiliation in a web of interpersonal relationships which completed his socialization, assured him of effective association with his fellow men, and protected him against social isolation.

In the traditional society, a boy went to work around the age of puberty, and began to earn his own living. It is customary to suppose and to say that when he had arrived at legal majority, and at a stage of sexual maturity and at economic independence, he had become a man. Very often, as it happens, he had indeed become a man, but neither because of sexual maturation nor because of economic earnings; for being a man was something that was *learned* by members of our instinct-deficient species and was not merely *arrived at* by physiological growth, or by getting a job. In fact, the society had a system for training boys to become men, and the completion of this training was nicely timed to coincide with physiological maturation and with the acquisition of earning power. The way that a boy really became a man was, first, by identifying with his father or some substitute authority figure, and thus internalizing the purpose to occupy a man's role; and later by practicing to assume a man's role in a group of young males with whom he formed affiliative ties such that he experienced socialization. Without the internalization of authority, without the purposeful adoption of a role, without the interpersonal relations with other individuals, no amount of elapsed time, sexual potency, or earned income could make him a socialized man. These processes were as vital to the maintenance of the human society as instincts are to animal species. In fact they may be regarded as the equivalents of instinct in providing human beings with a set of the right reactions.

Once these processes were completed, man in the traditional

society might settle into a world to which human adjustment was probably easier than it is to the industrial world of advanced technology. It was a more integrated world, and it had more continuity, and these features facilitate adjustment. It was a familiar world. The child had seen it all during his childhood, and, as Alexander Mitscherlich remarks, "One of the characteristics of the peasant tradition is that, no matter what the affective climate in the home may be, the life of the parents takes place before the child's eyes. No important aspects of the life of adults surrounding him take place out of his sight or beyond the range of his experience. Thus he grows up quite naturally into a way of life consolidated by tradition, articulated with the seasons, and the course of nature itself." As Mitscherlich also remarks, in the technological society, we are constantly the pawns of complex, intricate social and economic forces which we do not understand—sometimes do not even perceive—but "the 'savage' knows infinitely more than the ordinary 'civilized' man about the economic and social conditions that govern his existence."

The characteristic social organization of the traditional agrarian society consisted of a limited number of rather unspecialized groups—primary groups, as Charles H. Cooley called them. Closest to the individual was the family, consisting of parents and their young children, with married children and other kin on the periphery, inside the family circle if it was an "extended" family, outside if it was a "nuclear" one. Beyond the family was the neighborhood, and there was also the church congregation. Overall, there was the community. For purposes of human adjustment the merit of these organizations was that they contained so small a number of members that one could learn to "know" them all. Also, church and neighborhood and kinship groups overlapped in their membership, and one grew to know the members in an integral way, that is, to know them as persons and not just the performers of specialized functions (as one knows, for exam-

ple, a bank teller or a dentist). Knowing a person meant en-
countering him in a variety of situations—at market, at work
on his farm, at baptisms, at funerals, at a shooting match, at
the tavern, perhaps in town meeting. It meant learning about
various aspects of his life—what were his antecedents, what
kind of husband and father he is, how he operates his farm,
how he behaves when he has had something to drink, what he
is like in a fight, or in a horse-trade. It seems reasonable to
suppose that interpersonal relations were stronger when one
knew the whole person to whom one was going to relate.

Not only were human relationships more integrated, but
various aspects of life were integrated also: the farm was both
a man's workplace and his home. His family members were
also his fellow workers, as his sons worked with him in the
fields, while his wife, with her cooking, her preserving, her
meat-curing, her soap-making, and her spinning and weaving,
processed the commodities that he produced. Even the pleasures of life were articulated to the family and the home: husk-
ing bees or feasts came at or after the harvest; when a man
went hunting or fishing, he took his older boys along and he
hoped to add food to the larder.

As long ago as 1887, in his *Gemeinschaft und Gesellschaft*,
Ferdinand Tönnics depicted the contrast between, on the one
hand, the communal type of agrarian society, with its integrated, organic character and its highly personal kind of relationships, and, on the other hand, the diffuse, rationalized, bureaucratic type of industrialized society with its separation of
work from the home, its separation of the industrial worker
from the product of his work (to Marx the root cause of alienation), and its separation of life into a congeries of fragmented,
unrelated roles—one at home, another at the office, another at
the club—and each in a universe cut off from the others.
Tönnies perhaps exaggerated the charms of *Gemeinschaft*, for
the traditional community can be repressive, harsh, and capri-
cious, but it is probably true that significant interpersonal rela-

tionships were more easily formed and maintained in an integrated life-situation, and that the cohesive strength of the web of human affiliations was stronger.

The cohesive integrity of the traditional communal society never was as strong as its idealizers have supposed, and it began, very gradually, to deteriorate in Western Europe as early as the fifteenth century. But it was a system with deep roots, and though subject to modifications, it survived as a dominant form into the nineteenth century. Since the nineteenth century, industrialization has gained momentum, and disintegration of the surviving integral structure has proceeded apace. This is well known, and it is commonplace to remark on the separation of the world of work from that of family life, on the fractionization of life's activities, and on the impersonality of contacts with people whom one never encounters except in one limited aspect—figures behind a desk or at the other end of a telephone line, or at a party with a cocktail glass in hand, or in an elevator.

These changes no doubt increase the difficulty, for an individual, of maintaining a coherent sense of identity and of adequate human relationships, but they do not strike directly at the very roots of the processes of identification, internalization of an authority figure, and formation of interpersonal ties. Yet there are other historic changes that do strike at these roots, and their impact may be even more damaging to the social fabric.

History may have transformed the life circumstances of adult males, drawing their home lives and their office lives into separate universes, bureaucratizing the human quality out of their contacts with their fellow humans, and allowing them to see only one facet of the personality of most people they meet. But such adults have usually already done as much or as little as they are going to do in experiencing the processes which will enable them to achieve identification and the capacity for interpersonal relationship. It is really at the pre-adult stage that the processes are crucial. Here historical change has impaired the social arrangements through which these processes were carried out, first by revoking the function of the father, and second by revoking the special monopolistic position of the young male group as a socializing agent and as a medium for the development of interpersonal ties. The changes in the position of the father are already rather widely recognized; the changes in the position of the group of young males are not.

The changes in the position of the father have been recognized rather fully by various writers, but a number of points need to be recognized here. The processes of industrialization, of the transformation to an advanced technology have separated the site of work from the site where children are reared; they have subdivided and technicized the processes of work in such a way that a child cannot understand them and very often even an adult performing the processes himself cannot understand them; they have also created conditions of constant change both in the products used by society and in the mode of production, so that the nature of occupational tasks performed by workers has, of necessity, been made very flexible, very readily adjustable. The continuity in the occupational content of jobs has been abolished. In sum, boys can no longer see their fathers' work; they could not understand it even if they could see it; and it might have no significance for them even if they could understand it.

These developments have gone far to render the father obsolete. He can no longer serve as a model for his children, especially his male children, when they are internalizing what they want to be like and are learning to be like the model. This is true for the overwhelming reason that he is not with his children; he is at some other incomprehensible place, unknown or known only by hearsay, as the office or the plant. But what is worse, the time when he is with them, after work or on weekends, which includes after all a considerable span, is exactly the time when he is functionless; he is not doing anything which they need or want to learn to do. And even if he did do all his work at home, it would still not have much relevance to his children, for both statistical likelihood and social expectation tell them that in any case they are not going to be doing what he is doing. He does have an economic function as a worker, but no function as a father, for the function as worker is now irrelevant to his children; it is kept out of sight so far as they are concerned; and father himself is kept out of sight except in the most meaningless intervals of his life, the intervals when he is idle.

Despite all these conditions, probably the majority of male parents continue to be fathers in somewhat the same sense in which the culture defined fatherhood. They continue to derive some authority from their role as economic providers; the conserving inertia of the culture continues to accord them some sanction derived from their traditional role—"Daddy's gone a-hunting"; and in a species as plastic as *Homo sapiens* there are many ways in which an adult male can help to fulfill the psychological needs of children.

But the deterioration of the role of father has gone so far that with significant frequency the child fails to identify with the father. This failure of identification may not seem important or even regrettable to many people who dislike authority and who confuse *rejection* of the father (failure to adopt him as a model) with *revolt against* the father (failure to continue to accept subordination). The confusion is very productive of real misunderstanding, for it leads those who are confused into a basic fallacy. This is the fallacy that the present rejection of the dominant values is nothing new, because sons have always revolted against their fathers. It is true that they have always revolted, metaphorically if not literally, but revolt did not mean rejection of authority at all; it only meant transferring the exercise of authority from father to son. Having transferred it, the son is quite ready to exercise the authority which he internalized almost in infancy by *identifying* with his father —which does not mean loving him, or promising never to resist him, but wanting to be like him. Rejection of the entire system is indeed something new and should not be confused with a relatively conservative purpose to take over the control of the system from father so that one can run it oneself.

A further extension of this fallacy is the belief that American society is basically radical, because it has repudiated the principle of authority, and has in fact politically slain the father—slaying him as George III in the American Revolution. The immigrant, too, refuses to yield to the traditional tyranny of the Old World father. But again, the War of Independence was a struggle for control, not a struggle to overturn the society. The "revolutionists" did not have revolutionary ideas. They had identified with a powerful father and they meant to be like him if they had to fight with him in order to do so. Revolt against the father by a young man is one thing; rejection of the father by an infant is something else. Revolt asserts a male role; rejection declines to adopt a male role. Revolt seeks to seize authority; rejection expresses an aversion to the exercise of authority by oneself or anyone else. Revolt is an expression of confidence in one's identity; rejection is a failure to attain identity.

When identification fails, as it sometimes will in even the most stable and traditional of societies, the link of generations is broken and the continuity of culture is threatened. To appreciate these hazards, let us turn briefly to the Freudian analysis of the parent-child relationship. According to this analysis, the relation of the male child to his male parent is at best ambivalent. His first strong tie, resulting both from his nurture at the breast and from his infantile sexuality, is toward his mother, and he jealously resents his father as a rival. Only by a resolving of the Oedipus complex and a lowering of the intensity of the attachment to his mother can the way be cleared for him to reach the point at which he wants to be like his father. The visible and functional strength of his father is important to this switch, and if they are lacking, the switch may not be made. But if it is not made, what happens then?

What happens, first of all, is that the Oedipus complex may not be resolved and the attachment to the mother may remain dominant. The child may reject the father *before* he has ever identified with him as someone to be like, which is a very different thing indeed from revolting against the father's domination after having previously identified with him as someone whose strength and competence may serve as a model for emulation.

Yet, though the father is no longer available as an object for identification, the impulse toward identification is strong. What will happen to it? It may be directed toward the mother as someone to be like, and the male child may internalize some of her qualities, including qualities which the culture has somewhat arbitrarily classified as female, such as tenderness, love of beauty, neatness, gentleness. If he goes even a little distance in this direction it may prevent his participation in the intolerant and fetishistic society of pre-pubescent boys, and therefore may lead to his exclusion from the opportunity to learn how to form strong interpersonal relationships. In short, it may lead to social estrangement. If he goes any considerable distance, it will lead to uncertainty or ambiguity in his adoption of a sex role, and since sexual identity seems basic to other levels of identity, it will mean severe confusion as to who he is—an even more insuperable barrier to effective interpersonal relationships and an even more certain path to social estrangement.

Identification with the mother, however, is not the only alternative to rejection of the father. The impulse to find a person whom one wants to be like is a strong one—perhaps a compensatory factor to facilitate learning in a species which lacks the guidance of instinct—and it can operate in several ways. It can, for instance, lead to identification with a substitute for the father—a person with the strength and prowess which the real father may lack. It can lead, when the rejection of the father is strong, to a negative identification with a figure who exemplifies qualities and values which are opposite those of the father. If the father symbolizes wealth, influence, and respectability, the son who rejects him may be compatible with those who are poor, oppressed, or disreputable. In the impulses of the present day to identify with the wretched of the earth, there may be altruistic compassion, but one is justified in suspecting also a component of negative identification. If, in the somewhat imprecise analogies between private life and public life, it was realistic to regard the popularity of General Eisenhower as a response to a father figure, it would be no less realistic to regard the cult of Mao-tse Tung as a case of negative identification. Negative identification is itself a highly motivated, compensation-seeking form of social estrangement. Sometimes, when identification with a person fails, a great psychological void remains, and to fill this void people incapable of genuine interpersonal relationships will identify with an abstraction. An important historical instance of identification with abstract power has been the zealous support of totalitarian regimes by faceless multitudes of people. The totalitarian display of power for its own sake satisfies the impulse to identify with strength, and the compulsive expressions of adoration for a Hitler or a Stalin serve as impersonal, one-way equivalents for the kind of personal and reciprocating relationship between authority and dependence which had its optimum manifestation in the ties between father and son.

All these deviations of identification—with a person (the mother) whose role the society forbids the male identifier to assume; with a negative figure; with no one at all; or with an abstract concept or "cause"—reflect, in various ways, the failure to form or the lack of capacity to form strong interpersonal relationships, and all are in fact forms of estrangement which express themselves in the individual's rejection of the society of which he needs to be a member.

As I have suggested previously, identification by a male child with the father is also identification with the male role and identification with the principle of authority. Further, it is a tremendously important form of relationship. But it is not exactly a social relationship in the ordinary sense, for there is too much of authority and dependence about it. The kind of social responsiveness which an individual needs has been provided by another instrumentality, namely, the small group, and in Western society, as already noted, especially by the groups formed by young males between the end of infancy and the end of dependency upon the parent.

The group of young males was a "play group," frequently engaged in acting out picturesque fantasies about robbers, soldiers, pirates, Indians, and other red-blooded folk. Most people have regarded it with amusement (as in *The Adventures of Tom Sawyer*) or occasionally, when they caught a glimpse of how cruel and how utterly tribal it could be, with horror (as in *Lord of the Flies*). But it has seldom been appreciated as the remarkably functional institution which it was. Its function was to teach boys to become men (manhood being a socially defined role, not a biological condition). This was a job which fathers could not do, because it included explorations of sex and forms of more or less dangerous behavior which the adult world could not sanction. Fathers were inhibited from guiding their offspring in these activities. But for all its fantasy, the young male group perceived with deadly accuracy what attributes the society really valued in men (prowess, toughness, the capacity to persevere under adverse conditions) and what ones it merely pretended to value (obedience, studiousness, chastity). Armed with this insight, the group ruthlessly ignored the extraneous values while concentrating on the essential ones.

It is not entirely clear why the young male group gradually lost its monopoly in the period between, perhaps, 1930 and

1960. The process of urbanization had an eroding effect, for the group operated at its best in the atavistic milieu of woods and fields. The increasing demands of school had some effect, as I shall discuss shortly. But perhaps, fundamentally, society ceased to be sure that prowess, stamina, and bravery were the main qualities it wanted. In bureaucratic organizations, adaptability and the capacity for smooth interaction and flexible adjustment were wanted; in technology and increasingly in the professions, learned skills which could be acquired only by discipline and by diligent application were at a premium. More and more, the challenges of society were of a kind that could be met by trained intelligence—less and less, by endurance and physical bravery.

One might suppose that the growth of formal schooling struck a decisive blow at the dominance of the young male group, for schooling assumed a larger and larger place in the scheme of things, by every kind of measurement. The school year grew from a brief, rural, post-harvest session to a protracted, custodial, nine-month year. The school day, formerly ending an hour or two after noon, stretched out toward dusk. The school career, once limited for most people to four or five years of grade school, began in the first two decades of the twentieth century to include four years of high school for vast numbers, and by the end of the Second World War, the masses were following the elite to four years of college.

In formal terms, school seemed to challenge all the values of the young male group, but the boys again quickly sensed the difference between accepted values and pretended values, and simply moved their group into the school context where it continued to flourish, in spite of the institutional growth of formal education and the steady proliferation of female teachers. Indeed, the incursion of females probably made it easier for them to hold their citadel against the pedagogues, for male teachers might have been harder to ignore. The boys recognized that they must make the loathsome concession of demonstrating a decent competence in formal studies, but they knew that learning to become a man still mattered more than any of the subjects taught in the curriculum. Accordingly they refused to accept the teacher as what sociologists call "a significant other." In the classroom they knew how to practice, without publicity, what is now publicized as non-violent resistance, and at recess they continued to play their rough, girl-excluding games. Later they formalized their own groups as fraternities or as athletic teams which gave the school an identity through sports that it could never gain through scholarship. In the social enclave of the school, the boys who enjoyed prestige, who were envied and emulated, were not the honor students but the three-letter men.

The young male group was always an informal, uninstitutionalized, evanescent organization, and it is hard to say what happened to it. But somewhere along the way, it lost its authority, which was once omnipotent and terrifying to those young males who could not easily meet its specifications. The athletic teams are now on the defensive. The military units are now on the defensive. The fraternities are now on the defensive. The hippie culture rejects all the values which the young male group held sacred, and for good measure it also rejects their maleness and their tribalism. The hippie culture has, no doubt, been far too much publicized, and it still expresses the values only of a minority. But it is not on the defensive. As the young male group lost its authority, society lost what may have been its most powerful instrument for the formation and structuring of interpersonal relationships in a web that gave strong cohesion to the society. It lost also a major instrument for inducing an acceptance of society's dominant modes.

By 1969, American society was in a late stage of very rapid transformation from an age-old agrarian system to a new system geared to advanced technological development. The demands of the new system had caused serious impairment of some of the processes by which a given aggregate of humans maintained the organization and the web of relationships which made them a society with a certain structured fabric, and not just an amorphous mass of atomized individuals. The transformation had caused an impairment of a long and persistent psychic relation between father and male child, by which the male child took the father as a model from which to learn and with which to identify, thus accepting a defined male role for the otherwise unspecified implications of his gender, and accepting also the concept of authority as something to which he would submit in some relationships and which he would exercise in some others. Because of the impairment, the society now produced a much increased number of people who were confused as to their identity and who disliked authority, not wanting either to exercise it themselves or to let anyone else exercise it.

The transformation had also caused an impairment of another long persistent relationship: the association of young males who formed endomorphic groups, within which socialization was furthered (i.e., cohesive interpersonal relationships were formed), and within which also further fitting of the individual to the socially-defined male role was achieved. Because of this impairment, the society was now more permissive and more tolerant of individual diversity, but also it now produced more people without strong interpersonal relationships, because the processes of forming such relationships, though less rigid, were also more confused. Further, the reinforcement of identity which a clear-cut role can provide was lacking, as roles were less sharply (and, of course, less arbitrarily) defined. This weakening of identity further weakened the capacity for effective interpersonal relationships which are fostered by an assured identity.

In both cases, individuals had been exempted from a somewhat prescriptive authority, and had gained greater latitude for diversity of self-expression. But this was at the cost of a weakening of the ties of interpersonal relationship, and even of an estrangement of individuals from the society.

Lacking the interpersonal ties which might have given them a real sense of membership with others, the estranged individuals felt a psychological need because of the lack. Some of them compensated for the lack by dropping out of the society and joining in a drug culture which gave them escape, and by the practice of congregating gregariously in masses with other estranged persons. In these gatherings gregariousness, physical closeness, and sexual intimacy were made to substitute for actual affiliative ties, for the interpersonal ties among the estranged were weak.

Other estranged persons, feeling the lack of ties by which to relate to society, identified negatively with individuals who symbolized a rejection of the society, or identified abstractly with ideologies which condemned the society and thus also symbolized a rejection of it. Many of these were intensely motivated and worked with other estranged persons in protests, demonstrations, and militant activities which, in still another way, expressed a rejection of the society. Among these also, it appears that while they were brought together by a shared rejection of society, the actual bonds by which they related to one another were weak.

Thus the society was faced by an unusually large proportion of estranged people who rejected membership in it. Most societies have, at one time or another, had to deal with extensive discontent, and they have done so by simple repression, silencing the voices of the estranged, or by channeling the discontent into substitute outlets such as religious revivals (releasing guilt feelings), or persecution of scapegoats, or the prosecution of wars (releasing aggression). But the American society was not able to control the discontent, partly because the society had renounced the idea of coercive controls and had depended upon consensual controls. The efficacy of consensual controls had depended upon the ascendancy of a group numerous enough and influential enough to exercise a moral sway which the society as a whole would accept. But the overthrow of the rural Anglo-Saxon, Protestant domination, beginning in the 1920's, and of the business leadership in the 1930's, had left a situation in which no consensual basis for control continued—and there was no alternative form of control available.

Further, the society lacked conviction sufficient to motivate it to rally vigorously to defend its own institutions. Many who were not actively estranged were immobilized, as it were by the fractionalization of life in the segmented system which an advanced technological society imposes. Many others felt the depersonalization of human relationships which the technological society also tends to produce. A great many more were acutely aware of the society's failure to control its own population, to preserve its own environment, to escape potential destruction by its own technology, to right its own wrongs. Such awareness dulled their defensive impulse.

Thus, the society proved apathetic in defending itself, and the estranged, sensing the lack of resistance to their discontent, expressed it by attacking the society, attacking it openly, conspicuously, aggressively, under the protection of the institutions which they were attacking. By this time it was clear that society was losing its capacity to assign roles, by which people can achieve identities. This meant that it was losing its capacity to socialize its members. Perhaps new instrumentalities for socialization will emerge, but this remains to be seen.

These would seem to be some of the forces at work and some of the circumstances which were pertinent in one of the severest cases of social estrangement that any society has ever experienced. The estrangement grew gradually from deep roots, long before the crisis of the blacks or the Vietnam War. It led to what was perhaps the most aggressive rejection of dominant values that any society has ever permitted without seriously attempting to curb the attack and without really defending the values under assault.

16

SOCIAL COHESION
AND THE CRISIS OF LAW

In this essay, David Potter turns his attention from the causes of today's widespread social disaffection to one of its most obvious consequences—deterioration in the effectiveness of law. What happens to government "by consent of the governed," he asks, when a sizable part of the population vehemently and often forcibly withholds its consent? The essay was Potter's contribution to a symposium on the question "Is the Law Dead?" held in the spring of 1970 at the Association of the Bar of the City of New York. His full title was: "Changing Patterns of Social Cohesion and the Crisis of Law under a System of Government by Consent."

WHEN WE ATTEMPT to appraise the place which law occupies in any given society, it is a good point of departure, I believe, to start by recognizing that the law is a uniform system of social control for the entire population living within a given jurisdiction. Its rules apply to everyone within the area of this jurisdiction. Other institutions may have rules which apply to parts of the population—churches, for instance, may do so, and labor unions, and they may impose penalties for violation of their rules. But these institutions do not apply uniformly to everyone, while, on the contrary, the law does. Since the law is uniform, it will, of course, operate most effectively when the population to which it applies is also uniform, or, as we might say, homogeneous. In treating the relationship of law to society, legal thinkers commonly assume that the population, or society, to which the law applies, *is* homogeneous—is a holistic community. One finds this assumption, for instance, in the criterion that obscenity can be defined by "prevailing community standards." This is well and good if there is one community which coincides with the jurisdiction. But suppose there is no community; or suppose there are two or more separate and somewhat antagonistic communities, all within the same jurisdiction. Then there can be no holistic "prevailing community standards," and therefore no criterion for the law—perhaps no social "legitimacy" for it.

This is a point to which I must return later, but first I should observe that this problem does not arise in all systems of government. Historically, even the potentiality of such a problem could scarcely have arisen more than two hundred years ago, for up to that time legitimacy was regarded as residing in a single ruler rather than in a multiplicity of people—in a unitary authority, rather than in a pluralistic one. Of course, as we all know, this theory had been modified in various ways, by making the ruler an institution ("the crown") rather than a man ("the king"), and by avoiding the enactment of laws that would arouse popular hostility. But still, authority, and also legitimacy were believed to come from above, and so long as this was true, the question of what happened to the legitimacy of law when it was vested in a society which might be deeply divided—that question did not arise. The kind of sanctions that would justify an authority as universal as that of the law seemed to be of so transcendent a nature that men tended to attribute a supernatural quality to them—the law was from the king and the king was from God. Such authority could hardly present problems of heterogeneity.

But the Americans of the late eighteenth century broke new ground by everlastingly rejecting the idea of authority from above, and by repudiating the notions of rank which had buttressed such authority. America, they decided, was to be a society of men equal in formal rank. Without rank, there could be no hierarchical class of "natural" rulers, and government was specifically declared to derive its sanction ("its just powers") from the "consent of the governed."

Among the innumerable writers who have celebrated the advent, two centuries ago, of the principle of government by the consent of the governed, it is remarkable how few have ever recognized that this principle contained a built-in and perhaps insoluble problem: When the governed include the entire body of citizens (and even non-citizens), it is inevitable that they will disagree on many matters and that policies which win the consent of some will never gain the consent of others—perhaps of very numerous others. Therefore, at an operative level, government by the consent of the governed really means government according to the wishes of some of the governed and contrary to the wishes of some others of the governed. The phrase "consent of the governed," under the cover of a false assumption that the governed will always and inevitably be an integral body, concealed the imminent hazard that government by citizens might simply mean government by any combination of citizens strong enough to overpower any other combination or combinations of citizens. In this sense, the principle of "consent" might become an ironic fiction to cover the process by which a more powerful component in society would trample upon the deepest convictions of a less powerful component.

There was nothing inherent in the doctrine of consent itself—nothing in the logic of the idea—which would have prevented such a travesty. In terms of theory, one might say that the United States became exposed almost two centuries ago to the potentiality that conflicting popular factions might destroy the society by dividing it into irreconcilable opposing groups, for there was no authority higher than the peoples' own consent, to restrain them. Once, of course, at the time of the Civil War, this potential hazard became a terrible reality. But it was only once, and otherwise, for two centuries, the hazard remained potential only. Thus, by now, when divisiveness endangers our public policy as never before, we are so accustomed to the routines of government by consent and so in the habit of assuming that consent can always be attained at some kind of price that we have ceased to realize that our mechanism provides no recourse for society in situations where consent is really withheld. This lack of recourse constitutes a vulnerability in our system—an acute, distinctive, but largely unrecognized vulnerability—which renders the society almost helpless in the face of divisions which cannot be reconciled. This vulnerability is peculiar to the system of government by consent and is basic to the present crisis of law in a divided society.

Historically, the system of government by consent succeeded so well that we are now most inclined to take it for granted at a time when we can least afford to take it for granted. At the beginning of the American experiment, there were men who felt acutely apprehensive about the cohesiveness of a system which gave a broad franchise to dissent and which sanctioned organized opposition to the policies of the government. Most of the Founders were decidedly uneasy about the danger of political parties, because they felt that the creation of parties would deepen divisions in the society and would perpetuate strife. Strife was generally regarded as likely to tear the social fabric, and traditional governments had customarily sought to suppress it. Now, the United States was about to incorporate political strife as a regular part of the system. Not unnaturally, some political sages viewed such a step with deep misgivings. Further, it was generally recognized that by sanctioning a high degree of freedom for individual citizens, the founders were releasing a force which might weaken the claims of the community as a whole—as an organism—vis-à-vis the claims of the unrestrained individual.

Thus, men recognized that democracy was a peculiarly fragile system, especially dependent upon the responsibility and self-restraint with which citizens exercised their freedom. Long after the Revolution, pundits continued to repeat these warnings and the public continued to nod approval of the repetitions. But the fact is, that after a time, while still affirming these propositions ritualistically, we ceased to believe them. One may say that the system worked so well that it inspired faith in democracy, or one may say that America got along so well under the system (which is by no means the same thing), that people ceased to worry about it. Certainly, the United States, under the Constitution of 1787 did grow with incredible rapidity in area and in population. It experienced a total economic transformation from a land of small farmers, producing food for their own use, to what some social analysts call a post-industrial society, with the immensely complex and interdependent economy that we have today. Democracy survived this transformation. It survived the transition from horse-and-buggy technology based on the muscle of men and animals, the power of wind in a sail, and water in a water wheel, and heat from fossilized plants, to a technology that could put men on the moon, and what was even more remarkable, could bring them back. Naturally, we began to think that if democracy can flourish under such varied conditions, and can contribute in a significant way to such remarkable achievements, it must be tough, adaptable, and resilient—not brittle or fragile after all.

Our confidence in the indestructibility of the democratic system was strengthened when we saw it survive crises which other, seemingly "stronger" systems might not have survived. To begin with, in the Civil War, more than a century ago, the nation faced a test of whether a democratic government could be, at the same time, strong enough to defeat its embattled adversaries, and weak enough (or limited enough) to ensure that freedoms would not be sacrificed by the very severity of the measures required to protect them. Abraham Lincoln was deeply concerned with this problem, and he spoke very feelingly of "the necessity that is upon us of proving that popular government is not an absurdity." Before he was assassinated, he knew that the government of the Union —a democratic government—had vindicated itself, and that Old World critics could never again speak with their former confidence when they said that a republic might be all right in times of tranquility, but that it would fall apart at the first real test of strength.

Eight decades after the Civil War, the "inefficient" and hopelessly civilianized American democracy administered total defeat to the most "efficient" and powerful military machine that the world had ever seen up to that time. Meanwhile, on many fronts—industrial, and technological, and scientific—the country had passed from triumph to triumph in a way that further assured Americans of the invulnerability of their system.

Yet, all the while, we had been operating on a principle of government by consent, of which it might plausibly be said that the reason we trusted it so completely was that we had never taken the trouble to understand it. When we thought about it at all, it was usually in the simplistic terms of "majority rule." The consent of the governed, operationally, we thought was the will of the majority, and even while upholding individual rights and freedoms, we have been chronically oblivious to the contradiction between the principle of majority rule and the principle of individual rights, just as we have been uncritically susceptible to such unsophisticated corollaries of the majoritarian fallacy as the "one man, one vote" slogan. But, as almost everyone would recognize, if he would only stop to reflect, the process of government in the United States has never been one of an omnipotent majority imposing its will upon a defenseless and unresisting minority. Rather, the process has been one by which the majority and the minority arrived at an understanding—not necessarily an amicable one, and indeed usually an arrangement by which the majority settled for less than it wanted to attain and the minority yielded more than it wanted to concede. Both accepted terms with which they were not entirely satisfied. While actual coercion was avoided, heavy pressure was frequently used, but even when pressure was heaviest a kind of understanding was involved, and this was what was meant by government by consent.

I doubt whether History or Political Science has ever done full justice to the subtlety and also to the pervasiveness of the arrangements by which the principle of consent—seldom totally voluntary, seldom entirely coercive—was woven into the fabric of our institutions. Politically, consent did not mean what we now sometimes mean when we speak of "consensus," and if my interpretation here should be damned as "consensus history," at least it is not consensus history of the orthodox kind. Consent did not mean either bland agreement on all questions, or a decision to confine public dispute to non-essential or trivial questions. It did not mean that there would be no conflict. On the contrary, many battles have been waged with heat and acrimony over issues that were thought to be fearfully urgent. For instance, in the struggles between Thomas Jefferson and Alexander Hamilton, Jefferson felt that he was saving the country, as he expressed it, from "monarchism and militarism." After Andrew Jackson's conflicts with the Bank of the United States and with the South Carolina nullifiers, he is said to have expressed regret, when he left the White House, for two pieces of unfinished business—he had neither shot Henry Clay nor hanged John C. Calhoun. In 1884, when Grover Cleveland was being nominated for the Presidency, one of his nominators declaimed: "we love him for the enemies he has made." So, we must certainly recognize many of the contests were real, and many of the rivalries were intense. Also, as Richard Hofstadter has recently asserted, many of the issues—the American Revolution, the Civil War, and many ethnic and immigrant divisions—represented conflict of the most genuine kind.

But if the principle of consent did not mean the elimination of conflict, what it did mean was that conflict should be limited. Adversaries might pit all their strength against one another, but they would not engage in remorseless attempts to destroy one another. There are many ways in which we have shown our purpose to avoid struggles leading to political extermination. The provisions in the Constitution against *ex post facto* laws and bills of attainder are pertinent examples. But far more telling, perhaps, is the habitual pattern of our political contests—notably our presidential elections. During these quadrennial episodes, the element of conflict has customarily been highly conspicuous. Almost every election was hotly contested, and if there were no important issues involved, the heat of the contest might be even more intense. Rhetoric, customarily, became very highly charged. Both parties talked big and denounced each other most abusively, and it was not unusual for one party to claim that if the rival party were elected it would be the end of republican government in the United States. Men made frenzied efforts to gain electoral victory, as if the future of mankind were at stake.

But after the election was over, what happened? We all know the scenario. The loser would send his congratulations to the winner; the newspapers which had supported the loser would begin to publish more flattering pictures of the winner than they had published during the campaign. One or two members of the losing party, after what we may call a decent interval, might agree to take positions in the new administration. When the Congress met, the majority party would assign a certain number of places on each committee to be filled by the minority party. They would do this as a matter of course, without even discussing whether to do so. Pretty soon they would be busily working out legislative compromises in the cloakroom while hurling rhetorical thunderbolts at one another on the floor.

In fact, the very structure of the parties themselves reflected this pattern of limited conflict, for the traditional two parties of American history—Federalists versus Jeffersonians, or Whigs versus Democrats, or Republicans versus Democrats, have been very unlike the ideologically "pure" splinter parties which have arisen so often in central and western Europe. The ideological parties have consisted of adherents from only one segment of the political spectrum, united in support of one particular doctrine, rather like small religious sects in this country. But the American political parties have been coalitions of conservative Southern Democrats and reformist Northern Democrats, or in the first half of the present century, of stand-pat Republicans from the East and progressive Republicans from the West, working together more or less reluctantly and with more or less internal friction.

Since both parties represented coalitions of men of diverse views, it followed that neither party was ideologically very different from its rival. Both tended to take what are called "moderate" positions and to avoid going very far to the Right or very far to the Left. This made it easier for them to reach accommodations with one another. So long as this relationship prevailed, it was always possible to evoke a spirit of unity between the parties as well as to rouse angry strife between them. In fact, this dualism became, as I have suggested, almost a ritual in which the parties were expected to assail each other vigorously in election campaigns, but never so vigorously that they could not be reminded, after the election was over, that what they shared as Americans far outweighed what they disagreed about as party members, and that the President once elected, ceased to be merely a partisan leader and became President of all the people.

Thomas Jefferson was the first President to articulate this view of our political system, and no President has ever stated it better. At his first inaugural in 1801, Jefferson, addressing himself to both his supporters and his recent adversaries stated a profound truth—a truth that was valid on several levels—when he declared, "Every difference of opinion is not a difference of principle. We have called by different names brethren of the same principle. We are all Republicans; we are all Federalists." At the lowest level this meant that each party constituted a kind of brokerage house, and that the brokerage houses can, as the phrase goes, "do business" with one another—a little opportunism along with the principle. At a higher level, it meant that once the contest was over, both parties would abide by the results of the contest, and the country would be spared the disruptive consequences of an endless feud. As Jefferson himself expressed it, since the "contest of opinion" had been "now decided by the voice of the nation," "all will, of course, arrange themselves under the will of the law and unite in common efforts for the common good. All, too, will bear in mind this sacred principle, that, though the will of the majority is in all cases to prevail, that will, to be rightful must be reasonable; that the minority possess their equal rights, which equal law must protect, and to violate would be oppression." At the highest level of all, the principle of consent was based not only on a contract, but upon the recognition of a reality. The reality was that areas of agreement were always present among the American people—that these areas were more important than the areas of disagreement, which are also always present, and that therefore the factors of union and cohesion must take a priority over the factors of dissension and disruption. This was what made it possible for Americans to maintain a system of consent, even though limited conflicts over specific issues were always being waged.

It had been a quarter of a century earlier that Jefferson had coined his immortal phrase about governments deriving their just powers from the consent of the governed. I would suggest that in the passages I have just quoted he was at last defining what consent of the governed really meant. It meant, above all, that conflicting parties would constantly remember that they could be adversaries without being enemies, would observe the distinction between differences of opinion

and differences of principle, and would work out more or
less voluntary solutions to their differences of opinion, recognizing the obligation of the majority to respect the rights of
the minority and the obligation of the minority to respect the
popular mandate held by the majority.

Such, as it appears to me, was government by consent—a
system which prevailed in the United States for well over a
century, and which is not yet terminated, though it is, I
believe, badly impaired. As we look back at it, we are apt
to romanticize it, and indeed, I may have idealized it somewhat in my description here. Therefore, I must point out, for
the sake of verisimilitude, as Mark Twain used to say, that
the system had some rather unlovely features. Sometimes, in
the quest for accommodation, it reduced principles to such a
negligible point that parties indulged in shameless bargaining,
and thought more about how to win elections than about
what to do with the elections they had won. "What are we
here for," asked a delegate to the Republican convention of
1868, "except the offices." Further, to mention a more serious flaw, the principle of consent exaggerated one of its own
chief virtues into a vice. The virtue was the principle of
compromise. The willingness to compromise was what enabled adversaries to get along with one another even when
they disagreed. Compromise of all kinds—between large
states and small states, between slavery and antislavery, between mercantile interests and planter interests, between advocates and opponents of national power—was what made
"a more perfect union" possible in 1787. Great compromises
again, in 1820, in 1832–33, in 1850, and finally at the expense
of the blacks, in 1877, had either avoided or liquidated major
crises in the Republic. Partly because of this experience, compromise was almost sanctified, and men who rejected compromise were often written off as "fanatics" or "zealots" who
refused the "tolerance" and the "give-and-take," of the American way. At times, it seemed that there was no principle

which could not be compromised if the parties to the transaction were sufficiently "reasonable."

The greatest flaw of all, in the system of consent, was one
that was perhaps least recognized. The system had a fatal
tendency to bring in those who could be conveniently included, but if there were groups whose voices would not
harmonize, it adopted the brutally simple expedient of denying them a voice altogether. These excluded groups were just
not regarded as, in the terminology of the sociologist, "significant others." Thus, the American Indians were denied a
voice. Negroes, both slave and free, were denied a voice.
Also, occasional strong efforts were made to deny immigrants
a voice. The denial of a voice to immigrants never succeeded
in a formal sense, but, realistically, many immigrants were
made to understand that they were on probation, and that if
they behaved themselves, their children might be admitted to
full membership in American society. Strange at it may now
seem, for many of them, this was enough, and they gave
patient support to a system in which they occupied a very
marginal position.

These major faults in the system of consent cannot and
should not be extenuated, and indeed they were so serious
that they might be regarded, in the eyes of some critics, as
completely vitiating the entire structure. I certainly do not
want to idealize it. I would not conceal the fact that compromise was often given a priority over principle, harmony over
morality, and agreement over clarity of decision. I would
not gloss over the fact that shameless bargaining and relentless arm-twisting were frequently employed to secure agreements in situations where direct coercion was taboo. But with
all its faults, the system allowed for a measure of internal
criticism and dissent such as few societies have known, and
it reduced the factor of direct physical coercion to about as
low a point as is possible in a complex and highly structured
society. In fact this avoidance of coercion was the chief

glory of the system, and the devices for obtaining consent were important primarily because they made the avoidance of coercion possible. To an astonishing degree in America, public affairs have been conducted on a basis that nothing could be done until it had been put into a form such that the opposition could be induced to agree to it. The use of the filibuster in the Senate, the copious devices for obstruction in both houses of Congress, the bicameral system itself, the arrangements for checks-and-balances, have all contributed to make it virtually impossible to enact a Federal law if an opposition group of appreciable size is irreconcilably determined to prevent it.

But this emphasis upon more or less voluntary consent is by no means confined to the political sphere. Throughout the society, we regard the use of force in almost any situation as a confession of moral failure, whether it involves the use of a birch rod in the school, or of militia in the streets. We even construct our buildings in a way which suggests our faith that people will accept the prevailing practices of the society without any duress to compel them to do so. In the past, tellers in banks sat guarded in little metal cages, but we have taken them out of these barricades and placed them behind low counters in rooms designed to look as little like a counting-house as possible. In the past, honest burghers built their houses with heavy, solid shutters at the windows to repel marauders, but today we have turned to building and living in glass houses whose walls can be shattered with a small stone. Where loans were once granted only in return for formidable mortgages, we now flood the mails with unsolicited cards extending credit with a bounty so overflowing that it sometimes extends beyond adults to infants, deceased persons, and domestic animals. In place of compulsion, we substitute agreement, but this substitution makes the necessity for agreement truly vital, so that when an important issue is in dispute, we are obsessively concerned that the negotiations, which may lead to agreement, shall never stop. The cessation of talk means crisis, and negotiations must go on, day and night. In a government by consent, the default of consent is the paralysis of authority.

Such was the system of government by the consent of the governed that prevailed in the United States for about two centuries. It never meant consent in the simple sense of spontaneous agreement by everyone. Sometimes the minority blackmailed the majority and sometimes the majority put intolerable pressure upon the minority. Always, certain disadvantaged groups were disregarded and left out. But withal, the fact remained that the majority refrained from pushing the minority to the point of actual resistance and the minority recognized an obligation, at a certain point, to abide by the terms of a settlement which they did not like—not an obligation to approve of it or even to agree to it, but at least to acquiesce in it, or as we say, "to go along" with it. Within this framework, men enjoyed remarkable opportunities to oppose the existing authority and to dissent from prevailing opinion. This system could operate without producing crises of social disorder because it was understood by all parties concerned that after the dissent had been heard and the issues had been canvassed, an arrangement would be worked out which the majority could accept as good enough and which the minority could tolerate as not utterly bad.

When the matter is viewed in this way, one might suppose the principle of consent succeeded simply because of the rationality or the tolerance of the American people—because men were logical enough to appreciate the philosophical elegance of this beautifully balanced political device, and tolerant enough to cherish the mutual concessions by which the invocation of *force majeure* was avoided. But in fact, human behavior is seldom this reasonable, and the ways and means by which society induces its members to do what is expected of them are never this voluntary. Government by consent may have succeeded partly because men recognized that submission to the majority is the price of democracy, and that compliance with society's basic creed is the price of freedom within the context of that creed. But it succeeded less for these reasons than for two others: first, the American people were remarkably homogeneous, and were well aware that the values which they shared were far more important to them than the values on which they disagreed; second, government by consent did not abolish the principle of authority —instead it substituted the equalitarian authority of the community as a whole for the hierarchical authority of a designated ruling class. It accomplished this transition by making conformity rather than obedience the device by which authority was enforced.

Social critics from Tocqueville to the present, have, of course, given a great deal of attention to conformity in American life. They have pointed out how strong, and sometimes relentless, the pressure toward conformity has been. They have deplored its effects in stunting the growth of individualism and creativity, and even in making a travesty of freedom. Many of these criticisms are quite justified, and I would not gainsay them. But they have already been stated over and over again with skillful insight and with strong emphasis. At the same time, certain other aspects of social conformity have been relatively neglected, except by some sociologists. To begin with, it has been poorly understood that conformity has an important constructive function, especially in a society which avoids the use of physical force or coercion. Every society has to have ways of coordinating the activities of its members, and this means that it has to have ways of inducing individuals to behave in ways in which they may not wish to behave and to do things which they would prefer not to do. This is almost what we mean when we speak of civilization. Some of the modes of inducing such behavior are quite formalized, and we have the law, the courts, the police, and the prisons. But on the whole, American society has relied less on formal authoritarian devices than almost any important society in history, and the force of law, for instance, has derived more from its claim to embody society's concept of justice than from its threat of penalties. In this situation of minimal direct coercive control, conformity has imposed the coordinating arrangements in American society which authority has imposed in other societies. Our society demands "cooperation" with the community rather than "obedience" to the rulers, but both "socialize" the individual to behave as his society expects him to behave. Erich Fromm has expressed the essence of socialization in an elegant and subtle formulation: "In order that any society may function well, its members must acquire the kind of character which makes them *want* to act in the way they *have* to act. . . . They have to *desire* what objectively is *necessary* for them to do. *Outer force* is to be replaced by *inner compulsion*. . . ."

This is, I think, a perfect statement of what conformity is all about. But men in Jacksonian America anticipated Fromm by a century with a less learned but no less perceptive formulation. With a kind of subtle crudity, they asserted that "this is a free country, and every man does as he pleases, and if he don't, we make him do so." This too, was conformity, and as I have suggested, I think that scholars have not given enough attention to the social function of conformity in an anti-authoritarian society.

But if they have neglected the function of conformity, they have neglected even more the means by which conformity was enforced. It is, I believe, partly because we have never adequately recognized what these means were that we fail to understand, today, why values which, as recently as a decade ago, appeared to rest upon granite foundations, have suddenly proved vulnerable to basic attack.

In brief, I would argue, conformity and also the whole

system of government by consent and law by consent, were based upon the sanction of community sentiment. But this statement can have no meaning until the term "community" has meaning, and the term "community" [1] is one of the most loosely used words in the language. If the etymology is to count for anything, a community ought to mean an aggregate of people, living in propinquity, who share the same basic values, attitudes, and outlook upon their social and physical environment. In brief, we might say that they share a common culture. But we all, apparently, have a tendency to believe that any aggregate of people in propinquity *ought to* have these shared qualities, or we wish that they did, and therefore we have gotten into the habit of speaking of any localized aggregate as a community, whether this aggregate has any shared values and attitudes or not. Thus we beg the question of whether it is a community, and we sometimes try to make it a community by pretending that it is one. I recently heard a university administrator, in the midst of a campus crisis, state "This disruption will end when the community decides that it must end, and no sooner." Of course, a public leader must assume the existence of a community, for, without one, there is nothing for him to lead. Also, sometimes, by a moving appeal, it is possible to invoke a spirit of community. But in realistic terms, the question was not whether the community would decide; it was the question whether a community existed to decide—whether the aggregate of people in the situation were enough of a corporate group to be able to reach a collective decision.

Because of this practice of confusing actual community with mere physical propinquity or formal membership in a

---

1. A community is usually more or less co-terminous with a society, but the two may be theoretically distinguished on the ground that a society is an aggregate of people who are interdependent in their activities, without any necessary compatibility of ideas, while a community implies shared beliefs and values as well as activities.

particular institution, it may be worth pausing to ask how the demographic, economic, and social circumstances of an earlier America contributed to the process of community-formation. Briefly, let us consider the situation a century ago. At that time, 34,327,000 Americans lived in rural areas, or in cities or towns of less than 100,000 population. Another 4,128,-000 lived in cities of between 100,000 and 1,000,000. There were no cities of more than 1,000,000. This is to say that demographically, about 88 percent of the population was distributed in a great multiplicity of small clusters of people. There were, in fact 611 towns with between 2500 and 25,000 population. There were only 14 cities of over 100,000 and only two over 500,000. These clusters of population were economically tied together by a network of railroads and river boats and canals, and they were politically unified by national political parties, a strong but much limited national government, and a strong spirit of American nationalism. National church organizations and publishing houses, with a small but nationally distributed market, gave a limited degree of centralization to religious and cultural life—or at least the more elite and self-conscious aspects of cultural life. But by modern standards, America's towns and villages were remarkably isolated from one another. America's system of roads and automobiles was still more than half a century in the future and the only practicable way to make any journey of more than 100 miles was to go by rail. Electronic communication was even more than half a century away, and the chief medium of public communication was the local newspaper. Even the smaller towns had their own dailies or weeklies, with no national columnists, no syndicated news, and a remarkable degree of self-sufficiency. The local editor, the local clergyman, the local political leader, were not overshadowed by the quick accessibility and the technological dominance of the cities.

Population clusters of this kind tended to form strong cohesive communities. Their spatial isolation defined them as units. Their small size was conducive to a high degree of personal acquaintance and frequent contact among the people. The limitations of their technology intensified their cohesiveness, for the orbit of social interaction was effectively circumscribed by a circle whose radius was the distance that a person could conveniently walk (or, if a farmer, drive his wagon)—to the corner grocery, to the neighborhood school —or to the druggist a few blocks away. Their orientation to the physical environment gave them a good bit in common, for in a society which still relied primarily upon agriculture and did much of its work outdoors, they shared a common concern with the weather and a common adjustment to nature —to the phases of the moon, the rhythm of the seasons, the fatefulness of drought and flood and untimely freezes. The social institutions which flourished within a population cluster of this kind also greatly reinforced the cohesiveness of the cluster itself, for they were what the sociologists call primary institutions—family, church congregation, neighborhood— which emphasize the personal bond of relationship among their members and the loyalties of one for all and all for one.

The strength and cohesiveness of the communities of this world we have lost (to use Peter Laslett's term) are so well recognized that there is no need for me to dwell upon them. In fact they may have been too much sentimentalized and exaggerated. But there is a further point, quite crucial to the concept of consent which I believe has not been sufficiently recognized. This is the fact that the traditional community was a preclusive community. As I have observed, it certainly did not lovingly embrace everyone and draw together all the human beings within its orbit. It restricted active participation to the "significant others" and it openly excluded Negroes, slighted immigrants, and made life difficult for any square pegs that did not fit into its round holes. But even for those who were excluded, the community exercised such a strong gravitational force that though they had been rejected, they usually displayed compulsive impulses to qualify as insiders by adopting the values and the behavior of the insiders. For instance, the few Negroes who had attained middle-class status rejected Negro *mores* and zealously imitated the follies as well as the values of white middle-class life. As Milton Gordon has summarized it, the outsiders were culturally assimilated though not structurally assimilated: They tried to be like insiders though not accepted as insiders. To state this another way, they gave their allegiance to the *dominant* community and this meant that there could be no competing community.

Of course there have always been dissenters—men who did not want to pay the price of community membership. It is possible to identify a few of these in almost any community, and American history is rich in its record of dissent. But in the traditional community which I have been trying to sketch, the outlook for a consistent dissenter was bleak. The community frowned upon his deviance and it had a whole arsenal of social weapons, ranging from social snubs to outright ostracism, with which to whip him into line. It could easily isolate him and make him feel his isolation, because the population of the community was small and did not provide enough dissenters to form a socially self-sufficient group (or rival community) of their own. As for other dissenters in other communities, the dissenter might get some meager psychological support from reading what they had to say (Elbert Hubbard, H. L. Mencken, Brann the Iconoclast, Bob Ingersoll), but they were too remote to protect him from the dreadful anxieties of the socially isolated. He could not join them in the togetherness of sit-ins, be-ins, or marches on Washington. His lot was a lonely one, and indeed the brooding spirit of loneliness which pervades nineteenth-century American literature may be a reflex of this loneliness of the dissenter.

Thus, the community was not only holistic in the positive sense of being strong, cohesive, and integrated, but it was monolithic in the negative sense of inhibiting the development of social units which might deviate from the patterns of the dominant community. The basic American social structure until nearly the middle of the present century was a world of tight and tiny local communities, heavily insulated against external influences, but strikingly resembling and reinforcing one another because of their generally homogeneous character. Such communities exercised a unitary cultural control over all who lived within their orbits. Men who marched to the beat of a different drummer paid a high price for their singularity and were therefore few.

It was the fundamental structuring of American society into such communities that formed the functional basis for an informal system of conformity. And it was the prevalence of the system of conformity that made possible the formal system of consent as the basis for government and law. It is true, no doubt, that political philosophy encouraged both the forbearance of majorities and the acquiescence of minorities, both of which are essential to a consensual system. But the very notion of majorities and minorities is meaningless without the concept of a whole—a community—of which majority and minority are both parts. What, after all, is a majority? It is a number greater than half, just as a minority is a number less than half. But this must mean more than or less than half of a whole. If a large number tries to control a smaller number, and they are not parts of a whole, but are separate peoples, we regard the control as tyranny. If they are parts of a whole, and the whole is a community, then, under the doctrine of majority rule *and* consent of the governed, the control, if it does not violate basic individual rights, is legitimate. It is hard to say precisely why the fact of community makes such a vital difference, but it must be partly because of a recognition that the community is more or less homogeneous. Perhaps it is only a restatement of this same point in a more specific way to say that there is a recognition that the values on which the members of the community agree are more important to them than the matters on which they disagree, and therefore that the matters of disagreement must be subordinated to the matters of agreement, which means that conflict over the matters of disagreement must be limited.

Fundamentally, there are two ways of looking at the system of control by communities, whose outlines I have tried to sketch. From an adverse point of view, it can be regarded as a system of majoritarian control by a dominating group which demanded blind conformity and used the informal penalties of social disapproval and isolation to exercise a coercion just as forcible as the authoritarian control of an earlier time, which had used flogging, ear-cropping, and imprisonment to exercise a more naked coercion. This is a view with which all the most vociferous critics of conformity and the "establishment" would accept. On the other hand, it can be regarded as a system which encouraged men to comply with accepted standards of decent behavior, to recognize the importance of the values they shared, to settle their disagreements with a minimum use of force. It also encouraged them to base the legitimacy of law upon public consent. No matter which of these views one adopts, it is clear that the power of community sentiment was crucial and that such sentiment was not generated by just any kind of community. It was generated by somewhat isolated and autonomous communities which were more or less homogeneous to begin with, and in which particular factors of size, technology, primary institutions, and general orientation strengthened the cohesive effect.

To say this is to say that if this particular kind of community disappeared, the means by which the consent or conformity of the reluctant was procured might disappear also, and with it the sanction for the kind of government and the kind of law which a system of consent makes possible. It is to say further, that the unique vulnerability of a consent society, of which I spoke earlier, would be exposed, and

that many of the institutions of the society would be revealed to have no defenses. They would be exposed to assault—both verbal and physical assault since this country has
largely renounced the kind of coercive legal controls with
which most countries still defend their institutions. Being
based upon the assumption that any opposition from within
will always be limited opposition, and that any internal issues
are always negotiable, the system of consent provides no
mechanism for the contingency of unlimited opposition and
non-negotiable issues.

What I am contending here is that the system of consent
succeeded historically because the American people lived in
population aggregates of a certain kind. These aggregates
formed communities which were homogeneous with one another, strongly cohesive, and equipped with the means of inducing virtually everyone in the aggregate to accede to the
decisions of the dominant elements—decisions which were in
turn modulated by the right of those who were acceding to
demand certain concessions. Most of all, communities of this
kind were able to monopolize the field of social organization
in such a way that no effective communities incompatible
with the standard type of community could be created. The
consent that followed was not really the consent of millions
of individual persons; it was the consent of many hundreds of
individual communities. But what I would contend further
is that the traditional kind of community has deteriorated or
even disappeared. As it has done so, it has left the field open
for the emergence of a number of different kinds of communities—each with something of the strength, cohesiveness,
and self-sufficiency which result from personal association and
shared values. But these new-style communities, far from
being traditional or standard or homogeneous with one another, frequently hold values in conflict with one another's—
even values antithetical to one another's. In a social structure
of conflicting communities, there is no longer a sanction for

consent, and the whole system of law and government based upon consent faces a supreme crisis.

It is almost too well known for me to go into any detail about what happened to the nineteenth-century constellation of more or less autonomous, small communities. The automobile greatly lengthened the radius of men's mobility. This fact itself destroyed countless cherished community institutions. It also greatly increased the distance between men's work and their homes, and thus began to shatter the integration both of their personalities and their lives. Technological changes reared secondary environments—the office, the university, the ghetto—which stood between man and the primary environment. These secondary environments diminished the shared experience which exposure to the primary environment had offered. They also made possible the concentration of large populations in cities. By 1968, 63 percent of the population of the country lived in places of more than 250,000 population. The impersonality of city life, in turn, gave men an anonymity which was sometimes welcome, sometimes unwelcome, but, in either case, which relieved them of the personal impact of social pressures and social expectations. At the same time, city life was more secular than the church-oriented life of the rural community, and this secularism encouraged a skepticism in the higher learning—a skepticism that began to strip away the mystique with which a religious society will always sanctify its civil institutions—the constitution, the flag, the majesty of the law, the mandate of the people.

By the 1950's the solidarity of communities was fractured, their cohesion was diluted, and their power over individuals was but a shadow of what it had been. As patterns became diffused, the processes of socialization for children became blurred. Boys who had identified fairly readily with fathers who plowed a furrow on the farm, could not take their cues so readily from fathers who were away most of the time, engaged in incomprehensible work at places which one had never seen. Boys and girls whose sex roles were no longer codified all too frequently wound up feeling uncertain about their identities. Communities were divided in voice, bewildered by the rapidity of social change, bullied by "experts" who told them what to believe, and silenced by the voices of the electronic media, which came from the metropolis and to which they could not talk back. As instruments of social control, communities became faint shadows of what they once had been. They could no longer speak to the dissenters in tones of authority, nor could they monitor the behavior of deviant individuals.

But these changes are well known and what I would like to focus upon is a less recognized and perhaps more important aspect of this revolution in the patterns of social relatedness. This is a change in the scale of society, which has destroyed the power of traditional communities to control dissenters by isolating or ostracizing them, and has now given to those who reject or are rejected by the community, a power to form communities of their own. This change is vital, because when the traditional community loses its power to deny the blessings of social relatedness to those who reject it, the principle of social control by communities is left with no effective means of enforcement.

The readiness with which alienated or non-conformist groups can now form communities of their own is cogently suggested by a comment of Daniel Bell's in the spring 1970 issue of *The Public Interest*. Bell asks how many constitute the "mass" of the radicals, and he cites *Fortune* surveys which indicate that as many as 30 percent "in the elite schools" may be significantly radical. But then he adds: "A more important consideration, however, and a crucial one for all our problems is less the percentage than the change of scale. In an arena of ten thousand students, five percent comes to 500, and these can form a powerful striking force."

No doubt this is true, but the power of the striking force which they can form is perhaps less important than the strength of the community that they can form. A community of 500 is large enough to give the person who joins it a sense of belonging, large enough to protect him against the snubs and slights and disapproval of the larger society, large enough to isolate him from out-groups, as all communities do with their members. Five hundred strongly cohesive people can devise standards of dress, speech, and belief for their own group, and impose these as rigidly as if they were the most orthodox of conformists. David Riesman has touched this point rather effectively in his observation that "The Bohemians and the rebels are not usually autonomous; on the contrary, they are zealously tuned in to the signals of a defiant group that finds the meaning of life in a compulsive non-conformity to the majority group."

We still speak of the Bohemians and the rebels as dissenters, which means that we are still held in the grip of the illusion that there is one "community" which includes everyone except those who opt out and float about as displaced persons on the margins of society. But the fact that large numbers of people, living in propinquity, on campuses, in communes, in Bohemias, or whatever, may share common values and even impose standards of conformity upon their members means that these people are not dissenters at all. Rather, they are conforming members of new kinds of communities. Not only new kinds of communities, but communities which are committed to a cultural separation from communities of the standard kind. To embark on an extended scrutiny of these new social organisms is beyond the scope of this essay, for all we are immediately concerned with here is the impact of these changes upon a system of law based upon consent and uniformity. But the fact that they are communities, and communities of a special kind is beginning to be recognized. J. Milton Yinger has already written about what he calls a "contra-culture," and Theodore Roszak about a "counter culture." The "spirit of Woodstock" is a manifestation of an urge toward community in these new groups. This spirit in some ways is very different from the spirit of traditional communities. For instance, the traditional community was highly structured by a network of explicit commitments and loyalties binding individuals to one another in an intricate cohesive pattern. The spirit of the commune is much more an unstructured diffuse sense of "love" toward everyone in general and no one in particular. But in many respects, we have new communities whose relation to the traditional community is as negative as their culture is negative toward the traditional culture, and if we are to speak of contra-cultures or counter cultures, we might as well also speak of contra-communities and counter communities. It is such social entities as those which now withhold the consent which has been vital to our non-coercive society and which thus present a challenge to the legitimacy of law such as this basic institution has never before faced in America.

In sum, we have lived for some two centuries in a society which has minimized the use of physical compulsion at all levels and has used less compulsion than almost any society in history. Socially we have abandoned chastisement for children, both at home and in school. We have abolished, in law and almost in practice, the domination of husbands over wives. We have operated with a Congress in which it has remained almost impossible to enact a law to which a handful of Senators are deeply and irrevocably opposed. We have operated with a court system in which there is no good way to induce the accused to let his trial proceed if he is not willing to let it proceed. The unanimity with which, in the past, accused persons accepted this system was so total that we were not even aware of the naked vulnerability of the courts until the Chicago Seven disclosed it to us.

Having rejected compulsion as a means of social control, except in the cases of punishment of palpable felons whose offenses were condemned by almost everyone, we became desperately dependent upon "agreement"—perhaps under pressure, perhaps reluctant, perhaps secured by bullying or bartering or bribery—but still, with some measure of voluntarism or at least acquiescence in the result. Since agreement was the alternative to deadlock and paralysis, we became compulsively addicted to negotiation. I suppose that most legislation is negotiated before it is enacted, and that more legal disputes are negotiated than are ever brought to trial. In important disputes in the area of labor relations, we insist, above all, that the parties must never stop talking; and if the matter is urgent, they must negotiate around the clock. Since our only truly instrumental device for resolving disputes is by talk, the prospect that the contestants might actually quit talking is too awful to contemplate. Agreement or what passes for agreement *must* be reached, because if agreement fails, our system offers no recourse.

For two centuries, this system of government by consent operated, sometimes creaking loudly, sometimes brought to a dead halt, sometimes imposing injustice and hardship upon groups who were forced to the mockery of pretending to accept by agreement what they were compelled to accept by irresistible pressure. But on the whole, the system worked reasonably well, not because it is intrinsically workable, but because the dominant communities wanted it to work. People truly regarded the points on which they agreed as more important than the points on which they disagreed. When they did disagree, it was as adversaries, and not as enemies. We were all Republicans and all Federalists, and for all its imperfections, the operation of the system might well have gratified Thomas Jefferson.

But today, we face confrontations with men who believe in revolution—believe in it, in a good many cases with genuine conviction. They do not want to reach agreement. Their demands are, by stipulation, non-negotiable. Their adversary may give in, but they will not let him agree. Often their terms are stated in a way carefully designed to make agreement impossible.

Thus we approach the answer to a question which most people never recognized as a question and to which those who did recognize it hoped never to have to learn the answer. What happens to law based upon the norms of the community if there is no prevailing community but only a multiplicity of conflicting communities? What happens to the principle of consent if the social structure has no center which can even speak the voice of consent?

The answers are far from clear. But perhaps it is important to remember that while consent requires what Richard Hofstadter has called an attitude of comity on the part of conflicting parties, and while even minimum comity seems unattainable in many confrontations today, still the principle of consent was never predicated upon the idea of bland agreement and readiness to avoid issues for the sake of superficial harmony. It was predicated upon the idea that adverse parties can limit their conflict and can recognize the values they share, even while contesting the points on which they disagree. Whether the communities and counter-communities of America in the 1970's may be able to hold such a balanced view in the heat of the antagonisms and extremisms that now prevail is questionable indeed. But if it is possible to contest social issues without destroying essential institutions, it will have to be done by the difficult feat of combining tolerance with idealism. We need to look at people as individuals rather than as types. We need to remember with Thomas Jefferson that "every difference of opinion is not a difference of principle," to recognize that a principle is not necessarily a moral absolute, and to remind ourselves frequently that an adversary need not be a mortal enemy.

INDEX